Dismantling Conspiracy Theories

INNOVATIONS IN INFORMATION LITERACY

About the Series

This series for librarians and information literacy instructors provides information on the newest ideas and findings emerging from the field of information literacy, from teaching methods to emerging technologies to promising collaborations.

Books in the series engage in dialogues surrounding matters that are both conceptual and practical to librarians and instructors who are interested in teaching information literacy with local, cross-cultural, and international appeal.

The books are aimed at librarians at all types of institutions, from academic to public libraries, and also to non-library faculty members and teachers who are interested and invested in the conversations and advancements in information literacy.

About the Series Editor

The **Innovations in Information Literacy** series was conceived by and is edited by Trudi Jacobson, MLS, MA, Distinguished Librarian Emerita, University at Albany Libraries. From 2021-2024, she was an Extraordinary Professor in the Research Unit Self-Directed Learning, Faculty of Education, at North-West University in Potchefstroom, South Africa.

Trudi Jacobson co-chaired the ACRL Information Literacy Competency Standards for Higher Education Task Force that created the ACRL Information Literacy Framework for Higher Education. She received the Miriam Dudley Instruction Librarian of the Year award in 2009. She was the recipient of a 2024 Divergent Publication Award for Excellence in Literacy in a Digital Age Research for *Metaliteracy in a Connected World: Developing Learners as Producers* (ALA, 2022), written with Thomas P. Mackey.

Titles in the Series

Dismantling Conspiracy Theories

Metaliteracy and other Strategies for an Information-Disordered World

Katie Greer and Stephanie Beene

ROWMAN & LITTLEFIELD
Lanham • Boulder • New York • London

Published by Rowman & Littlefield
An imprint of The Rowman & Littlefield Publishing Group, Inc.
4501 Forbes Boulevard, Suite 200, Lanham, Maryland 20706
www.rowman.com

86-90 Paul Street, London EC2A 4NE

British Library Cataloguing in Publication Information Available

Library of Congress Cataloging-in-Publication Data Available

Library of Congress Control Number: 2024941282

ISBN 978-1-5381-7698-6 (cloth)
ISBN 978-1-5381-7699-3 (paperback)
ISBN 978-1-5381-7700-6 (electronic)

Contents

Acknowledgments

With a book like this, there is always a support network that helps turn a concept into a reality. We are fortunate to have a wonderful group of colleagues, friends, and family who have supported this project since day one. Without their constant support, we may have gone down the rabbit hole ourselves.

A project like this demands a lot to do it justice, and when things got crazy and our expertise ran short, our "phone a friend" Shawn McCann came through. Thank you to him for his chapter on AI and information disorder—it would not have been nearly as cool if it were just left to us.

Thank you to the many colleagues, too many to name, who inspired us and engaged with us on this research. We especially want to thank Clarence Maybee and Rachel Fundator at the Institute for Information Literacy at Purdue for the grant that helped support our work, and our cohort grantees for inspiring us. We are grateful for the guidance from the team at Rowman and Littlefield, including Trudi Jacobson, Charles Harmon, and Lauren Moynihan. Beth Wallis, thank you for your time and energy reading chapter drafts. Thank you to Joe Pierre, Will Sommer, and Karen Zack, who generously allowed the use of their work.

Stephanie would like to thank members of her University of New Mexico research group, the Container Conundrum: Amy Jankowski, Alyssa Russo, and Lori Townsend, all extremely supportive from the very beginning. Your thoughtful insights about trust and online information helped shape this research.

Katie would like to specifically acknowledge Tom Mackey, her wonderful first- and second-year PhD mentor, who has continued to inspire and support her work. This project would not have happened without the support (and occasional interventions of) family: her husband, Scott, who ensures she is fed, watered, and as rested as possible; mom Laura and grandmother Sara; children Caleb and Grace; and, of course, the chihuahuas, Fox and Kreacher.

Stephanie would also like to acknowledge the role of her husband, Nathan, who has heard more about QAnon and conspiracy theories than he ever bargained for; her newborn Edward, who made his appearance during the writing of this book; and her furbaby Hayley, who always keeps her laughing. Extended family listened and offered insight as well—this project took a village!

Lastly, thank you to all those who are "doing the work" in the face of this information crisis, some of whom we know and many of whom we have cited. This long list includes Chris Conner, Matthew Hannah, Sarah MacMillen, Robert Spinelli, and so many more.

Preface

"There comes a moment in every new Q follower's life when the person closest to them realizes they aren't joking."—Will Sommer

We began our journey as coauthors during our work on the Association for College and Research Libraries' Visual Literacy Task Force. That project spanned 2018 to 2022. One of the concerns of the task force was how visual literacy could begin to address some of the most intractable facets of information disorder—although we hadn't yet encountered the concept of information disorder itself. At the time, QAnon was gaining media attention (LaFrance 2020). During a casual conversation about research consultations with students and patrons, Stephanie mused to Katie, "What if we had a consultation with someone into QAnon?" Katie commented about the effect of combating what seemed to be a very overwhelming rising tide of conspiracism, which felt like standing in front of a tsunami with a bucket. Stephanie responded, "We should write about that!"

So we began writing about conspiracies, QAnon, and what librarians could or could not do about it. Over 2020, a year of lockdowns, quarantines, isolation, and confusion around the pandemic, we furiously wrote against time—QAnon was rapidly changing, and the media coverage was expanding. Our article, "A Call to Action for Librarians: Countering Conspiracy Theories in the Age of QAnon," published just days before the January 6, 2021, insurrection, served as our attempt to organize and make sense of conspiracy ideation and conspiracy theories, formally introducing the phenomenon of QAnon to the field of librarianship. Thanks to the timing of our article's release and the zeitgeist of the time, what had been a research tangent became our research agenda. Nonetheless, its reception surprised us. We were invited to give several presentations and interviews, including as plenary speakers in Athens, Greece, for the 2021 annual Qualitative and Quantitative Methods in Librarianship meeting. This plenary talk focused on our follow-up research, conducted in the fall of 2021, a nationwide survey of library workers who were encountering conspiracy ideation, titled "Library Workers on the Frontlines of Conspiracy Theories in the U.S.," published in 2023. We received a 2022–2024 grant from the Institute of Information Literacy at Purdue University on information literacy challenges, which united us with other scholars working on conspiracy phenomena and their intersections with information literacy. This grant funded our research and the publication of a 2024 article on splinter influencer groups and networked conspiracist communities, "When Belief Becomes Research: Conspiracist Communities on the Social Web."

Over the years of this research, we have had many, many moments of "What have we gotten ourselves into?" We've stuck with it thanks to encouragement from others and probably just a little innate stubbornness. This book is the culmination of so much reading, exploring the dark corners of the internet, and many conversations with friends and colleagues. We are indebted to our community of scholars and fellow librarians for their enduring support and for pushing us to consider new directions. While the research sometimes felt like falling down our own version of the rabbit hole, we kept in mind the importance of tackling this societal problem from a pragmatic application of current literacy frameworks. Even so, we recognize the limitations of this approach, as much of the work to pull people away from or prevent conspiracy thinking proves enormously challenging. We will always encounter those who cannot be persuaded to think differently. We ourselves have engaged in many of these frustrating conversations with loved ones over the years of conducting this research. If you, dear reader, have also encountered family, friends, neighbors, or patrons endorsing conspiracy theories or QAnon, you are not alone—in fact, shockingly, about 25 percent of the U.S. population ascribes to at least one tenet of the QAnon conspiracy theory (Todd, Murray, and Dann 2021). While conspiracy research itself is a relatively new field, there is a growing wealth of resources and literature, and the field is rapidly evolving in a zeitgeist of anxious conspiracy ideation—proliferated via new and emerging information-sharing technologies.

The information age has introduced a wealth of opportunities, but also what scholar Matthew Hannah (2021b) has termed "the information dark age," with the rise of QAnon and other "superconspiracies" (Barkun 2003). Information professionals in an information-disordered society must draw on disciplines external to librarianship to shift information literacy praxis, especially as they encounter patrons exhibiting conspiracy ideation. Librarians have enormous potential as information experts to shape our information society and its citizenry. However, our profession must better understand the challenges and opportunities we face in this evolving information landscape. This book explores the issue of information disorder in our society, how conspiracy theories shape citizen engagement with information and reality, and integrates current metaliteracy, visual literacy, and information literacy frameworks. While it can still feel like standing before a tsunami, we hope this book will arm readers with more than a bucket.

WHAT READERS CAN EXPECT

This book explores the intersections of information and visual literacies, metaliteracy, and conspiracy ideation. There have yet to be books that focus on the information professional's role in combating or preventing conspiracy ideation. In addition, it provides a desperately needed look at the problems of our information-disordered society, the rise of superconspiracies like QAnon, and how information professionals can help shape societal engagement with information. Here we define our information-disordered world and how we got here, the fraught relationship between trust and distrust of information and how this relationship interacts with conspiracy ideation, the historical roots of QAnon and other conspiracies, the evolving political and technological landscape, and what roles educators and information professionals can play in combating conspiracism. Although there is increasing coverage of the information disorder problem in the news and social media, it is an increasing problem encountered in U.S. libraries.

The primary audience for this book is librarians and information professionals, including academic, special (e.g., law, medical, government), and public professionals, archival librarians, visual resources professionals, and others. There is increasing coverage of this problem in the news and social media but more needs to be written for this audience, and it is an increasing problem encountered in U.S. libraries. As a secondary audience, we expect that high school, college, and university educators may also be interested in what we have written here, as these readers share the goal of developing critical thinkers for the future—and have certainly encountered their fair share of conspiracy theories. Academic librarians have positioned themselves as educators over the past two decades due to the "instructional turn" of the profession. Even though this burgeoning discourse is fraught with challenges for implementation, librarians embrace challenges. As a field, we educate the public in a variety of literacies and information access, and we continue to fight for these liberties even as the information landscape changes.

OUTLINE AND SCOPE

Part I, "Our Information Disordered World," sets the stage for our investigation of information disorder in the current information landscape. Chapter 1 explores how social media and big tech have entirely changed how we find, access, use, and think about information. Evaluating information remains a crucial step in this process, but as the information landscape has shifted so quickly, many are left without the skills needed to effectively decide what and whom to trust. As such, chapter 2 takes a deeper dive into operationalizing "information disorder" in this new landscape, particularly on social media. It is in chapter 3 that we explore the literature on conspiracies and conspiracy theories, utilizing the superconspiracy QAnon as a case study because of its relevance to the present moment and its unique qualities, explored throughout the book. This first section surveys scholarly literature from history, psychology, political science, and education, among others, while also scanning the most current discourse on technology and social media.

Part II, "A Matter of Trust and Distrust," delves into psychology, neuroscience, and library literature to explore current thinking on biases and human nature, trust evaluations, and the role affect, or emotional response, plays in these trust assessments. We first explore in chapter 4 the research from various disciplines on why humans might be prone to conspiracy ideation. Chapter 5 explores how notions of authority (e.g., how we determine authoritative information, expertise, competence) have shifted in this evolving information landscape, including how cognitive authority and parasocial relationships impact trust. We examine how these facets have been featured in information and metaliteracy frameworks and how the field of librarianship is shifting toward a more complex and nuanced understanding of trust. This section is wrapped up in chapter 6 by offering pragmatic strategies for readers to build trust with others, and techniques for nudging them away from conspiracy ideation, whether in person or online. We hope readers will glean some specific tactics to use during instruction and daily encounters with students, patrons, neighbors, family, friends, and colleagues, both in-person and online.

Part III, "How Conspiracy Theories Exploit Distrust in a Post-Truth America," begins in chapter 7 with a historical lens to examine the tropes and narratives that conspiracy theories exploit, over and over again, throughout time and space. Not only is this history important, it is our hope that if people better understand the hallmarks of conspiratorial narrative structures, they might be less likely to fall for the next, newest conspiracy theory. Chapter 8 brings us back to the present, where we explore conspiracy theories on social media and the participatory nature of the social web. We investigate the rise of online amateur sleuths, gateways to QAnon such as the health and wellness industries, and how conspiracy theories are proliferated through these subcultures. Finally, we offer some tips for breaking out of the social media cycle, knowing what we now know about the addictive properties of social media platforms and their potential harm to our mental and emotional well-being. In chapter 9, we examine how conspiracy theories have driven political and community activism, including those that impact libraries and educational institutions, such as coordinated book banning efforts, first amendment audits, and the increase in violent threats against elected officials. The final chapter of this section introduces readers to assessing the spectrum of conspiracy ideation and methods for counteracting it, including inoculation theory, prebunking and debunking techniques. Again, we provide examples of how to employ these tactics in various contexts.

Finally, Part IV, "Emerging Issues and Strategies," concludes our explorations with some big, controversial topics impacting librarianship and education. We problematize the notion of neutrality in these fields, but especially librarianship. Our friend and colleague Shawn McCann graciously contributed chapter 12, exploring AI and the conspiratorial worldview. Closing out the book is chapter 13, where we problematize the current methodologies used by information professionals and other educators against an information-disordered landscape, and posit some strategies and future directions. This final chapter, while offering some hope for future directions, really serves as a more intensive "call to action for librarians"; as with our initial article, we are hoping that the communities of practice out there will take this book as a prompt for furthering research and knowledge in these areas.

HOPE IN THE SHADOWS

We have spent years thinking about this material, and to be honest, at times it feels no less overwhelming than when we just understood QAnon as a weird buzzword popping up in weird corners of the internet and fringe political groups. And yet—there is hope. Forums such as reQovery or QAnon Casualties on Reddit exist for those who have made it out to tell their stories, or for those who are helping loved ones escape to share their tips and techniques. Many of their success stories are rooted in the strategies we exhort throughout this book—utilize empathy and care, build trust, go slowly. Human intuition for those in need, combined with the professional frameworks and research that we have gathered in this book, provide hope within the shadows—we can find a new future, together.

To end this preface, a caveat. In another book in this series, *Knowledge as a Feeling*, Troy Swanson (2023, xxvii) wrote the beautiful disclaimer that "delving into outside disciplines is a dangerous game, and I am sure that I have made my fair share of errors and misunderstandings. [. . .] I hope that you grant me forgiveness and understanding where I have screwed up." Like Troy, we have done our best here to weave together disparate scholars and disciplines, but there is always more to learn, include, and consider. We hope this book serves as a starting point for further researchers and writers to build on, as we all work together to tackle the problem of conspiratorial thinking in our society.

Part I

Our Information-Disordered World

1

An Unprecedented Information Age

Humans have always found a way to communicate; whether through paint, words, gestures, or expressions, we manage to share our stories with others, giving our ephemeral musings life outside of ourselves. Andrew Pettegree, in his 2014 tome, *The Invention of News: How the World Came to Know About Itself*, asserted that, throughout the ages, information "gained credibility from the person who delivered it," whereas written news of any type was viewed with suspicion because it could be tampered with and was not easily verified (2). Information delivered verbally by a trusted confidante was far more likely to be believed. In his foundational text on cognitive authority, Patrick Wilson (1983) examines how we determine an information source's trustworthiness based on its perceived authority, credibility, and trustworthiness. Today, we still rely on personal recommendations in a world replete with secondhand information.

To be sure, information and its transmission have changed rapidly, with broad implications. We live in an unprecedented moment, unimaginable to our ancestors, in which the amount of information available to anyone with a mobile device and an internet connection is staggering. On the one hand, this amount of information empowers us; on the other, it can be isolating and disruptive.

Scholars agree with this paradox. One of the more popular descriptors of our era is the Information Age (Kline 2015), also known as the Computer Age, Digital Age, Silicon Age, or Media Age, linked to the development of the transistor in 1947. Other popular characterizations are the Information Economy (Godin 2008) or Fourth Industrial Age (Haag 2002; Matthews, McLinden, and Greenway 2021), coined in the early aughts, with the latter describing an ongoing present. In the library literature, readers may have encountered the terms Information Landscapes (Lloyd 2006; Savolainen 2021) or Information Ecosystems (Kuehn 2023), phrases describing a rapidly evolving information ecology. So far, these have all been positive or neutral terms; scholars have also described our era in overtly negative ways, such as an Infodemic (Stephens, Poon, and Tan 2023; Revez and Corujo 2022), a term that blends *epidemic* or *pandemic* with *information*; an Information Dark Age (Hannah 2021b); an era marked by Surveillance Capitalism (Zuboff 2019; Chaudhary et al. 2022); or the Attention Economy (Ciampaglia et al. 2015; Odell 2019). Still others have renamed our time a Post-Truth Era (Fister 2017; McIntyre 2018; Mackey and Jacobson 2018) or a Misinformation Age (O'Connor and Weatherall 2019). Yet another representation of our time, which will be the focus of the second chapter of this book, is the concept of "information disorder" (Wardle and Derakshan 2017; Filimovicz 2023) No matter with which designation one agrees, all share the notion of information saturation.

To understand how we arrived at this moment, we will briefly consider previous information revolutions that underpin the current moment. While much of the book will concern itself with social media titans like YouTube, Facebook, Twitter, Instagram, and so on, the story of our information era builds on and is shaped by historical precedents. Concepts like corroboration and verification, objectivity, and social networks—all are birthed and refined in previous generations through older technologies, recycled, and made acute by social media, smartphones, on-demand technology, and algorithms.

THE PAST INFORMS THE PRESENT: HOW WE GOT HERE

The speed of innovation and connectivity is so fast that even Big Tech's industry leaders have warned the public about the dangers of machine super-intelligence (Roose 2023). Objects now talk to each other and us. Cities and countries fight ransomware, deep fakes, and cybercrime on the dark web. Social and streaming media is fragmented and sometimes encrypted. Information is targeted, on-demand, and catered to preferences, tastes, likes, and dislikes. Algorithms learn.

This chapter is organized into the four information waves, the last of which is ongoing. Each section highlights technologies and moments in time. To that end, the first information wave chronicles the invention of the printing press and the rise of newspapers. Our designation of the first information revolution goes largely undisputed in the scholarship (Eisenstein 1980; Wheeler 2019, 27–54; Gleick 2012, 399). The second information wave is also largely undisputed: The Industrial Revolution ushered in a vast electronic and analog network of interconnectivity through the telegraph and telephone (Wheeler 2019, 55–86). With the onset of the space race, the Manhattan Project, and satellite technology, the post-war period focused on television, the birth of 24-hour news, and personal computing. Indeed, we argue that the conspiracy theories around the Kennedy assassination and the moon landing would not have the potency they continue to have today without the ubiquity of television. Finally, the ongoing fourth information wave ushered in the social web, Google, smartphones, and social media.

THE FIRST INFORMATION WAVE: THE PRINTING PRESS AND THE BIRTH OF NEWS AND CORROBORATION

The printing press and movable type represented a new era of information storage, retrieval, preservation, and transmission (Eisenstein 1980). As a machine, the printing press represented a "decisive point of no return in human history" (Gleick 2012, 400). The printing press made production cheaper and more accessible, producing far more copies of treatises to disseminate.

What we now call "the news" became a commercial commodity after the invention of the printing press, between 1450 and 1530 (Pettegree 2014, 2). These eighty years represent a time of technological innovation, when publishers began experimenting with far shorter and cheaper texts. For the first time, the news became a part of popular culture.

As the news industry matured, so did the practice of corroboration (Pettegree 2014, 3). Throughout the sixteenth and seventeenth centuries, readers developed complex heuristics for deciphering the truth: excluding reports based on personal worldviews, focusing on events of consequence, and weighing conflicting reports to discern a consensus (4). At times, it was determined that eyewitness accounts were so conflicting that the "facts might never be known" (5).

By the end of the eighteenth and beginning of the nineteenth century, partisan reporting became competitive between newspapers, and the distinction between news and opinion became blurred (Pettegree 2014, 367). Pettegree terms this era "the great age of the newspaper" (371), which would last about a century and a half, when the contest for power within Europe and the United States sowed the seeds of the catastrophic conflicts of the twentieth century.

This period, often called the Progressive Era, was also the rise of muckraking in journalism. Yellow muckrakers, with which most readers are familiar, ridiculed and demonized those they set out to expose, using sensationalistic language and presenting binaries (e.g., good versus evil, black versus white) to convince audiences of unverified facts: "Articles were a mixture of emotionally charged and exaggerated language, dramatic conspiracy, salesmanship, and personal attacks . . . with only a pinch of verifiable evidence" (Klein 2019, 1, 2, 32).

Oddly enough, the notion of objectivity arose out of this era of muckraking. For instance, the fledgling *New York Times* stood apart from New York's yellow journals, writing that they would be run "without fear or favor" (Hartman 2023). Their editorial section was downplayed while they focused on verified news and legal coverage. Such was the skepticism at the *Times* that when rumor swept newsrooms of the "unsinkable Titanic," they "reflexively questioned it," allowing them to get the scoop when the Titanic's radio went silent (para 2).

Another invention that helped objectivity was the telegraph, ushered in by the second information wave. A group of newspaper publishers banded together to create the Associated Press in 1846, using the telegraph as their communication medium (Wheeler 2019, 14). This shift brought a more diverse readership and advertising base, where it became economically wise to "offend as few people as possible by offering balanced reporting" (8).

THE SECOND INFORMATION WAVE: A NETWORK WROUGHT BY THE INDUSTRIAL REVOLUTION

In 1851, the first telegraph ran alongside railroad tracks to communicate with stations, where railroad employees doubled as telegraphers (Wheeler 2019, 39). Samuel F. B. Morse conceived of a system of dots and dashes representing words in 1832, now known as Morse code. This binary code is foundational to the iterative technological innovation that led to later computing.

The telegraph would prove revolutionary. It was the first medium to separate information from its container, and thereby reformatted news delivery. It changed people's expectations of how and when they would receive personal and professional information. It also led to the telephone.

The name most associated with early telephones is Alexander Graham Bell, who invented a way to put sound on telegraph wires (Wheeler 2019, 48). In 1925, the American Telephone & Telegraph Company (AT&T) founded Bell Laboratories, a ground zero for innovation, employing engineers and scientists who continued to improve on these foundational technologies. In 1915, the first transcontinental phone call between New York and San Francisco transpired, while the first transatlantic phone call between the United States and the United Kingdom occurred in 1927.

Wheeler argues that the telephone's importance was not its analog technology but its "ubiquitous backbone for connecting computers" (Wheeler 2019, 56). Bell Labs also contributed to early computing through the engineers and mathematicians they employed. Among the scientists who worked at Bell Labs were Thomas Edison, Alan Turing, and Charles Shannon, who developed a theory of information (Gleick 2012, 7). This theory would lead to the transistor, magnetic storage, and early computing.

THE THIRD INFORMATION WAVE: TELEVISION, THE BIRTH OF 24/7 NEWS, AND PERSONAL COMPUTERS

After World War II, scientists converged at two coveted research labs in the United States: Bell Laboratories and Los Alamos National Laboratories, the site of the Manhattan Project. The former gave us the transistor, and the latter the atomic bomb. This era was that of the Space Race, with NASA being established in 1958, and the era when television (TV) became ubiquitous. The birth of 24-hour news occurs in this information wave, a vital prelude to social media and the on-demand era to follow. Personal computers and the first protocols and experimentations of the internet are also hallmarks of this age.

Television

The post-war years signaled a boom in TV's popularity, with 1952 to 1960 marking an era of rapid cable and network TV expansion. Some monumental events that endure in the American cultural narrative occurred during the next decade, including some of the most enduring conspiracy theories.

For example, from 1961 to 1963, President Kennedy became the first television candidate and president, with his assassination covered by four days of coverage in 1963, unprecedented at that time. Theories around his assassination endure today. In 1966, TV coverage of the Vietnam War expanded as fighting increased, and the United States became increasingly polarized (Sterling and Kittross 2001, 760). Later, 1968 was a big year, with heavy coverage of the aftermath of Dr. Martin Luther King Jr.'s assassination, the subsequent protests, and the assassination of Senator Robert Kennedy. The Apollo 11 mission put a man on the moon, live and broadcasted worldwide, in 1969 (which also led to subsequent conspiracy theories). In 1973, the Watergate hearings were carried on live TV for several weeks, while the following year, Nixon's impeachment hearings were broadcast live, as was his resignation.

That is a tumultuous thirteen years, all on television. Never had so many *watched* the same events—at the same time. This new media fed an untapped hunger for live visual programming. The next five years brought 24-hour news coverage, with CSPAN and CNN going on-air in 1979 and 1980, respectively. These channels were essential precursors to the influential TV personalities of the 2000s, decentralized internet personalities, and social media influencers in the years to come.

The 1980s also marked the beginning of the Satanic Panic, which coalesced with concern over violence on TV. The new medium helped spread the now-discredited practice of recovered memory therapy, in which people claimed to remember torture or sexual assault in occult or satanic abuse rituals; in the most extreme cases, allegations involved a conspiracy of a global satanic cult that included the wealthy and elite, in which children were abducted or bred for human sacrifices, pornography, and prostitution (discussed further in chapter 7). Through talk shows and news, TV helped spread the message. In 1982, a ten-year review by the National Institute of Mental Health found a connection between media messages and viewers' subsequent vigilante actions against neighbors, friends, and family (Sterling and Kittross 2001, 764).

By 1988, Time Inc. and Warner Communications had merged to become the world's largest entertainment company. In twelve years, they would provide internet service through America Online (AOL) by way of the cable that wired America's TVs and computers.

Personal Computers and the First Internet Protocols

In 1942, a patent dispute case ruled that "the computer as a concept [was] un-patentable and thus freely open to all" innovators (Computer History Timeline, n.d.). Inventions were abundant. For example, one of the earliest examples of a reference to machines "thinking" occurred in 1950, in Edmund Berkeley's book *Giant Brains*, where he noted, "We shall now consider how we can design a very simple machine that will think" (Berkeley 1956). Five years later, the term *artificial intelligence* was coined at a summer research workshop at Dartmouth College (McCarthy et al., 1955). By 1975, the first DIY kits for building computers at home were marketed and sold, and in 1981, IBM's personal computer was released, and portable and desktop computers continued to be innovated throughout the 1980s and '90s. The term *internet* was born in 1969, with the Defense Department's early precursor, the Advanced Research Project Agency Network (ARPANET), which connected mainframe computers from four U.S. research institutions for scientists to share data (Wheeler 2019, 60). The TCP/IP protocol was born in 1983, which solved a critical information retrieval problem by sorting information in a network. Tim Berners-Lee and the World Wide Web would be the next giant leap.

OUR ONGOING FOURTH INFORMATION WAVE: WELCOME TO SOCIAL MEDIALAND

With rapidly advancing technological change, our world continues to be utterly transformed. Society entered a new reality once social media and the Big Tech titans rose in ubiquity. Indeed, it is hard for the youngest among us to imagine a time before swiping, selfies, influencers, and emojis.

The fourth wave represents another paradigm shift, beginning in 1990 with Tim Berners-Lee, who developed a means to identify and retrieve information from the internet, coining the phrase "World Wide Web" (WWW). Building off the affordances of the internet, he created three components that we take for granted today: the URL (i.e., the web address), the common publication language (HTML), and the language to transfer and display information (HTTP). With this trio, a web browser can retrieve specific data records a user requests and display them properly. At this point, the web leaped from obscurity into the mainstream. As Gleick opines, "An unindexed Internet site is in the same limbo as a misshelved library book. This is why the successful and powerful business enterprises of the information economy are built on filtering and searching" (Gleick 2012, 410). To create this structure, those enterprises utilized Berners-Lee's architecture. According to pop culture analyst and *New Yorker* columnist Jia Tolentino, author of *Trick Mirror: Reflections on Self Delusion*, this early period of the internet was characterized by static "screenfuls [*sic*] of texts and graphics"; the later Web 2.0 would become an interactive portal where "what you did on the internet would become intertwined with what everyone else did, and the things other people liked would become the things that you would see" (Tolentino 2019, 4; DiNucci 1999, 221–22). This era of rapid innovation and interactivity paved the way for social media applications.

Beginning in 1993, an exponential yearly increase in domain registrations ensued (Gleick 2012, 391–92). The online bookseller Amazon launched in 1995, beginning its reign in reshaping online retail. AOL became dominant in 1996. The volume of internet traffic had grown by a factor of ten each year; AltaVista had been building and revising an index to every page it could find on the internet—by 1996, there were tens of millions of them (422).

Then came Google. In 1998, Larry Page and Sergey Brin were Stanford graduate students building a search-engine prototype. "Their idea was that cyberspace possessed a form of self-knowledge, inherent in the links from one page to another and that a search engine could exploit this knowledge" (Gleick 2012, 423). Gleick discusses how they re-envisioned the internet of their predecessors:

> They visualized the Internet as a graph, with nodes and links. . . . They considered each link as an expression of value—a recommendation. And they recognized that all links are not equal. They invented a recursive way of reckoning value: the rank of a page depends on the value of its incoming links; the value of a link depends on the rank of its containing page. (423)

Page and Brin's work revolutionized searching and dominated the web—"to google" something became synonymous with searching for something online. Indeed, the verb "to Google" entered the Oxford English Dictionary (OED) five years after Page and Brin's first prototype.

If that rate of change seems mind-boggling, the next thirteen years are a flurry of innovation. In 1999, LiveJournal, an early blogging and social networking site, initiated the blogging phenomenon, even though the OED did not officially recognize the word *blog* until 2003, the same year WordPress was released. MySpace was also launched that same year alongside 4chan, although MySpace was quickly eclipsed by the public launch of Facebook in 2004. Flickr was released in 2004, followed by YouTube and Reddit in 2005. Twitter launched in 2006 alongside Facebook's Newsfeed. Tumblr launched in 2007, then Pinterest and Instagram three years later. Snapchat and Twitch came a year later, in 2011. The popular dating app Tinder, which features swiping, launched in 2012. Vine and Slack were released a year later, alongside 8chan, a decentralized English-language imageboard (4chan and 8chan will be discussed more in chapter 3 of this book). Social media transformed everyone into a creator, able to publish photos and videos on the web, especially with the advent of modern smartphones with the iPhone in 2007. By 2010, around five hundred billion images were uploaded to the web, while YouTube streamed over a billion videos daily (Gleick 2012, 397).

The now-famous message "Move fast and break things" was ubiquitous throughout Facebook's company culture, according to Wheeler, who toured the company's offices in the early 2000s: "The gospel was everywhere: in hallways, stairwells, break areas, and workspaces" (Wheeler 2019, prologue). Everything on Facebook's campus felt unfinished, uncannily mirroring the heady days of internet start-up culture (71).

When Facebook unveiled its Newsfeed in 2006, it seemed innocuous enough. There was just one problem. There was no way for users to gauge legitimate news stories from propaganda amid baby and pet photos, posts, and advertising. The world had become flattened, and the endless scroll beckoned. By then, the first smartphones had hit the market, and Newsfeed was optimized for smaller screens and interfaces.

Additionally, Facebook continued to iterate on its reaction emojis for everything in its Newsfeed, with new reactions—wow, love, ha-ha, sad, and angry—a flattening of human emotion mirroring the flattening of the information that whizzed by. Facebook's algorithm ranked emoji reactions five times higher than a mere "like"; therefore, the more profitable and viral content was also more controversial (Oremus and Merrill 2021). The platform also became addictive for users, as more highly emotive content kept them engaged with the site longer. Likes, clicks, and shares skyrocketed. According to the Pew Research Center, in 2021, 69 percent of Americans used Facebook, a number only bested by YouTube at 81 percent. Of those who used Facebook, 70 percent visited it daily, and almost half visited it more than that; 36 percent of Americans got their news from it (Gramlich 2021).

Facebook's competition, YouTube, had a rocky start but rose to prominence under Google's leadership. According to Mark Bergen, author of the 2022 tome *Like, Comment, Subscribe: Inside YouTube's Chaotic Rise to World Domination*: "YouTube [has] become one of the most dominant, influential, untamed, and successful media businesses on the planet. In less than two decades (Bergen 2022, 389)." Like other social media platforms, it has weathered its own scandals (Tufekci 2019) but remains dominant, with 2.5 billion users worldwide as of 2023 (Oberlo 2023). An entire generation has been raised watching YouTube instead of television (Bergen 2022, 384; Madrigal 2018). As the web transformed, so did online video. YouTube was the second most popular search engine after Google in 2023. Even as TikTok chipped into its profit margins in 2021, YouTube remained a key source of entertainment, information, and revenue. Influencers rose to prominence there. Indeed, the title of Bergen's book mimics the phrase of virtually every influencer at the end of their videos: "Like, comment, subscribe."

By the mid-2000s, the influencer industry was blossoming. During the 2008 economic recession, when many people were out of work but online, blogs were popular, and entrepreneurship was transferred to online pursuits. Emily Hund and Olivia Yallop describe the commodification of the self, the blurred line between labor and leisure, and the allure of authenticity that influencers promise, external to "traditional expertise" (Yallop 2021; Hund 2023). Seen on Instagram, YouTube, TikTok, Twitch, Facebook, and more, influencers build a personal brand to reach millions—it can be a lucrative and time-consuming job (Bancchor 2023). Wading through influencer culture, it can be challenging to know what is fact. Going back to Patrick Wilson's theory on cognitive authority, we might feel reassured about secondhand recommendations and rely on the heuristics of authority, credibility, and trustworthiness of the information. However, Wilson created his theory before the internet and certainly before influencers and the relativism they have unleashed. Influencers are a marketable asset. Their worth is in gaining sponsorships and followers, not in adhering to the truth. They do not necessarily fact-check their claims, which can be difficult to verify. With the information ecosystem replete with unverified or unverifiable claims from social media authorities, we can feel like we are in a hall of mirrors, a metaphor used by both Gleick (2012) and Tolentino (2019).

In this environment of trick mirrors, "selecting the genuine takes work . . . the answer to any question may arrive at the fingertips . . . and still we wonder what we know" (Gleick 2012, 426). Some of the reason for this confusion are the very systems of recommendation built into social media platforms. Alternately known as filter bubbles, echo chambers, rabbit holes, or feedback loops (Thorburn 2023), these terms refer to algorithms tailored to our likes, tastes, and preferences that limit what we see, who we socialize with online, what products we buy, and so on. Technology makes our world vast yet cliquish. The internet has made "everything close, and everything far, at the same time. This is why cyberspace can feel not just crowded but lonely" (Gleick 2012, 424–25).

A CONTINUING HALL OF MIRRORS

It was late 2022, and Elon Musk had just acquired Twitter (now called X). Over half of Twitter's content, disinformation, and hate speech moderation teams left or were fired (Ortutay and O'Brien 2022). Banned accounts were reinstated, increasing hate speech by over 500 percent (Associated Press 2022). As Twitter's demolition has continued, it can be hard to remember its dominant role in the information environment during the COVID-19 pandemic (Villasenor 2022) and various protest movements (Huang 2011, Emerging Technology from the arXiv, 2013; Australian National University Newsroom 2022).

In Tolentino's meditation on the internet, she muses on its transformation and, in turn, our own: "Platforms that promised connection began inducing mass alienation. The freedom promised by the internet started to seem like something whose greatest potential lay in the realm of misuse" (Tolentino 2019, 7). In building an ecosystem that monetizes the self and exploits attention, avoiding the world the internet has created can be hard, if not impossible. Tolentino and Wheeler make this difficulty abundantly clear—from an economic standpoint to a personal newsgathering one. How does the internet distort our sense of reality and blur opinion and verified fact? "Everywhere, the true rubs shoulders with the false" (Gleick 2012, 419). How does the internet teach us to overvalue our opinions, talk only to those who agree, and incentivize us to dive deeper down the rabbit holes of misinformation? The rest of this book will explore these questions in more depth. In 2020, a much-anticipated Project Information Literacy Algorithms study was released, with a memorable quote by a student: "It's a horrible totalitarian hellscape, but it's kind of the best we can reasonably expect" (Head, Fister, and MacMillan 2022). Is it, though? As librarians and educators, let us work together to build the tools, resources, skills, and dispositions with which we can equip tomorrow's learners so that they may expect better, create better systems, and better navigate an information society that will continue to evolve rapidly.

2

Understanding Information Disorder

In the bleak, empty days of the pandemic Katie spent a lot of time, as did many, doomscrolling through social media and relentlessly refreshing government websites for updated numbers. As the months went on, however, things on her feed got very weird. "The entire pandemic was planned!" asserted a mom she barely knew from her son's social circle. "Masks are only making us sicker from breathing recycled air!" screamed another mom. Neither of them are scientists. A good friend she had known for years claimed that her mother-in-law's death certificate included COVID "just for the money they will get." The "live science" of the ongoing pandemic meant that sometimes information would be superseded or shifted as new data emerged. The changing recommendations would then be shared across social media, but often mockingly: "They don't know what they are doing"; "It's clear they are just trying to control us or withhold the real story." What was happening? How was so much bad information being spread so widely?

In the early days of the internet, it was much easier for sketchy content to be something about which one could say, "I know it when I see it." Gimmicky banners, poorly designed pages, an overload of links and pop-ups—all those visual cues instantly signaled the user that they had stumbled upon something that was not, perhaps, the finest available information. We are in a new age, however, in which anyone and everyone can have a respectable-looking platform through which to sell their own unique snake oils. As content "goes viral" on social media, or as rumors are shared by even presumably reputable news organizations, the blurring of truth gets worse, and the shaping of society by disordered information starts to have very real consequences. What *is* information disorder? How and why is it produced? How, exactly, did we even get here? These questions, of course, could be entire volumes on their own, but this chapter will attempt to provide a succinct summary of the key issues.

DEFINING INFORMATION DISORDER

Our Information Age is one in which affordable, connected, and social technologies allow for almost anyone in the world to locate, access, use, create, and share information that is immediately accessible to others. Hanson writes of this information environment that it is "often characterized by the speed of the exchange of information as well as the social capital it has for the user; that is, the value of the information is established by the person who receives and uses (or chooses not to use) it" (Hanson 2016, 207). This definition, with its emphasis on the social capital of information, has important implications, as the ability of the user to define for themselves what "good" or "important" information means has pivotal consequences for the information landscape. As Lewandowski and van der Linden describe it, the plethora of bad information out there "undermines democracy by calling into question the knowability of information altogether" (Lewandowsky and van der Linden 2021). The combination of access to information and the amount of information available to even a casual user of technology is unprecedented in human history, and is not without its consequences.

Much ado has been made about "fake news," the "infodemic," and misinformation—so much so, in fact, that these terms have been stripped of all value. One journalist estimated that President Donald Trump used the term "fake news" on Twitter 596 times, as of late 2019 (McAfee 2020, 17). Social media fact-check warnings and other flags put in place to help users distinguish credible from non-credible information sources may help, but it also may be that by that point the damage has been done (Hameleers 2022; Vinhas and Bastos 2022). While everyone seems to be in agreement that "Houston, we have a problem"—it is growing ever more difficult to distinctly and meaningfully define that problem.

A Council of Europe report by Claire Wardle and Hossein Derakshan (2017), *Information Disorder: Toward an Interdisciplinary Framework for Research and Policy Making*, provides a framework for understanding information disorder. In their analysis of information disorder and information pollution in our society, the authors defined three levels of information pollution:

- Mis-information is when false information is shared, but no harm is meant.
- Dis-information is when false information is knowingly shared to cause harm.
- Mal-information is when genuine information is shared to cause harm, often by moving into the public sphere information designed to stay private (5).

Misinformation, the most benign of the three, often presents as rumors or speculation on current events. Sometimes it is disguised; for example, a "native ad" on a reputable site—if you've scrolled through a news site recently and come across a strange section that includes product recommendations and such, you've seen these. They are usually labeled in tiny print as "sponsored content," but many people may not see or know about this red flag for biased material, because they look so much like the actual news stories.

Users—accustomed to scrolling, liking, and sharing quickly in the social media timeline—usually do not take the time to vet content that they are sharing, relying instead on the shortcuts of cognitive authority ("I trust this person's content because I know them," etc.). The flattening of expertise on the internet also indulges the temptation to expound one's opinion, no matter the topic; the social sharing of those posted opinions then turns an idle musing from the average citizen into internet gospel. The internet newsletter *Garbage Day* astutely pointed this trend out during the early days of Russia's invasion of Ukraine:

> Online platforms flatten the content uploaded to them, assigning engagement metrics to videos of shelled cities and fleeing civilians, prompting other users to share or comment or, worse, find their own content to add to the trending topic. The hashtag #nuclearwar is trending on Twitter right now. If you click in on it, it shows you the top content tagged #nuclearwar. If you click on one of the posts, in giant letters, Twitter asks you to "tweet your reply." What's your take on nuclear annihilation, the bird site wonders thoughtlessly. (Broderick 2022)

Renée DiResta further clarifies that misinformation "is a word that's generally used to mean things that are inadvertently wrong," with the distinction that much of the time the information is being shared "with a highly altruistic motivation. [The sharers] want to inform their community" (Beres et al. 2023).

In contrast, mal- and disinformation are created and often proliferated with nefarious intent. The scope of these two can be as small as the doxing or internet bullying of a personal enemy, or as large as the strategic use of troll farms by Russia to destabilize political enemies (Kelly and Samules 2019; Meister 2016). Malinformation, as defined by Wardle and Derakshan, contains at least a kernel of truth, but that truth is often distorted or cherry-picked to advance a harmful agenda. Wardle and Derakshan assert that disinformation is completely falsified, a problem that has always existed but has reached new heights as artificial intelligence (AI) and deepfake technologies spread and evolve.

Wardle and Deraksham further assert that information content is not the only concern when considering information disorder. The elements of information spread need to be considered: the information producer, or "agent"; the information message itself; and the consumer of the information, or "interpreter." All three collude to perpetuate information pollution in the information landscape (Wardle and Derakshan 2017, 22). Due to the emphatically affective nature of the information landscape, the subjective interpretation of even an innocuous piece of information can serve to create information disorder; this occurs often in the context of conspiracy ideation. Xie (2021) explores this aspect of the information landscape further, explaining that

> [i]n other words, the information is *the interpretive meaning* of the content together with any relevant contextual information available to the recipients. [. . .] Consequentially [*sic*], people come to different conclusions and have varied responses even with the same information. (12, emphasis added)

Subjective interpretation of information builds on the production and dissemination process, and all should be considered together: "[I]t's important to consider the different phases of an instance of information disorder alongside its elements, because the agent that creates the content is often fundamentally different from the agent who produces it" (Wardle and Derakshan, 2017, 23). Wardle and Derekshan explore the Russian troll farms in this context: Writers might create the disinformation content, which is then shared out by the agentic social media troll accounts. The consumer/interpreter of the message then shares or reproduces the content, making changes or editorializing, sharing the new version, and continuing the cycle. And the driver of the sharing part of the cycle? More often than not, it is rage.

AFFECTIVE STATES AND THEIR DISCONTENTS

Affect often is equated with emotion, but it includes so much more: all of the minor and major forces that act upon a being. It is the relation in relationship, the moment of connection as a concept is understood, "where the patho-logy [*sic*] of a body meets the pedagogy of an affective world" (Gregg and Siegworth 2010, 12). Theorists speak of it as a neutrality or a "bloom-space," a thing that is as-yet rather than as-is:

> Affect marks a body's *belonging* to a world of encounters or; a world's belonging to a body of encounters but also, in *non-belonging*, through all those far sadder (de)compositions of mutual in-compossibilities [*sic*]. Always there are ambiguous or "mixed" encounters that impinge and extrude for worse and for better, but (most usually) in-between. (Gregg and Siegworth 2010, 2)

There does seem to be a consensus that the cognitive and the emotional, or the emotional aspect of affect, are intertwined and occur *simultaneously* in response to sensory input and thinking; in other words, we react before we fully evaluate (if we ever do) (Beane 1990; Davidson 2003). Understanding this is critical to being able to identify information disordered content—pausing and parsing our emotional reactions is a crucial first step.

It is important to acknowledge additional research connections between affect and our current information landscape. Brian Massumi (2010) writes of "The Future Birth of the Affective Fact," connecting the concept of threat and, specifically, future threat, as one that affects information consumption and behavior in the present (and past):

> The could-have/would-have logic works both ways. If the threat does not materialize, it still always would have if it could have. If the threat does materialize, then it just goes to show that the future potential for what happened had really been there in the past. In this case, the preemptive action is retroactively legitimated by future actual facts (56).

Massumi opens his essay by describing a newspaper headline in the early 2000s screaming about "the next pandemic"—a threat that had no present reality (post-2020, many of us read this with very real panic), and yet was newsworthy because of the emotion-driven information landscape. This idea of affect reaching forward and backward in time and space is extremely relevant when considering how emotion-driven algorithms and social sharing function together to spread mis- and disinformation. Threat, completely imagined or not, is a major part of the disinformation landscape.

Threat is often connected to, and drives, *moral outrage* in the social media environment. Moral outrage "is a powerful emotion that motivates people to shame and punish wrongdoers" (Crockett 2017, 769) who have transgressed, or are perceived to have transgressed, a moral norm. The expression of moral outrage serves to identify the outraged as a conformist, part of the "in-group," and to collectively shame and punish the outlier. Moral outrage is a strong emotion. It hearkens back to our prehistoric tribal past when strong group identity meant better survival. And, as Max Fisher (2022a) perceptively notes, because this ingrained behavior is so strong, it can be and has been manipulated:

> Which is exactly what despots, extremists, and propagandists have learned to do, rallying people to their side by triggering outrage—often at some scapegoat or imagined wrongdoer. What would happen when, inevitably, social platforms learned to do the same? (87)

While many put the blame squarely on social media algorithms for our information-disordered mess, the truth is that humans are biologically and culturally primed for the manipulations of social media. In other words, the social media environment with its memes, its videos, and its easily (some say addictively) scrollable timelines, is perfectly designed to take advantage of our foibles.

HOW DID WE GET HERE?

Sensationalism, of course, is not new, and anyone who remembers the lurid covers of the *Weekly World News* at checkout stands of the past will understand that even the most outlandish material—probably because it is so outlandish—will sell. The more things change, the more they stay the same (Brotherton 2020). The television and social media landscapes have been shaped around this profit ideal, with outrage and opinion prioritized over ethical journalism.

> Americans now consume the news the way they watch football, baseball, or even professional wrestling. They tune in to hear their favorite host or to hiss at the person reading the teleprompter as they explain what happened on a given day in Washington. (Zelizer 2017, 176)

With the rise of cable news channels beginning in the 1980s, creating more competition, and the repeal of the Fairness Doctrine in 1987 (which until that time had provided at least some checks on wild partisanship in the news media), the hallowed fourth estate of journalism was broken in the name of profit; as Dan Pfeffer (2022) opines, "[T]he traditional media, which are charged with telling the story, are culturally and psychologically unable to do so" (21). News became about personalities, bombastic overproduction, and, tellingly, outrage. All social media had to do was pick up the baton.

In *Filling the Void: Emotion, Capitalism & Social Media*, Marcus Gilroy-Ware (2017) discusses the use of humor and other affective tactics used by traditional media to obtain and retain viewers, noting especially the "sidebar of shame" on the *Daily Mail*'s website, one of the most popular news sites in the world (43). Humans are drawn to content that seizes us emotionally, whether that be cat videos or, much further down the rabbit hole, stories of children being victimized by a global satanic cult. Social media companies have taken the lessons learned from psychology and traditional media and capitalized on them in a big way, creating a global industry worth billions and engineering a new way of being in the process:

> An ever-growing pool of evidence, gathered by dozens of academics, reporters, whistleblowers, and concerned citizens, suggests that its impact is far more profound. This technology exerts such a powerful pull on our psychology and our identity, and is so pervasive in our lives, that it changes how we think, behave, and relate to one another. (Fisher 2022a, 11).

The effect, multiplied across billions of users, has been to change society itself.

Capitalism drives social media, which is easy to forget when the services are "free" to users and they have effectively integrated so fully into our lives. The early promises of social media were many: more connectedness, a more informed public. And yet, the reality has been a nightmare: political instability, radicalization, epistemic bubbles, and an overall disconnection from reality and each other reality and each other. To drive engagement and maximize the time people spend on social media platforms, the companies have incorporated the infamous algorithms to customize each user's experience on the site, showing them what the algorithms think they will most want to see, or rather, what would promote the most engagement. The algorithms exploit our innate need to belong, our need to feel part of an "in-group" (which presupposes an external Other), our need to enforce societal mores, and our need to be stimulated. In between several horrifying examples of how social media outrage has spilled over into reality to disastrous and deadly consequences, Max Fisher (2022) makes the following observation:

> Social media, by bombarding users with fast-moving social stimuli, pushed them to rely on quick-twitch social intuition over deliberative reason. All people contain the capacity for both, as well as the potential for the former to overwhelm the latter, which is often how misinformation spreads. And platforms compound the effect by framing all news and information within high-stakes social contexts. (152)

Perhaps more terrifying, the algorithms typically rely on machine learning, meaning roughly that once it is put in place, an algorithm is designed to learn from its successes and adjust itself accordingly. As a result, the engineers of social media, those who are supposed to be in control, might have very little idea what is going on behind the curtain (Fisher 2022a, 105). The medium massages the message, and the message is designed to promote "incentives and conditions of interaction for content creators that are similar to markets" (Golino 2021). The more the algorithm can keep you online, the more money the platform makes.

There are thousands of resources out there that explore in detail the how and the why of the algorithmic news feed on social media platforms and its effects; within those are several key ideas from psychology, sociology, and media studies that are important to understand when considering our information environment and why information disorder is so prevalent, which are briefly explored below.

THE PSYCHOLOGY OF SOCIAL MEDIA AND INFORMATION DISORDER

Compensatory Internet Use

The anxieties of modern life often drive people to escapism, which can take the form of unhealthy coping mechanisms such as alcohol, drugs, food addiction, or—the internet. Kardefelt-Winther proposed the compensatory internet use theory in 2014, after finding that the literature on internet addiction did not sufficiently explore the motivations or rewards for users that drive problematic internet use, writing, "Exploring motivations in conjunction with psychosocial well-being allows us to elaborate on *why* someone goes online by contextualizing the motivation for excessive use in the presence of psychosocial problems" (353). Social media provides compensations for users that they cannot (or feel they cannot) obtain in their "real" lives; as the world collectively learned during the COVID-19 pandemic, when other avenues of connection are unavailable, social media can allow users to maintain a semblance of socialization (Zhao and Zhou 2021).

CONFIRMATION BIAS AND THE ILLUSORY TRUTH EFFECT

As will be explored throughout this book, our brains are lazy and prefer short-cuts; confirmation bias and the illusory truth effect are just two biological heuristics that are relevant to the spread of information disorder. Confirmation bias, defined as "a type of cognitive bias in which one tends to look only for evidence that confirms one's beliefs and to ignore or pay less attention to evidence that contradicts one's beliefs" (Sullivan et al. 2009) is a pervasive tenet of information disorder. News and research are cherry-picked and taken out of context, bent to fit the users' preconceived notions; for example, despite a quote being entirely miscontextualized (or even falsified), the reference allows for a veneer of trustworthiness. The factoid reinforces the bias; the bias is confirmed. No further critical thought is needed.

The sharing of information that affirms our biases then plays into another neurological quirk: the illusory truth effect. Put simply, the more times people are exposed to a piece of information, the more they are likely to believe that information is true (Arkes, Hackett, and Boehm 1989). The pervasive parental directive to eat more carrots because they will help with eyesight is one example of this effect—this folk wisdom dates to an intentionally fake World War II propaganda campaign, and yet how many of us pat ourselves on the back for getting our vitamin A (Smith 2013)? Even when we know better, we can still be victims of this psychological card trick: A recent study found that "prior knowledge does not protect against illusory truth. [. . .] In other words, simply knowing that something isn't true is no guarantee that you won't be duped by a false headline when it's repeated over and over" (van der Linden 2023, 21–22).

Importantly for the consideration of information disorder's spread, a 2023 study found that the illusory truth effect also drives information sharing; having seen a piece of information previously, users are more likely to then share that information, believing it to be true, rather than pausing to properly evaluate the information (Vellani et al. 2023). The phenomenon of "going viral" thus becomes a self-feeding loop—a post is seen by a user, then shared by that user because it is familiar, and the cycle repeats.

SOCIAL IDENTITY THEORY AND THE SOCIAL VALIDATION FEEDBACK LOOP

Social identity theory, first developed in the 1960s by Henri Tajfel, posits that bias and divisiveness can, in a social setting, be attributed to groupthink rather than individual personalities. Experimentation has shown that "mere categorization into groups can produce a distinctly consequential social identity, and that social identity based upon group membership is the psychological foundation of intergroup conflict" (Callero 2007). In the social media environment, Lüders, Dinkelberg, and Quayle argue that "humans (in interaction with algorithms) strategically exploit the affordances of online platforms to pursue social identity goals," specifying that the affordances allow users to "1) connect large numbers of users and build up efficient online communities, 2) consensualize group-normative representations, and 3) express and align emotions" (Lüders, Dinkelberg, and Quayle 2022, 3–4). Although much of this research is still new, the emerging picture seems to be that online groups, harnessing the anonymity or constructed selves of online personas, become more salient than the actual individual characteristics for the group members, and may in turn affect offline behavior.

Social media companies have designed themselves around social identity theory—consider Facebook Groups, for example—and utilize (among other things) what psychologists term a "variable reinforcement schedule" to ensure that users stay engaged. If your phone buzzes in your pocket and it's a friendly notification from Facebook that someone has liked one of your comments, that provides you with a small hit of dopamine that makes you want to keep engaging. Much like Pavlov's infamous canine, "we are conditioned neurologically to want to think about that like or that share. And it comes on a variable reinforcement schedule, meaning we don't know when the next ping is going to come" (Martin 2020). The variable reinforcement schedule trains our brains to keep checking in on the app, keep scrolling, keep commenting. The "us vs. them" mentality of social identity theory coalesces and is fed by filter bubbles and epistemic echo chambers—amplifying and weaponizing information disorder in the process.

STATUS THREAT

The groupthink of social identity theory is relevant to another useful term from psychological and sociological research—status threat. In exploring the election of Donald Trump in 2016, Diana C. Mutz (2018) attributed much of his popular support to status threat, a condition in which

> perceived threat makes status quo, hierarchical social and political arrangements more attractive. Thus, conservatism surges along with a nostalgia for the stable hierarchies of the past. Perceived threat also triggers defense of the dominant ingroup, a greater emphasis on the importance of conformity to group norms, and increased outgroup negativity. It

is psychologically valuable to see one's self as part of a dominant group; therefore, when group members feel threatened, this prompts defensive reactions. (4331)

As mentioned above, threat is an extremely relevant affective motivator. In the United States, the dominant culture has been white, male, and Christian for much of its history, and since World War II the United States has been a dominant global power—and yet, as Mutz notes, demographic shifts, globalization, and the perceived rise in power of other nations makes the dominant group very uneasy. They feel their status is threatened—and they don't like it: "For white Americans, the political consequences of racial and global status threat seem to point in similar directions with respect to issue positions: opposition to immigration, rejection of international trade relationships, and perceptions of China as a threat to American wellbeing" (Mutz 2018, 4332). Misinformation and disinformation about the Others, spread through the affordances of social media, are welcomed wholeheartedly by followers as confirmation and affirmation of their unease, subverting any critical analysis of the information that may have otherwise occurred.

THE NEW TOOLS OF INFORMATION DISORDER: ARTIFICIAL INTELLIGENCE AND DEEPFAKES[1]

Doctored and falsified audiovisual media is nothing new—with the advent and popularity of photography came staged Civil War photographs (McBurney 1999), "spirit" photography, and other tricks to subvert the camera's objective eye, and as video technologies advanced, so did special effects. As our technological capabilities grow, however, new and troubling tools have arisen, which rely on artificial intelligence (AI) and allow users to manufacture convincing video and audio material. "Deepfakes," as they are known, "are the most prominent form of what's being called 'synthetic media': images, sound and video that appear to have been created through traditional means but that have, in fact, been constructed by complex software" (Briggs and Moran 2021). Deepfakes have been around for several years, with a popular forum on Reddit in 2017, in which users swapped the heads of female celebrities onto pornographic content, often cited as one of the first mainstream manifestations of their disinformation capabilities. A popular TikTok channel, deeptomcruise (https://www.tiktok.com/@deeptomcruise/) provides a more family-friendly demonstration of deepfake capabilities.

With a social media economy dependent on generating increasingly outrageous content in order to get coveted likes and shares, the rise of numerous deepfake technologies that are increasingly user-friendly for those with little technological skills has many concerned:

What makes deepfake videos especially worrisome is the relative ease and accessibility with which adverse actors can manipulate moving images. With virtually no technical expertise, individuals can produce untraceable, deceptive videos and distribute them online from almost anywhere in the world. Altered videos have the power to propel a terrorist group's agenda or reword a politician's speech. (Nour and Gelfand 2022)

On Monday, June 5, 2023, Russian television, radio, and social media were hacked and a deepfake was spread that depicted Vladimir Putin declaring martial law and announcing that Ukraine had invaded (J. Jones 2023). Just one of numerous examples of political deepfakes, this represents a particularly concerning incident, as it was spread via official, trusted (and apparently not secure enough) channels. Some of our own media entities doubtlessly have similar security flaws, adding an additional layer to the concern that journalists and politicians have already voiced about the potential for (and reality of) the misuse of these technologies. Rob Brotherton does provide a more reassuring view of these technologies, noting that similar fears have arisen each time new tools, such as Photoshop, were developed and made commercially available; people adapt and, in the end, "just aren't as gullible as the feverish concern about deepfakes makes out" (Brotherton 2020, 219).

In addition to fake video content, textual tools such as ChatGPT, which rose to prominence after its launch in late 2022, can be used to create and spread false information, often without the users realizing they are doing so. ChatGPT, like many AI tools, is programmed to keep the user engaged and happy (sound familiar?) and may resort to outright storytelling to do so. Already many who are not technologically literate have suffered the consequences—such as an unfortunate lawyer who relied on ChatGPT, thinking it was just another research tool, and was caught citing fake cases in court (Bohannon 2023). With the additional problem of demonstrated racial, political, and other biases in these systems (Alba 2022; Knight 2023), the dangers for how these tools could contribute to the information-disordered landscape only grow (and will be explored in detail in chapter 12).

Although the state of today's information landscape may be overwhelming, the old adage "knowledge is power" still holds. By continuing to monitor and understand the information landscape, and teach others about the pitfalls, we can create a more information-literate and metaliterate society.

NOTE

1. Katie would like to acknowledge her LIB2500 students and their "information age explorations" presentations for many of the sources used in this section, including but not limited to Katelyn Cavenaugh, Ashton Rains, and Natalya Reid.

3

Conspiracy Theories and the Rise of the Superconspiracy QAnon

It was dusk, and Stephanie and her husband were walking their dog. Rounding the corner, they met a dark-haired woman, whom we will call Shannon, with a standard poodle. She was friendly, and immediately the dogs were friends. As the dogs frolicked, the humans began to chat—the usual things. A pleasant feeling settled over them on the warm fall night: new dog playmates, new friends. Suddenly, Shannon mentioned, "Have you heard of the ReAwaken America Tour?" Stephanie looked at her partner. She knew, from her research, this was QAnon. Her heart sped up, but she hoped her face remained blank. She'd never been very good at keeping a poker face. Her partner said, "Uhhh, no, I don't think so." Shannon explained, "Well. It's big. With a lot of important people. A lot of bad things are happening, even to Christians. They will be surprised when they discover the bad things that are happening. Like satanic abuse. And linked to our space programs and things." Stephanie counted her heartbeats while anxiously watching her, concentrating on keeping that poker face. Her husband kept saying "uh-huh" like a metronome. This can't be happening, she thought. Shannon detailed how her life had unraveled from one thing to another, how she planned to relocate to Florida, and how she was recruited to work for an alternative news network because the mainstream media is "a part of it." Before departing, she handed Stephanie a business card. She used to be a lawyer with a private practice. They had chatted for three hours.

When we encounter people espousing conspiracy theories, knowing how best to respond can be difficult. Here, we introduce concepts to ground us on that journey. We also introduce the superconspiracy QAnon, to which Shannon obliquely referred. Readers may have become better acquainted with QAnon since the January 6, 2021, U.S. Capitol insurrection, when Americans were introduced to the "QAnon Shaman," Jacob Chansley.

This chapter discusses the differences between *conspiracies*—real-life collusions between people who sometimes get charged and tried before the law—and conspiracy *theories*, which are unproven, larger-than-life plots between obscure groups. Conspiracy theories are more akin to whispered rumors around the proverbial water cooler, even if they have a nugget of truth. What is so engaging about conspiracy theories? Why are they so enthralling? In this chapter, we touch on the answers to these questions by exploring the psychological concepts of conspiracism and conspiracy ideation and how these concepts interact with conspiracy theories.

CONSPIRACIES VERSUS CONSPIRACY THEORIES

The discourse surrounding conspiracy theories often becomes convoluted: When does something move from a conspiracy to a conspiracy theory? As scholar Michael Barkun (2003) has observed: "Despite the frequency with which conspiracy beliefs have been discussed . . . , the term conspiracy itself has often been left undefined, as though its meaning were self-evident" (3). Here we examine conspiracies, including their legal definitions as verifiable and corroborated facts that are proven through evidence and upheld through the historical record. We compare these to conspiracy theories, which are unverifiable, overarching narratives claiming that individuals or groups exert inexplicable power over events, often in multiple places across time and space, in one sinister, secretive plot. Then, we investigate why conspiracy theories appeal to followers. Lastly, we examine the specific traits of conspiracism.

The word *conspiracy* derives from the Latin term *conspiratio*, with the word coming into English during the Middle English period in Chaucer (Oxford English Dictionary 2023). Today, the free Wex Legal Dictionary provided by Cornell University's Legal Information Institute defines a conspiracy as "an agreement between two or more people to commit an illegal act, along with an intent to achieve the agreement's goal" (Legal Information Institute, 2022).

Interestingly, the terms *conspiracy theory* and *conspiracy theorist* did not appear in English until the twentieth century (Oxford English Dictionary, 2023). Conspiracy theory was first used in 1909, and conspiracy theorist in 1964 (Oxford English Dictionary 2023). Conspiracy theories move the needle from the realm of fact to that of the fanciful. While a conspiracy is a plot that necessitates two or more people colluding in secret, a conspiracy theory assumes that this group of people has the power to influence unexplained events—behind closed doors. According to the Oxford English Dictionary, this collusion is "typically political in motivation and oppressive in intent" (Oxford English Dictionary 2023).

Authors of a 2022 annual review on conspiracy theories, Karen Douglas and Robbie Sutton, offer that conspiracy theories are "social constructs" because they are "moral, even political claim[s] about what the public should believe" (Douglas and Sutton 2022, 286). Essential to their argument is that conspiracy theories "do not merely represent social realities but have the potential to create them" through proliferation, perpetuation toward marginalized communities, and collective sense-making (286). They define conspiracy theories as beliefs comprising claims in which "two or more actors have coordinated in secret to achieve an outcome . . . of public interest, but not of public knowledge" (287).

Psychologist Rob Brotherton further provides a rubric to identify conspiracy theories. First, they are unverified claims at odds with the mainstream consensus, and they grow and thrive *because* of their oppositional nature: "In conspiracist rhetoric, the mainstream explanation is usually termed the official story, with 'official' serving as a disparaging label for the facts" (Brotherton 2013, 10). Conspiracy theories are sensationalistic and assume everything is intentional, nothing is coincidental, and the world is divided into "good . . . struggling against evil" (Brotherton 2017, 11). They are built around low standards of evidence or "gaps or ambiguities in knowledge," such as perceived "unanswered questions remaining to be solved" (12). Lastly, conspiracy theories are epistemically self-insulating "against questioning or correction," as seen in the phenomenon known as "cascade logic," which implicates more people and data the longer it exists (12). The most successful conspiracy theories morph and evolve to stay relevant to followers.

Michael Barkun, in his 2003 foundational book, *A Culture of Conspiracy: Apocalyptic Visions in Contemporary America*, builds on this last point. He helpfully provides a framework for conspiracy theories, providing three categorical distinctions, which we have used in our previous research (Beene and Greer 2023). We rely on this framework again here, especially in considering the phenomenon of QAnon. Event conspiracies are those limited to a discrete occurrence or set of circumstances, with one of the most famous examples being the Kennedy assassination (Barkun 2003, 6). Systemic conspiracies, on the other hand, are those conspiracies with "broad goals usually conceived as securing control over a country, a region, or the world," and "while the goals are sweeping, the conspiratorial machinery is generally simple: a single, evil organization implements a plan to infiltrate and subvert existing institutions" (6). According to Barkun, famous systemic conspiracies surround the alleged machinations of Jews, Freemasons, the Catholic Church, international capitalists, and communism (6). Superconspiracies, then, are "conspiratorial constructs" in which "event and systemic conspiracies are joined in complex ways so that conspiracies come to be nested within one another" (6). Super-conspiracies are complex, evolving, and amorphous belief systems in which a "distant but all-powerful evil force" manipulates "lesser conspiratorial actors . . . invisible and operating in secrecy" (6).

CONSPIRACISM AND CONSPIRACY IDEATION

The conspiracist worldview draws directly from these characteristics and frameworks. Barkun explains that a conspiracist worldview implies a "universe governed by design rather than by randomness" (Barkun 2003, 4). As described by Douglas et al., this assumption of agency helps us understand why there is a tendency for conspiracy theorists to perceive intentionality where none is likely to exist (Douglas et al., 2016).

According to the conspiracist lens, nothing is as it seems; conspirators obfuscate their identities, activities, and/or the truth, and the appearance of innocence does not guarantee that anyone or anything is benign (Barkun 2003, 4). Since conspiracy theories are inherently unproven, the theory is always a work in progress. According to the conspiracist worldview, a lack of evidence alludes to truth, and "an outright denial by the accused conspirators" can further bolster their assurance of their guilt (Brotherton 2017, 42). Conspiracy theories lack evidential trace and assume the gullibility of both followers and the public, lacking consideration of other causes for events (Douglas and Sutton 2022). Everything is connected, and patterns are everywhere: "The conspiracy theorist must engage in a constant process of linkage and correlation to map the hidden correlations" (Barkun 2003, 4). Seeking out such patterns is human nature, but conspiracists take it further—scholars have upheld that conspiracists seek connections and causal relationships between random occurrences (Wagner-Egger et al. 2018). In his book *Suspicious Minds: Why We Believe Conspiracy Theories*, Brotherton calls this "anomaly hunting," where each anomaly is imbued with "profound significance" (Brotherton 2017, 40–41).

Thus, a suspicious mindset is necessary for conspiracism to gestate, defined by paranoia and distrust. Those who fall prey to one conspiracy theory tend to believe in others (Brotherton, 2017, 49). Likewise, someone who doubts one may doubt others. According to psychologist Ted Goertzel (1994), the content of a conspiracy theory matters less than the fact that it is one. Conspiracy theories seem to act as self-perpetuating belief systems, where the mere belief in the plausibility of one will open the door to others, with the opposite also being true.

In their dramatic and sweeping accounts, conspiracy theories promise followers they will "expose some remarkable and hitherto unknown 'truth' about plot[s] with nefarious and threatening aims" (Byford 2011). Like true-crime aficionados and amateur sleuths, conspiracy theorists follow tantalizing clues, unlocking bits of mysteries. Armed with insider knowledge and fighting perceived injustice, followers can feel they are on a unique quest. Researchers have found a correlation between people with a chronic need to feel unique and their belief in conspiracy theories (Lantian et al. 2017).

In contrast to the drive for uniqueness and individualism, the need for relationships and belonging is human nature. This inclination to belong to a group can also be a powerful motivator to find others with similar beliefs, including those with like-minded conspiratorial leanings. It has become easier in our interconnected, socially networked, mobile world.

Beyond the social web, conspiracy theories lure people in because they often contain nuggets of truth. And because of conspiracists' relentless theorizing, scholar Joseph Uscinski points out, some of these theories have been proven true (Uscinski 2018). Some scholars have shown that marginalized communities with a warranted distrust of authorities (Fredericks et al. 2022) may be particularly prone to conspiracy ideation, such as Black Americans' vaccination suspicions in light of ethical misconduct in examples such as the Tuskegee syphilis study or Henrietta Lacks's cell line (Parsons et al. 1999; Simmons and Parsons 2005).

Importantly, Brotherton and other psychologists emphasize that conspiracy ideation falls along a spectrum, from those beginning their exploration into conspiracy theories to devotees who reject all mainstream accounts (Pierre 2020). Skepticism, like belief, is not binary. Individuals' beliefs in conspiracy theories depend on whether and how they and others in their communities have been exposed to these ideas, and what and how alternative theories are made available to them (Pierre, August 21, 2020).

THE SUPERCONSPIRACY *DU JOUR:* QANON

QAnon began as a conspiratorial worldview claiming that an underground cabal of Satan-worshiping pedophiles and sex-trafficking elites, primarily leftists with globalist agendas, including Democrats and celebrities, were working against former president Trump and his allies. It has since morphed and evolved, spreading globally. Though this phenomenon has capitalized on the affordances of the internet and social media, it has recycled far older tropes that lay dormant in American conspiratorial culture (which are explored further in chapter 7) (Uscinski and Parent 2014; Aaronovich 2010; Walker 2013). The zeitgeist of the last eight years further perpetuated QAnon, which has incorporated numerous other conspiracy theories and tropes. As of this writing, the world is grappling with the end of the COVID-19 pandemic (Associated Press, May 5, 2023), existential climate change (Shaftel, n.d.), inequity (Turchin 2023), backsliding democratic institutions (Fisher 2022b), and artificial intelligence (Allyn 2023). It may not be surprising that conspiracy theories are thriving.

Conspiracy theories themselves may not be new, but the internet has enabled fringe thinkers to "find their people," and "the power of the social web" allows groups to spread from "a niche or regionally-specific cult to a global movement" (Kotsonis and Brooks, 2020). One of the more concerning aspects of QAnon has been its ability to morph as it gathers followers, a defining feature of superconspiracies (Barkun 2003).

FROM A MESSAGE BOARD TO A MOVEMENT

In our previous research, we traced the rise of the QAnon movement up to the moment before the January 6, 2021, Capitol insurrection (Beene and Greer 2021). The following is an abbreviated synopsis of that previous research, updated for where QAnon stands in summer 2023.

In the early days of the internet, QAnon was born on an image message board called 4chan, where users posted anonymously as "anons." From 2003 to 2008, the chans stood in stark contrast to the burgeoning social media of the time. They are especially known for their /pol/ (politically incorrect) boards, which attracted self-described incels (involuntary celibate males), men's rights activists, White nationalists, conspiracy theorists, and angry, disaffected young men defining themselves by their lack of employment and education (Beran 2019). From 2006 to 2015, several chan boards began competing for membership and prominence, much like other social media. In 2012, a programmer named Frederick Brennan launched a new unmoderated imageboard named 8chan (Beran 2019). The permissiveness led to exponential growth, with the type of members that other chan boards had disallowed. It also attracted the person (or persons) who would become Q.

In 2015, Brennan sold 8chan to Jim and Ron Watkins, who are QAnon enablers, minor political actors (View, Rockatansky, and Feeld 2022), fervent conspiracy theorists, and trolls (Vogt and Goldman 2020). A year after its sale, the chan boards were thrust into the limelight through a confluence of political mayhem and what became known as "pizzagate." Hillary Clinton's campaign manager, John Podesta, found his email account hacked, with its entire contents posted on 8chan. Infamously, a vigilante citizen stormed a pizzeria, Comet Ping Pong, with an AR-15, ready to free enslaved sex-trafficked children from a basement. Upon his arrest and discovering there were no children—and no basement—Edgar Maddison Welch responded that his "intel had not been one-hundred percent" (LaFrance 2020, 29). How are these two actions—a hacked email account and a vigilante arrest—connected?

An unfolding participatory conspiracy theory existed on the seedier side of the internet, where Welch increasingly spent his time. The 8chan community had begun to "decode" the emails, using CP as shorthand. CP had long stood for child pornography, but it now also stood for Clinton and Podesta, Comet Ping Pong, and cheese pizza (Beran 2019, 218). In the imageboard world of competitive memes and a race-to-the-bottom of distasteful jokes, "ordering cheese pizza" became shorthand for "ordering child pornography," which became inextricably linked with Clinton and Podesta and the pizza parlor. It took on a life of its own:

> To anyone remotely familiar with chan culture and its winking meme signals, it was clear that the "pizzagate" conspiracy theory was a joke. . . .

But remarkably, in a post-fact world where conspiracy was more fun and useful than reality, the report spread like all the other Clinton conspiracy theories [at the time]. . . . In this environment, it was easy to pick up the banner on Twitter and insist that pizzagate was real. (Beran 2019, 219)

In other words, insider jokes were the genesis of many of today's conspiracy theories.

In another example, these boards often served as gathering spots for anyone interested in Live Action Role Play (LARP) online, where users act out a role in a constructed and evolving script. In 2016, several participants were LARPing as government officials leaking secrets (e.g., HighlevelAnon, FBI-Anon, CIA-Anon, and White-House-Insider-Anon) (Vogt and Goldman 2020). Nobody paid much attention to a new member who "started posting on the /pol/ board, initially not giving any information about themselves, just posting these sort of bizarre polemics that were mostly comprised of rhetorical questions . . . with a paranoid whiff to them" (Goldman and Vogt 2018). The community dubbed the user Q for the top security Q clearance they claimed to have. In 2016, even Brennan, the inventor of 8chan, was incredulous: "When I first heard about Q, I just thought that it was . . . somebody having a laugh and tricking people . . . posting vague Nostradamus-like messages" (Vogt and Goldman 2020).

Because QAnon posted around sixty times over three or four days, the chan community took note, and the ideas began to spread. The posts were based around the premise that QAnon was an intelligence or military insider with "proof" that investigations into former president Trump were all a façade (Goldman and Vogt 2018). Former president Trump, the belief continued, was "a brilliant 4-dimensional chess player" engaged in a strategic prosecution of left-leaning elites who also "run a child sex and torture ring [and were] in collusion with basically every person who has been a part of a right-wing conspiracy over the last ten years" (Goldman and Vogt 2018). Uscinski asserts, "There's nothing new to [QAnon conspiracy theories], and in fact, it's just a bunch of other long-standing conspiracy theories mushed together into one" (Brooks et al. 2020, 25:44–25:45).

One of the core QAnon claims that has had staying power since 2016 is that indictments have already been handed down but are sealed, and that Trump and his allies have been tracking bad actors until the "Great Awakening." As QAnon followers converged around this messaging, some began proselytizing interpretations of Q's messages on mainstream social media. The QAnon movement jumped over to YouTube, where videos garnered millions of views, and Reddit boards gathered tens of thousands of members. QAnon spread to Facebook, Twitter, YouTube, Instagram, Telegram, and other social media platforms, sneaking into preexisting groups with seemingly harmless slogans like "Save the Children" (Roose 2020b). Disinformation expert Joan

Donovan describes QAnon as "a densely networked conspiracy theory that is extendible, adaptable, flexible and resilient to takedown" by social media platforms (Donovan 2020, para. 16).

Internet users continue to drive the conspiracy. Journalist Adrienne LaF-rance interviewed QAnon adherents to discover that some spent six hours per day poring over Q's messages for clues to the conspiracy puzzle. "The purpose of this whole community is [that] you have to do your own research . . . and that makes this theory something you can tailor to fit whatever you want it to be" (LaFrance, 2020). Perhaps because it invites people to participate in a conspiratorial game that conjoins pieces of the world in a maddening, never-ending distortion, what started as one conspiracy theory quickly morphed into something more sinister: a superconspiracy.

EVERYTHING, EVERYWHERE, ALL AT ONCE: QANON BECOMES A SUPERCONSPIRACY

While the QAnon movement began as obscure messages posted on the internet's fringe, it spread rapidly in eight years, capitalizing on people's "greatest dreams, impulses, and worst nightmares" (Goldman and Vogt 2018). By September 2020, polling showed that almost half (47 percent) of Americans said they had heard of QAnon (Mitchell et al. 2020). QAnon was as popular in the United States as major religions by May 2021 (Russonello 2021). By the end of November 2022, QAnon had seeped into almost every demographic and sphere of American life, making the core tenets of its worldview impossible to escape (PRRI 2022).

Returning to Barkun's definition, superconspiracies exist because they morph and evolve to stay relevant. More than any current conspiracy theory, QAnon has exploded on the scene as a movement, a worldview, a conspiracy of everything (Rothschild 2021). Are you against vaccinations? QAnon's got a home for you. Have you always had a sneaking suspicion that the Earth is flat? Welcome to QAnon. Have you ever been suspicious of Catholics? What about the Jews? Or elites? Let QAnon tell you what's *really* going on. There is a gateway for everyone. Jacob Chansley, the now-infamous "QAnon Shaman," was known before the January 6, 2021, storming of the U.S. Capitol as someone who was into New Age spirituality, alternative healing, and pseudoscience (Meltzer 2021). He was considered to be a little out there sometimes, but not dangerous (View, Rockatansky, and Feeld, 2023). Initially receiving one of the longest sentences for his role in the Capitol insurrection, he was released early from prison, partly on good behavior, partly for a mental health evaluation; since his release, he has started a podcast peddling Q-laced rhetoric and QAnon merchandise, and is running for a seat in Congress as a Libertarian (Kim 2023; Gilbert 2023; Roy 2024).

Fueled by the internet's particularities, the QAnon brand has become mainstream. As Jeffrey Goldberg, a journalist at *The Atlantic*, observed in 2020:

"The rise of mainstream conspiracism is the result not just of bad information or bad politics or bad thinking, but of systems built to stoke paranoia and to profit from mistrust" (Goldberg 2020). Jeff Sharlet found as much in his multiyear tour of America, where he describes a throughline of conspiracism, dividing communities and cultures. In *The Undertow: Scenes from a Slow Civil War*, he immersed himself in a men's rights activists' conference, hobnobbing with such disaffected White men as the incels who had populated the chan boards and sourced QAnon (Sharlet 2023, chapter 5). From there, he became acquainted with numerous Americans on their social and political views, often infused with QAnon theories, fealty to former president Trump, and prosperity gospel evangelism. Another journalist, Will Sommer, found the same throughline in his deep dive into QAnon, *Trust the Plan: The Rise of QAnon and the Conspiracy That Unhinged America.* Sommer warns all those who ignored QAnon for too long before the eruption at the Capitol. We must be prepared for superconspiracies like QAnon, which he describes as a "totalitarian, violent . . . repackaging of older conspiracy theories" (Sommer 2023, 220). As we learn more about how these types of conspiracy theories proliferate, hopefully we can be better prepared—and stop them before a democratic crisis occurs.

SEEDS OF HOPE

Stephanie's relationship with Shannon has been deepening and evolving since that first night at the park, and their conversations rarely veer into QAnon territory now. It's unsure whether that's because they try not to discuss politics and instead focus their conversations on lighter topics, like their dogs and the weather. Now and then, it does skirt politics, and Stephanie will test the waters with insertions of critical thinking told through stories of people she knows or narratives of family life. Sometimes Stephanie will introduce adjacent conspiracies to ascertain whether Shannon also believes in them, as research suggests is common. As we progress in this book, we will discuss why Stephanie is using these specific techniques and not others, how and why she is establishing trust before inserting any moral dilemma narrative or storyline with critical thinking, and how this technique of "nudging" can be used—with friends, family, loved ones, even library patrons. We will discuss this and more in the sections to come.

In our polarized society, it can be easy to stick with conversing with like-minded individuals. As librarians and educators, we don't have that luxury. For those flirting with conspiracy theories, the impulse to self-insulate is strong (Sullivan, Landau, and Rothschild 2010). The following sections of this book will examine the balance we must walk as librarians and educators in our relationships with our students and patrons, and how we might begin to stem the tide of conspiracism.

Part II

A Matter of Trust and Distrust

4

Why Are We Like This? Lessons from the Applied and Social Sciences

You're at work, heading to the break room for some much-needed caffeine. It was a rough night and you can barely keep your eyes open. As you walk in, two of your coworkers, whom you consider friends, huddled near the coffeepot in the corner, startle and immediately stop their conversation. Fake smiles are pasted on their faces as they perfunctorily greet you and then make excuses to rush away. What was that about?

Later in the day, you walk by your boss's office to see, through the windows, a gathering of nearly your entire department. Seeing you, your boss waves and everyone glances over to watch you walk past.

You leave that day feeling unsettled. Clearly, your coworkers are working against you in some way—but how? And why? You spend the next few hours mentally picking apart the last few months at work—every project, every encounter, every rumor—looking for red flags or patterns. Several scenarios start to coalesce. There was the rumor of the company being bought out— you're probably slated for the inevitable round of cuts. Or you're being removed from your pet project; there was that awkward sort-of-argument the other day with one of the stakeholders.

By Friday, three days later, you are hypersensitive to everything in your environment and overwrought from mental exhaustion. You read each email several times to determine what hints are accidentally being given; you parse each meeting and conversation afterward for hidden meanings. It is clear to you that groups working against you threaten your status at the company; you're just waiting for the official fallout. So at lunch, as you head to the office kitchen to get your frozen meal, you are shocked to walk into a room festooned with decorations and all of your coworkers: It's your milestone birthday celebration, a week early (as they explain to you, laughing) so that you'd be unsuspecting as they planned it.

Although the above example is of a rather innocuous conspiracy theory, it illustrates how easily affective states such as alarm, alienation, or fear drive us into seeing patterns, collusion, and possibilities that don't exist in reality. While some research seems to indicate that a conspiratorial worldview is more common among those with lower intelligence or who are less educated, the truth is that roughly 50 percent of the U.S. population ascribes to at least one conspiracy theory (Oliver and Wood 2014). Hofstadter referred to a "paranoid style" approach to history and society, a sort of anxious teleologism that assumed causal conspiracy for all events (Hofstadter 1964). Hofstadter's work, as built on by scholars in the decades since (Goertzel in 2010 coined the term "conspiratorial mindset") has perhaps biased the academic and popular conceptions of conspiracy theorists as those who are pathologically paranoid, spouting nonsense that we, the rational ones, can dismiss out of hand.

And yet. Is it really the case that conspiracy theories, by their very nature, are built on "crippled epistemologies" (Sunstein and Vermeule 2009) and, therefore, they (and their adherents) should be dismissed out of hand? Some argue otherwise, positing that conspiracy theories should not be treated as a generalizable category unto themselves, but rather should be assessed individually on their own merits (or lack thereof) (Dentith 2014). As discussed in chapter 3, there is a difference between conspiracies and conspiracy theories. One need only consider Watergate, the events of 9/11 (to be clear, the actual events, in which a terrorist group conspired to attack the United States, not the conspiracy theories that have promulgated around the event), or the widespread NSA spying program as revealed in the leaks from Edward Snowden to acknowledge that, in fact, conspiracies do happen, and have happened throughout human history. The motives for conspiracies can be inferred easily—power, money, control, revenge. But for each real conspiracy, there are innumerable alternate explanations and theories for events, both historic and contemporary.

Why are we like this? Is there something inherent to our very physiology and psychology that causes us—some more than others—to eschew rational explanations in favor of things like alien lizard overlords? In our article "A Call to Action for Librarians: Countering Conspiracy Theories in the Age of QAnon," we attempted to answer for ourselves and our profession the questions of "What exactly is this QAnon thing anyway?" and "What should librarians know about conspiracy theories?" (Beene and Greer 2021). The library science literature at the time did not have a significant amount of material relevant to conspiracy ideation, especially given what was at the time an increasing intrusion of the QAnon mindset into the public sphere. In this chapter, we will reiterate some of our findings from other disciplines, as well as delve into what newer research is telling us about the how and the why of conspiracy ideation.[1]

BORN THIS WAY: THE BIOLOGICAL AND NEUROLOGICAL UNDERPINNINGS OF CONSPIRACY BELIEF

The human ability to use causal inference to understand the cause-and-effect of events in our environment (i.e., to be a "why specialist," as Justin Gregg describes in his book *If Nietzsche Were a Narwhal*), is possibly unique to humans (Gregg 2022, 37). Our constant questioning has created an impressive body of knowledge and continues to do so—but it also comes at a cost when we make wildly incorrect inferences based on faulty cause-and-effect reasoning. Gregg mentions as exemplars the long history of humorism in medicine, the internal combustion engine (which has contributed to our current climate crisis), and the theory of "polygenism," in which different races developed "from separate lineages of early hominids or had been created separately by God" (Gregg 2022, 52)—a nice, neat, and completely incorrect evolutionary basis for racism. Our need to find causal explanations for events can lead us down the rabbit hole of conspiracy ideation.

The tendency to suspect a conspiracy, even where there may be none, is as old as our species, argues behavioral scientist Jan-Willem van Prooijen (2019). For prehistoric humans, often in conflict with each other, the tendency toward a suspicious mindset served as an adaptive evolutionary behavior:

> [A]ncestral humans were easily suspicious of a different tribe nearby, which might well have saved their lives. They would migrate into safety before the other tribe committed a lethal attack. Modern humans are still easily suspicious of different groups—but now these different groups might consist of medics, scientists and pharmaceutical companies, leading people to refuse life-saving vaccines or treatments. Or they might consist of ethnic minorities, amplifying xenophobia, discrimination and exclusionary policies. (van Prooijen 2019)

Basically, we evolved a sense of paranoia to protect ourselves. This sense of paranoia malfunctions in the current world, seeking targets that do not exist because we no longer need to worry about being eaten by wild animals. Raihani and Bell explore the phenomenon of paranoia as an evolutionary mechanism but go further in trying to understand why there is such variation in conspiracy ideation. They propose a "coalitional perspective," citing research that shows higher-than-average conspiracy ideation in groups that "are involved in higher-than-average rates of coalitionary aggression, such as gang members and army veterans" (Raihani and Bell 2019). The additional stress and situational contexts trigger more paranoia. In addition, they note contextual factors including isolation, unstable living situations, or being a member of a marginalized group; each of these contexts carries a higher risk of paranoia. Likewise, different developmental periods, such as adolescence, and pathological factors such as drug use or dementia can also play a part.

While our evolutionary adaptations and biological mechanisms do have a role to play in conspiracy ideation, it is important to note that these factors are not deterministic. Psychologists, in fact, are moving away from a predispositional, deficit model of thinking about conspiracy ideation in favor of an understanding that is far more nuanced and holistic. Essentially, these arguments boil down to the age-old "nature vs. nurture" dichotomy.

THE PSYCHOLOGY OF CONSPIRACY IDEATION

The psychology of conspiracy ideation is a relatively new field in the discipline, with acknowledged gaps. That said, the published research so far reveals a fascinating—and often frustrating—picture of the conspiratorial mind, which we began exploring in chapter 3. Brotherton and French (2015) surmised that

> a literature is now beginning to emerge pointing towards individual differences and cognitive factors which may be associated with endorsement of conspiracy theories, including such variables as agreeableness, authoritarianism, openness, mild paranoia, confirmation bias, the conjunction fallacy, illusory pattern perception, the proportionality bias, and projection.

Writing a few years later, Douglas, Sutton, and Cichocka (2019) summarized the literature on conspiracy ideation by organizing the research into three motivational factors: epistemic, explanatory, and social. We borrow this frame for our discussion.

I THINK, THEREFORE, I OVERTHINK: THE EPISTEMOLOGY OF CONSPIRACY IDEATION

A common thread that runs through each of the three motivational factors is that of causation. If we consider personal epistemology (one's understanding of knowledge), conspiracy theorists tend to turn to conspiracies because they offer neat little explanations for events that otherwise might not be well understood. "People want to know the truth and be certain of that truth. They are also curious and want to find out new information" (Douglas, Sutton, and Cichocka 2019). This curiosity fulfills a psychological need. The human desire for knowledge and closure is evident in Abraham Maslow's famous theory of motivation; although he wasn't quite sure exactly of its place and underlying mechanisms, he included "the desire to know and understand" as one of the driving desires for his famed hierarchy of needs (Maslow 1943). Safety, for example, is one of the foundational needs in the hierarchy—and, as we have explored previously, conspiracies thrive in times of uncertainty or chaos as scared people seek meaning during instability. Our minds want consistency and closure. Conspiracies shape themselves around the gaps in our knowledge or the events that loom so large and overwhelming (such as 9/11 or the global COVID pandemic) that the official explanations seem unsatisfying. The means are arranged to justify the end in a teleological mental exercise. For conspiracy communities, that usually includes hidden knowledge revealed only to them; the QAnon community exemplifies this mindset through their mantra "Trust the plan."

Conspiracy theories subvert a human need to find meaning and patterns in our experiences of the world, and they exploit our innate cognitive biases. Consider, for example, the very common experience of pareidolia, in which one sees an image or a pattern in something that does not actually exist. For example, Figure 1 reproduces a meme asking, "Is it a chihuahua or a blueberry muffin?"

Figure 4.1 Chihuahua or muffin meme by Karen Zack (KarenZack.com, @ teenybiscuit on Twitter/X). Used with permission.

With a quick glance at the images, how many of the muffins can your brain reasonably see as chihuahua faces? Faces in trees, religious images on toast, figures in the stars—human brains are excellent at imagining connections, and this tendency doesn't just have to be visual. If you dive into a conspiracy thread, you will find many "clues" that are being deciphered from incredibly disparate sources. Not only does this exploit (perhaps manically) the pattern-finding drive, but it also points to another commonality among conspiracy theorists: the tendency to see connections and meaning where they do not exist. In QAnon, reliance on the numerology system known as gematria is one of the most extreme examples (Ratzabi, n.d.). Hebraic in origin (thus giving the system a gloss of "ancient knowledge"), gematria assigns numerical values to letters. Words are analyzed for their total value, and then words or phrases with the same numeral value are listed so that meaning can be derived from the combinations. Wild theories then abound. In an analysis of QAnon and alternative spirituality practices, Christopher T. Conner includes an illustrative post using gematria to suggest that Donald Trump and John F. Kennedy Jr. are the same person (Conner 2023).

As with the paranoia that may be activated by unstable situations, conspiracy theories tend to thrive among populations that are marginalized or threatened. Threat, as mentioned in chapter 2, is an extremely powerful motivator, triggering a response that leaves the mind vulnerable to disinformation. Green et al. observes that "there is much to suggest that QAnon conspiracy beliefs might take root from [. . .] existential threat motives" (Green et al. 2023, 34). This conclusion is echoed by Jan-Willem van Prooijen, who argued that existential threats also need "a salient antagonistic outgroup that promotes conspiratorial suspicions during sense-making processes" (van Prooijen 2020).

Epistemology is also at the heart of a socio-epistemic model of belief in conspiracy theories as proposed by psychiatrist Joseph M. Pierre (2020). Noting that the research published thus far attempts to understand all conspiracy theories under a general umbrella of understanding, despite their varying themes, Pierre proposes that conspiracy ideation occurs because of two interrelated forces: epistemic mistrust and misinformation processing (Figure 2). Epistemic mistrust (a lack of trust in authoritative information) and its causes will be explored extensively in chapter 5. Pierre's "misinformation processing," illustrated in Figure 2, encompasses several factors, including personality and psychological tendencies, cognitive biases, and poor information literacies.

Importantly, Pierre's model integrates psychological underpinnings with the societal; as he concludes, it offers "a potentially normalizing account of conspiracist ideation based on a reciprocal relationship between mistrust and belief in misinformation" (Pierre 2020, 631). This is echoed in Douglas et al.'s conclusion that

> there is evidence that conspiracy theories appeal to individuals who seek accuracy and meaning (or both) but perhaps lack the cognitive tools or

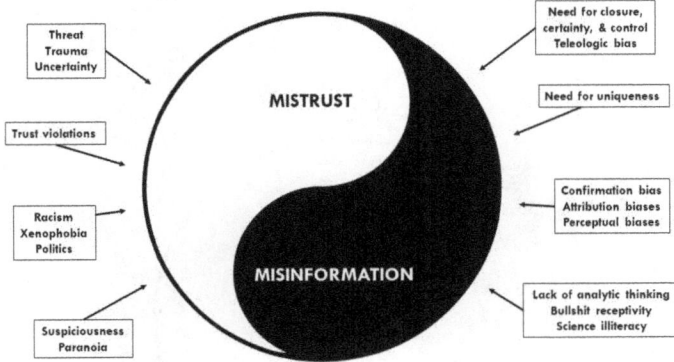

A Two-Component "Socio-Epistemic" Model of Belief in Conspiracy Theories

Pierre JM. J Soc Polit Psychol 2020; 8:617-641

Threat
Trauma
Uncertainty

Trust violations

Racism
Xenophobia
Politics

Suspiciousness
Paranoia

MISTRUST

MISINFORMATION

Need for closure,
certainty, & control
Teleologic bias

Need for uniqueness

Confirmation bias
Attribution biases
Perceptual biases

Lack of analytic thinking
Bullshit receptivity
Science illiteracy

Figure 4.2 Joseph Pierre, "A Two-Component 'Socio-Epistemic Model of Belief in Conspiracy Theories," (2023). Used with permission.

experience difficulties that prevent them from finding these via other means. Conspiracy theories therefore appeal to people who are looking for the truth but *seem to lack the skills to look in the right places* [added emphasis]. (Douglas, Sutton, and Cichocka 2019, 65)

Librarians, with their expertise in information systems and information literacies, can train the public in exactly these skills.

EXISTENTIALISM AND CONSPIRACY IDEATION

The "dizziness of freedom" generates anxiety, wrote Kierkegaard (2014). It could be argued that the Information Age has led to an existential crisis, as people are overwhelmed with conflicting thoughts, ideas, and potent disinformation. Anxiety drives conspiracy ideation, with one theory specifically linking attachment anxiety, or anxiety centered on one's relationships, to conspiracy ideation:

Endorsement of conspiracy theories could be another means to catastrophize life's problems for people with attachment anxiety as an attempt to garner attention and support from friends, family, and partners. (Green et al. 2023, 34)

Even negative attention, for those who suffer attachment anxiety, is considered good attention, serving as a force that will help reinforce or reinvigorate social bonds that feel unstable.

As people's concepts of themselves and existence veer into credulity, and as they fall down the conspiratorial rabbit hole, they don't see themselves as being

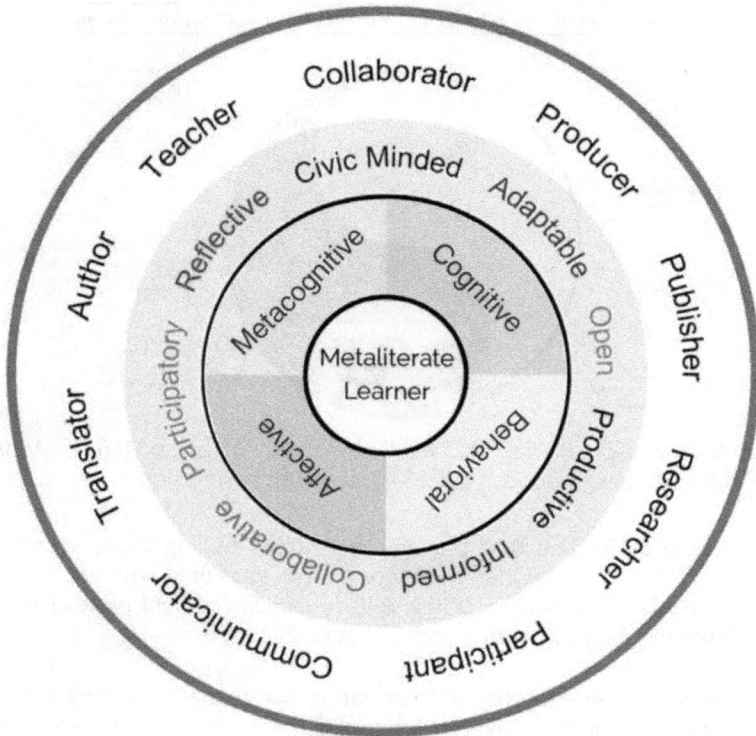

Figure 4.3 Integrated Metaliteracy Model. Image from Thomas P. Mackey and Trudi E. Jacobson, Metaliteracy in a Connected World (Chicago: ALA Neal-Schuman, 2022), 23.

outliers. In fact, it is human nature to project our own thoughts and motives onto others' behavior, assuming that others around us feel, think, and believe the same way we do (Douglas and Sutton 2011). When twenty TikTok videos on one's algorithm reinforce those assumptions, it can be harder and harder to consider that we might be wrong. These biases serve to protect us from existential crises: We create, in our minds, a sense of belonging and safety because we are part of the (possibly imagined) in-group. We also favor our own reasoning, falling into a "myside bias" in which we have a personally skewed worldview and therefore evaluate information in terms of our own feelings and beliefs (Stanovich, West, and Toplak 2013). This bias is evidenced by news coverage from different sides of the political spectrum about the same topic; a report on the same event, with the same end results, will have very different discussion points depending on the source and audience.

Safety and belonging are incredibly salient to conspiracy theorizing. As has been mentioned, often the political party on the losing side will see an uptick in conspiracy theories. Again and again, research has shown that those who are isolated and anxious, or who feel threatened somehow, are far more likely to accept a conspiracy theory as the source. Consider, for example, the global pandemic in 2020. A new disease, mandated lockdowns globally, hospitals overflowing with the sick and dying, and it often felt like each new day brought updated guidance on what individuals should be doing to protect themselves. Those who lived through those days, many of whom were stuck inside and cut off from most human contact and "normal" life, probably all experienced some form of existential vertigo. Many wanted answers, and many wanted a scapegoat to blame for the situation that was affecting (and continues to affect) not just public and mental health but relationships, livelihoods, and entire ways of living. Is it any surprise, then, that Dr. Anthony Fauci, the then-government spokesperson for pandemic policies and updates, became a target of so many conspiracy theories and violent threats? (Zak and Roberts 2022). The new narrative, for many, became not a situation of fear and instability, with more questions than answers, but rather one of coercion and control: "They" created the virus, "they" are exaggerating its dangers, because "they" want us to be powerless. Once the vaccine came out, especially since it was the first vaccine outside of research labs to utilize mRNA technology, it was only a slight jump to combine existing anti-vaccine conspiracies with the conspiracy narratives of the pandemic. With this added piece of the conspiracy puzzle, it of course made sense to insist that Democrats and the global cabal were using microchips in the vaccines to further control and track us, or to make us sicker, etc. Shadows of QAnon integrated into the story as well, even though the Trump administration's role in "Project Warp Speed" to develop the vaccine, and his triumphant announcement of its rollout, has been conveniently suppressed in the narrative.

By turning to conspiracy theories, those who are anxious or who feel powerless have the perception of control. They can feel secure in the knowledge that only they and a small group of fellow insiders have. In the case of a movement such as QAnon, the believers become active agents as well, perceiving themselves as "digital soldiers" to help the goals of the supposed "white hats" working to overthrow the satanic global elite. The conspiracy theory thus provides a purpose, a reason for being, that may otherwise be absent in the believer's life. We must note, however, that existential crises do not always precipitate conspiracy ideation; research has found that at times, they increase trust in prevailing systems (Kay et al. 2008).

A COMMUNITY OF BELIEVERS: SOCIAL MOTIVES FOR CONSPIRACY IDEATION

It cannot be stressed enough: Extreme conspiracy ideation is a disease of loneliness and isolation (Allen et al. 2023). Loneliness causes physiological problems as well: Americans' longevity has decreased precipitously and chronic illness is claiming more Americans in their prime (Center for Disease Control and Prevention 2021). Thus, conspiracy ideation could be considered among these other contemporary epidemics. When we are part of a social group, we have an increased sense of safety and control (Rose 2022, 55). Many times those who adhere to conspiracy theories end up with only their conspiracy community, as family and friends distance themselves, which serves to further entrench them in their beliefs (Hornsey et al. 2023).

The conspiracy community can also fulfill psychological needs beyond those of just belonging. Douglas, Sutton, and Cichocka (2019) discuss how conspiracy theories

> [allow] blame for negative outcomes to be attributed to others. Thus, conspiracy theories may help to uphold people's image of the self and their in-group as capable and honest but as harmed or impaired by powerful and immoral others." (67)

The binary thinking of us vs. them, or good vs. evil, that is common to conspiracy ideation reinforces itself through group identity and collusion. Again, we are more powerful as a group—as are our emotions. Todd Rose writes that "neuroscience confirms that we actually feel pleasure when we see the rivals of our in-group lose" (Rose 2022, 33). Consider, for example, when your preferred candidate wins an election or your sports team beats their major rival. The anticipated schadenfreude is evident in many memes shared in conspiracy communities, lauding the day when the "normies" will know what the group members have known for a long time.

Then there is the phenomenon of mass hysteria, in which large groups of people subscribe to the same delusions. Examples of such include the Salem witch trials and the Satanic Panic of the 1980s. In his study of social delusions, Robert E. Bartholomew connects these instances of large-scale mass hysterias to the zeitgeist; our delusions reflect our current anxieties (Bartholomew 2001, 227). He further observes that "[h]uman perception is a selective and organizational process that is based more on inference than reality. [. . .] People continually test reality by comparing their perceptions with those of others [resulting in] observations that do not reflect the real world but reflect the socially constructed world of the observers" (Bartholomew 2001, 233). William J. Berstein, in his book *The Delusions of Crowds* further elaborates on this social construction of reality, noting that because of the human propensity to prefer narrative over hard facts, all it takes is a compelling story in a conversation for critical thinking to go out the window (Bernstein 2021, 16).

BELIEF WITHOUT SUSPICION; OR, ARE THEY JUST GULLIBLE?

A discussion of social motives for conspiracy ideation brings up an obvious question: Are these people just gullible? If you have seen some of the material we have—miraculous "medbeds" that will age people backward and cure all ills, a major QAnon influencer who claims he is actually JFK Jr., for example— you could reasonably deduce that, yes, people are just incredibly gullible. In the next chapter we explore the notion of trust—what it is, how it is constructed, and how forces like affect influence who and what we trust—but gullibility is a separate construct from trust and functions slightly differently. We can trust without being gullible, as Rotter (1966) clarified:

> [If] we redefine trust as believing communications in the absence of clear or strong reasons for not believing (i.e., in ambiguous situations) and gullibility as believing when most people of the same social group would consider belief naive and foolish, then trust can be independent of gullibility. (4)

Research has shown that those who are generally trusting are actually no less gullible than those who are distrustful (in fact, those who have low trust may actually be more prone to gullibility). (Rotter 1966).

A 2022 paper theorizes "populism gullibility" (van Prooijen et al. 2022). Populism, which has grown around the world in recent years, is a political movement that espouses a good guys vs. bad guys duality. Populism "oversimplifies complex societal problems through catchy one-liners" or suggests solutions that don't make rational sense, being "incompatible with the constitution or international treaties (e.g., populist movements within various EU member states that promise to lower their country's financial contributions to the EU or to close the borders for immigrants entirely)" (van Prooijen et al. 2022). These ideas probably sound very familiar from recent history and from the tenets of QAnon, which is a populist conspiracy theory. The study found that those who conform to populism tend to be more gullible:

> [P]opulist attitudes predicted increased credulity of politically neutral news items (regardless of whether they were broadcasted by mainstream or alternative news sources), receptivity to bullshit statements, and supernatural beliefs. Furthermore . . . these findings were mediated by increased faith in intuition. (van Prooijen et al. 2022, abstract)

Populism, of course, is not the sole predictor of gullibility, but in a world in which populism continues to be a major political force, it serves us to be aware that there is a concomitant tendency to believe, well, anything, especially if the information in question is salient to our personal beliefs or interests.

Relevant to this discussion is the now-infamous "Dunning-Kruger effect," based on an initial study by Justin Kruger and David Dunning in 1999. Those who are novices or untrained in a subject area will tend to overestimate their abilities. It is only with further training that they can recognize their own limitations and understand how to surmount them. Until they have that training, however, they are at a disadvantage, continuing to make errors that are often quite impactful.

> [W]hen people are incompetent in the strategies they adopt to achieve success and satisfaction, they suffer a dual burden: Not only do they reach erroneous conclusions and make unfortunate choices, but their incompetence robs them of the ability to realize it. (Kruger and Dunning 1999, 1122)

These errors impact all facets of life, as the authors illustrated with the example of bank robber McArthur Wheeler, who wore no disguise while committing his crimes because he was convinced that putting lemon juice on his face would render him unable to be recognized on video (Kruger and Dunning 1999, 1121). Although a kneejerk reaction to this anecdote might be that Mr. Wheeler is just laughably gullible, the example points more to not just a lack of knowledge leading to naive credulity but specifically a lack of scientific and information literacy. Faulty metacognition might also be a mitigating factor in decision-making; in the Dunning-Kruger effect, there is no reflection on one's limitations. In other words, the metacognitive process is not primed to recognize when gaps exist in one's knowledge.

In the Information Age, in which influencers have become the authoritative voices, the Dunning-Kruger effect will often drive the spread of misinformation, as Della Lena (2023) suggested in his study of individual and social learning networks:

> [P]otentially the most harmful agents are those who have poor individual learning in the specific subject, but, at the same time, are well respected and/or influential. Indeed, poor individual learning makes them more susceptible to misinformation and their influence over others makes them a powerful channel for spreading misinformation. (12)

Della Lena provided the example of a politician promoting misinformation on social media that is then taken up and spread exponentially by others within the social network.

To dismiss conspiracy theorists as hopelessly gullible, therefore, is to fall prey to our own Dunning-Kruger effect. Gullibility as a concept is far more nuanced and contextual than its popular understanding. The intersection of conspiracy ideation and gullibility is even more complex. As we move forward in understanding the *why* and *how* of the psychology of conspiracy theories, it is imperative that we do not dismiss out of hand the cognitive fallacies that lead to those beliefs. By digging a little deeper, we can more effectively help those enmeshed to find their way out.

LESSONS FROM EDUCATIONAL PSYCHOLOGY

To escape from the rabbit hole will require education, whether that be casual, through ongoing conversations, or in a formal setting, as librarians are increasingly called upon to do. As Cook and Klipfel exhort, "Understanding the science of learning is particularly important for instruction librarians in academic libraries who are being increasingly called upon to take on robust teaching and learning roles on their campuses" (Cook and Klipfel 2015, 35). We cannot effectively teach if we do not understand what learning means, and how it happens.

Cognitive psychology histories often start with the work of Jean Piaget (1896–1980). As one of the first to empirically study children's cognitive development, he, along with his research assistant Bärbel Inhelder (1913–1997), proposed a "stage theory of cognition" (Martin and Torok-Gerard 2019, 33), which posits that there are several unique stages that learners pass through on their way to cognitive maturity. The stages were linked to physiological changes during childhood and adolescence—the maturing brain—but the learning processes that stem from their work have implications for learners of all levels. Piaget's model proposes that cognitive development is continuous and progressive; much like the threshold concepts of the *Framework* (see chapter 5), once a stage has been reached, it is a permanent shift. The process of learning in these stages, according to Piaget, occurred as a cycle of assimilation, accommodation, and equilibration (Jardine 2014, 136). Assimilation occurs when a learner connects a new experience to previous knowledge, organizing the environment into what is already known and familiar. This sometimes results in errors, as learners will apply previous knowledge incorrectly. By observing learners and how they are using the process of assimilation with new concepts, we can determine what gaps they have in their learning. For example, students often will cite any resource they find online using the citation format for a website (Greer and McCann 2018). The knowledge of how to access and use resources online exists, and the knowledge that sources must be cited exists, so they are combining those past experiences as they utilize an online article from a database or an ebook, but they are missing an understanding of what type of information they are using, and the affordances that various information offers, by flattening everything into the website model (Russo et al. 2019).

Accommodation occurs when the learner adjusts their mental models in response to new information. This occurs over time and can take repeated instructional sessions and practice before the proverbial lightbulb goes on. Anyone who has instructed students in using phrase searching, for example, only to see them putting quotation marks around every single keyword, can now breathe easy—it's not the instruction, it's the fact that learning does not occur immediately.

Lastly there is equilibration, the stabilization and comfort with one's new knowledge and understanding of the world. These processes don't necessarily occur linearly, but are cyclical and ongoing, with "an all-embracing" equilibration being the end goal (Jardine 2014, 139). Stability and comfort are the products of this process—the learner has crossed a threshold, reached a new stage, and the experience which previously required assimilation and accommodation is now familiar and understood.

Piaget's theories provide a grounding for cognitive development that theorists have continued to build upon. Mezirow's transformative learning theory, which has been explored extensively in the information literacy literature, utilizes the concepts of assimilation and accommodation (Hess 2018; Kos and Špiranec 2014). Lev Vygotsky's social development theory rejected the tidiness of Piaget's work for a messier model that incorporated humans' lived experiences and how those are brought to bear on the learning experience in social interactions. For Vygotsky, the school is "a meaning making site" (Connery and Curran 2014, 154), and the effective teacher will adapt the classroom to allow for the individual cultural meanings and experiences that each student carries with them to be embraced in the learning process.

Vygotsky is perhaps most well-known for his Zone of Proximal Development (ZPD), which posits a continuum between a learner's development level and the level they potentially can achieve when working with a peer or mentor who is at a further developmental level. The ZPD underscores the importance of social interaction for learning and the fact that no learner is a blank slate—concepts that are utilized by theories of constructivism, critical information literacy, and many others. This social constructionism, which "emphasises social processes and how individuals seek to interpret or construct meaning against social, historical, and political processes that influence the particular discourse in which they engage in" (Lawal and Bitso 2020, 232), is used by Lawal and Bitso to examine Reijo Savolainen's model of Everyday Life Information Seeking (ELIS) in information literacy instruction, ascertaining that

> the research context of IL and ELIS in everyday life information seeking has allowed for a shift in focus from the individual as a unit of analysis to the broader socio-cultural context. The social constructionists' approach reflected in Savolainen's ELIS model thus provides a potential theoretical framework for studying the holistic information experiences of the individual in his or her given social context in a way that aligns with and contributes to the wider discourse of IL in diverse contexts. (Lawal and Bitso 2020, 237)

These concerns are echoed by Troy Swanson through the application of personal epistemology to information literacy and knowledge construction. Personal epistemology "seek[s] to understand how individuals understand knowledge, how this understanding impacts knowledge construction, and how this impact can be applied to educational practice" (Swanson 2006, 94). Swanson emphasizes the role of belief in personal epistemology, which connects to the affective theories and implications for information behavior discussed in chapter 2. Personal epistemology also "tends to operate in the metacognitive plane, while information literacy operates in a plane defined by actions" (Swanson, 2006, 107). The role of metacognition in information behaviors is a crucial component of metaliteracy, discussed below.

The work of these scholars represents only the tip of the proverbial educational psychology iceberg, but they illustrate how a broader understanding of learners' cognitive processes can help move the field of information literacy forward. It behooves us to continue to integrate the work of other fields into our own as we continue to evolve as educators and seek to address the challenges of the information landscape.

HOPE IN THE GAPS

The pedagogical model metaliteracy, developed over the past decade by Thomas J. Mackey and Trudi Jacobson, functions as a response to the rise of social media and the more active, participatory role that learners play in the information landscape (Mackey and Jacobson 2014). The framework serves as a useful tool in the fight against information disorder and will be explored throughout this book. It explicitly acknowledges the social construction of knowledge and the role of emotion in information behaviors by framing the metaliteracy goals and objectives through the four domains of learning: cognitive, affective, metacognitive, and behavioral (https://metaliteracy.org/learning-objectives/). The metaliterate learner is conceptualized as having various characteristics and roles as they interact with the dynamic information landscape.

Thus the metaliterate process exists not as a single loop, of learner to information item and back, but rather as a web with the learner at the center, as that learner shares out content, teaches others through conversation about the information process, collaborates in social spaces, and creates their own content, among other activities.

Scholars as diverse as psychologist Joseph M. Pierre and philosopher Matthew R. X. Dentith now consider conspiracism as a normal function of being human—with the caveat, of course, that there is a wide spectrum on which this occurs. The common stereotype of the crazy conspiracy theorist defies the biological and psychological realities; the initial research literature dependent upon the dominant deficit model, looking for specific etiologies of conspiracism, has shown inconsistent results (Pierre 2020). The growing consensus seems to be that, while there are definite psychological drivers and motivations for conspiracy ideation, those do not by themselves lead directly to conspiracism, but rather offer a more holistic view of the conspiracy theorist. It will be more effective, instead, to focus on critically analyzing the conspiracy *theory* itself.

Whatever the intrinsic or extrinsic motives, the conspiracy theory ultimately is ineffectual for most people in fulfilling psychological needs (Pierre 2020). Perhaps therein lies the hope—despite the conspiracy theorist's stubborn adherence to false realities, there is a space between the need and the conspiracy theory that may be leveraged, then carefully and slowly widened, to subvert the mental hold. This is a slow process and will not occur within a single conversation, but requires a relationship of trust.

NOTE

1. For more, our extensive bibliography may be viewed at https://www.zotero.org/groups/2545313/a_call_to_action_for_librarians.

5

Trust and Affect in the Current Information Environment

Researching conspiracy theories can be quite fraught and sometimes causes our brains to work in peculiar ways, as Katie discovered on a family trip to Florida in 2022. Having been immersed in QAnon and the visual iconographies of QAnon followers for years, she was alarmed to see a plane on the tarmac decorated in red, white, and blue with "Patriots" in loud font across each side. Katie is trained in visual and information literacies. She knows to think about context when evaluating information. Nonetheless, she was duped for a moment until someone with more sports knowledge than she has explained it was for the Patriots football team.

This vignette illustrates that even an advanced researcher trained in information and other literacies can be tricked by gut reactions. It has happened to all of us. Stephanie remembers sharing a video clip through the popular neighborhood app Next Door, only to have community members point out that the material was several years old. Why does this happen? Over the years, many neuroscientists and psychologists have pondered this same question (Swanson 2023). Chabris and Simons discuss the human mechanisms of pattern recognition, persistence and detail of memories, the role of intuition in decision-making, and how easy it is to pay attention to unimportant information while missing essential context. He argues that "everyday illusions . . . all make us think mental abilities and capabilities are greater than they actually are" (Chabris and Simons 2010, 228).

In fact, we might be so sure of something that we are shocked when we are wrong. The "feeling of knowing," a conviction that we *know* at the gut level, has been explored by numerous scholars (Pinker 2021; Kahneman, Sibony, and Sunstein 2021; Burton, 2009; Swanson 2023; Sloman and Fernbach 2017). Collectively, their research represents neuroscience, psychology, information-seeking behavior, and linguistics, building a more holistic picture of how the mind works when presented with choices. This body of research has also allowed us to understand better the role of emotions in decision-making. For example, Burton examines neural networks, the nature of thoughts, notions of objectivity and rationality, and the complex roles of intuition, faith, and belief in those mechanisms (Burton 2009). Likewise, Sloman and Fernbach argue that knowledge is a slippery concept, especially when considered as a component of community interactions and relationships (Sloman and Fernbach 2017, 1–19).

As librarians and researchers, we are interested in how various information formats and genres transform as they move through information systems. How do people evaluate, create, and trust rapidly changing formats, genres, and platforms? How do trust and information evaluation coalesce and diverge? How do our cognitive mechanisms differ, depending on prior knowledge and life experiences? As educators, we are interested in how learners navigate a rapidly changing information landscape. The previous chapter introduced Pierre's two-component socio-epistemic model of conspiracy belief; half of that model is mistrust. This affective and cognitive state is so vital for information evaluation, our general understanding of the world, and our knowledge, that we will spend this chapter discussing what trust is and how a lack of trust contributes to the disinformation environment. We also examine current information and other literacy models through the lens of trust, and conclude with the strengths afforded by the metaliteracy model for addressing trust and affect in a social information environment.

WHAT IS TRUST? A BRIEF EXAMINATION

What, exactly, is trust? Is it a gut reaction, a mindless thought exercise, or a careful calculation? What does it mean to "trust" someone or something? To live each day, we make a series of trust evaluations (or gambles): We trust that the food we eat won't make us sick (until we have food poisoning, at which point we may "distrust" a particular food or restaurant). We trust that traffic lights will cycle from red to green, and that people will generally adhere to traffic laws. We trust that the water we drink, bathe in, and wash our food in won't make us sick (and the ongoing water crisis in Flint, Michigan, foregrounded this issue for many Americans) (Buttigieg 2020, 45). To trust someone or something inherently creates vulnerability (DeSteno 2014).

Political scientists, psychologists, economists, and sociologists have all examined trust and its impact on social relations, daily decision-making, and confidence in democratic institutions. For example, in 2021, sociologists examined the mounting sociological scholarship that examines what trust is, where it comes from, and how it impacts social relations. They found that since the 1970s sociologists have argued that, without trust, "society as we know it could not exist" (Schilke, Reimann, and Cook 2021, 239). Today, the notion of trust remains at the forefront of sociological research, undergirding such societal concepts as solidarity, collective action, reciprocity, equality, social order, and democratic institutions. Similar to writers of psychological literature, sociologists place vulnerability at the center of trust, arguing that it entails "the willingness of an entity (i.e., the trustor) to become vulnerable to another entity (i.e., the trustee)." In taking this risk, the trustor presumes that the trustee will act in a way that is beneficial to their cause or their welfare, despite the trustee's actions being out of the trustor's control (Schilke, Reimann, and Cook, 2021, 240). Similarly, political scientists have long studied the role of trust in political entities, including democracy. For example, a 2018 *Annual Review of Political Science* focused on empirical evidence in the United States, addressing the long-term decline in trust in institutions and the potential causes, including partisanship, polarization, media priming, and more. Political trust expands the notion of social trust, which entails confidence in governing bodies and institutions. Indeed, they argue that "the longstanding puzzle of whether and when distrust of authorities begins to erode the legitimacy of democratic regimes has taken on new urgency in the wake of five decades of steady decline in political trust in representative institutions in the United States and Europe" (Citrin and Stoker 2018, 50). This statement is striking, especially considering it was written in 2018, years before the January 6 Capitol insurrection in 2021. Both Gallup and Pew survey results have found similar sentiments. For example, a 2023 Gallup longitudinal survey reported that the United States is experiencing historically low faith in its democratic institutions (Saad 2023), while a 2019 Pew Research Institute study reported that Americans believe their declining sense of trust in each other and institutions makes it harder to solve problems. Moreover, participants saw fading trust as a moral decline or cultural sickness (Rosenberg 2019).

These are complex issues that scholars have been studying for decades. The challenge is similar for information professionals who study the trustworthiness of information and trust evaluations: How do we determine whether information is trustworthy? How do we vest trust in an entity, a piece of information, or an authority? How does trust impact the use of information? In the following few sections of this chapter, we will delve deeper into these questions, examining cognitive authority and parasocial relationships, the role of affect when making a trust determination, and how information literacy and metaliteracy models have dealt with these issues.

WHY IS TRUST SO CRITICAL IN THIS INFORMATION ENVIRONMENT?

Before the Information Age, a person needing information might consult the local newspaper or the telephone book, or go to a library to access encyclopedias, atlases, almanacs, and other volumes of codified, edited information. Those sources were trusted because people understood how they were produced, and because of their solidity and perseverance—the *Encyclopaedia Britannica*, for example, was in print for over two hundred years, meaning that generations had referred to it to answer their information needs. There was, of course, still mis- and disinformation in the print age—chapter 1 mentioned some examples, and in chapter 7 we explore one of the most notorious examples, *The Protocols of Zion*. In general, though, the sources of information one used were those that one's friends and parents used or what teachers and librarians used and recommended. With the rise of the Information Age came far too many sources of information. In 2013, Facebook users shared over 600,000 pieces of content each minute; by 2022, that number had nearly tripled to 1.7 million per minute, with other platforms rising to outpace Facebook's growth and use (DOMO 2022). We are inundated with information, making it extremely difficult to know what and whom to trust. The metrics we used to use—currency, authority, relevancy—have become meaningless when information is produced and shared in real time, and authority is earned through the metrics of likes, comments, and shares. Add flashy productions, engaging personalities, and solutions that sound too good to be true but are hyped up just enough to override our skepticism—and you have an information environment that has warped trust and distrust and leads users down all the wrong rabbit holes while they take their followers with them.

This warping of trust creates confusion and anxiety and can cause people to withdraw from social supports and systems, seeking answers and placing trust in those who seem to be asking the same questions and seeking the same closure. Conspiracy ideation and trust are directly related. As people build community around the conspiracy theory and withdraw from their families and friends who do not adhere to it, they create insular support systems. They begin to trust each other and the information sources shared among group members, and promote cognitive authorities within the group. The closed-off trust system developed within the community can make it extremely hard to break through, as any questioning or nudges from the outside are met with reassurance and counterpoints from the in-group. Their definitions of traditional authorities do not align with societal definitions. Those who follow QAnon and its more outlandish offshoots strongly reject "elitist" knowledge (i.e., academic information) as part of their worldview, so traditional epistemologies and pedagogies cannot function alone to dislodge the conspiracy worldview. In-group trust is central to QAnon's mantra, encouraging those who doubt or falter to hold steady, to "Trust the plan."

The isolation and anxiety that fuel conspiracy theories about institutional malevolence are created by the very existence of those institutions. In his book *Mistrust*, Matthew Carey argues that as bureaucracies developed, so too did conspiracy theories; in most cases, the theory that develops "espouses or mimics the bureaucratic form that regiments the theorists' lives" (Carey 2017, 95). This parallelism makes sense: As institutions rise, as walls (physical or metaphorical) are built, there will always be those who come to be excluded or marginalized. Indeed, it has been suggested that the strength or weakness of societal institutions directly correlates to interpersonal trust: "Institutional distrust strips away a basic sense that one is protected from exploitation, thus reducing trust between strangers, which is at the core of functioning societies" (van Prooijen, Spadaro, and Wang 2022). Misinformation and disinformation create a cycle of distrust, first sowing the seeds and then reaffirming and deepening that distrust, weakening society.

When trust in traditional authorities is eroded, information evaluation suffers. Recently, we have seen new technologies such as generative artificial intelligence (AI) tools that can create videos and images that mimic reality so closely it can be challenging for humans to determine which are real and which are fake (explored further in chapter 12) (Mai et al. 2023). Many members of the general public do not have the technological knowledge of information systems and production to be able to parse out what is artificially created; we saw this in anecdotes from our survey of librarians encountering conspiracy theorists. One patron, for example, presented an image of Katy Perry with cat eyes as proof of her being part of the secret organization known as the Illuminati (Beene and Greer 2021, 11). The patron accepted and trusted the visual at face value, not realizing how easily photographs can be manipulated (they had probably received the image from one of their trusted social media contacts or groups or had seen similar images previously in those groups). A Twitter account known as "Trump History" (https://twitter.com/Trump_History45/) has been using AI to create images of former president Trump in historical moments. Some are obvious parodies, such as one in which he is shown creating the wheel; however, some images, such as a black-and-white photo of Trump shaking hands with John F. Kennedy, have been shared unironically and seem to have been taken seriously by commenters in some social media groups.

The consequences of distrust have larger societal effects, with some of the most visible fallout seen in public health and politics. Due to a problematic and now-retracted study in the *Lancet* linking the MMR vaccine to autism, parents since the late 1990s have distrusted vaccine efficacy and safety. As a result of this vaccine hesitancy, the childhood disease measles, which had been nearly eradicated in the United States (Orenstein, Papania, and Wharton 2004) has made a resurgence. A 2020 report on an outbreak noted that 9 percent of infected children required hospitalization, with one death (Feemster and Szipsky 2020). Fear of the COVID vaccines, due to either previous vaccine hesitancy or fear of the new mRNA technology used in the vaccines, led to a number of conspiracy theories and lower vaccine uptakes; as a result, a report in 2021 estimated that the Delta variant was 11 percent more fatal for those who were unvaccinated (Dyer 2020).

Political distrust can be seen in protests, voter swings from election to election, or, on the extreme end of the spectrum, insurrections and revolutions. In "Rethinking Political Distrust," Eri Bertsou describes the literature on political distrust as "consistently ambiguous," with some arguing that "citizen distrust of government is inimical to democracy" and others lauding it as a "welcome and necessary citizen stance to ensure democratic survival" (Bertsou 2019, 214). In what will sound familiar to those following along as we explore the commonalities of conspiracy theories, Bertsou concludes that a distrusting political attitude

> poses a danger when diverging interests are delineated between the citizenry and the political establishment as a whole. Populist rhetoric finds fruitful ground in conditions of distrust as it contrasts an "evil" elite that operates against the interests of "good ordinary people." (Bertsou 2019, 227)

Those of us who watched with horror the events of January 6, 2021, in the United States can attest that political distrust can have extreme consequences. The anti-vaccine movement and the adherents of the "Big Lie" conspiracy theory (which claims that the 2020 election was altered to force Trump's loss) provide vivid and alarming examples of how mis- and disinformation drive distrust and lead to consequences that affect us all. Motivated reasoning drives belief in bad information and conspiracy theories; people champion causes because they are meaningful to their personal or political value systems. One study has found, though, that trust can be a mitigating factor on motivated reasoning, concluding that "even when they want to protect their worldviews, people are bound by reality; if they believe the world is a trustworthy place, they are less able to convince themselves that political rivals are engaging in nefarious, secretive plots" (Miller, Saunders, and Farhart 2016, 838). As librarians, educators, and all concerned citizens fight against the tsunami of disordered information, we must focus on understanding trust's role in information evaluation and trust as a crucial component of our toolbox.

THE ROLE OF AFFECT IN TRUST EVALUATIONS

In the previous section, we mentioned the role of motivated reasoning in information evaluation—people trust information and people who conform to their closely held beliefs and values. It feels good to know that others share and reinforce our own ideals. It does not feel good to confront and explore information suggesting we may be wrong.

In chapter 4, we introduced affect and, specifically, the role that threat plays in the information environment. We now turn to the current state of social and cognitive psychology research that considers the role of affect in trust evaluations. Affect, for a long time, was denigrated or ignored in psychological and educational research (Forgas, Wyland, and Laham 2012). It was thought instead that emotion and mood were tangential to our rational, cognitive processes and could be suppressed or controlled; the (slightly toxic) adage of having a "stiff upper lip" was the legacy of that thinking. And yet, anyone who has cared for a two-year-old for any length of time can attest that mood and emotion absolutely drive how we think about and react to information. We improve, as we grow older, at negotiating social mores when it comes to our affective reactions—but they are still there. Who doesn't have moments of wanting to throw themselves down on the floor in a tantrum?

The late twentieth century saw the beginnings of the "affective turn" in psychology and education (Dernikos et al. 2020). In the information sciences, Kuhlthau's Information Search Process (ISP) model, developed in 2004, was one of the first to acknowledge that consideration of information behavior must include "'the total person,' where thinking is deeply intertwined with feeling and emotion" (Swanson 2023, 216). Although groundbreaking at the time, the model has faced criticism as research has advanced over the past twenty years. Scholars now agree that Kuhlthau didn't go far enough, as her model mostly treated emotions as separate, interruptive elements in the cognitive process and only focused on negative affective states, such as anxiety (Swanson 2023, 217). It is now generally agreed that there exists a bidirectional link between affect and cognition (Forgas, Wyland, and Laham 2012, 6).

In brief, two main influences affect how we think and judge: congruence and processing. Affect *congruence* explains how our emotions and moods negotiate meaning for us; our affective states bias our judgments. We may think of ourselves as utterly rational in our decision-making, but we are not. There are two models of affect congruence: affect-priming and affect-as-information. In affect priming, if our memories are triggered by something, the affective state that those memories contain will color our experience of whatever triggered the memory. Consider, for example, the feeling of nostalgia: Seeing or hearing something that reminds us of a pleasant period in our past will make that new experience bittersweet because of the associated memories. By itself, the new experience has no reason to create such affect. The affect-as-information model requires a more conscious acknowledgment of affective states, requiring you to ask yourself, "How do I feel about that," and incorporate the knowledge into your conscious thinking. The danger with affect-as-information is that you may apply your underlying state to your thinking, whether it matches how you feel about something or not. Minor irritations can be magnified if you are having a bad day or easily ignored if you feel euphoric. It is important to note that affect congruence is not always salient to our judgments.

The affect infusion model (AIM) was developed to explain the inconsistencies of affect congruence by postulating that its influence is contextual and depends on the cognitive strategy used (Forgas, Wyland, and Laham 2012;

Forgas 1995), leading us to examine the effect of affect on thought processes (as opposed to content). The literature on this is complex, but moods trigger different processing strategies. Some research suggests that "people in a positive mood tend to use more heuristic, superficial, and rapid and flexible thinking to make decisions," while "negative mood seems to trigger a more effortful, systematic, analytic, and vigilant processing style" (Forgas, Wyland, and Laham 2012, 11). In other words, when we are cranky, we are more critical.

Bless and Fiedler explored the question of mood influencing cognitive processing in detail, and their findings replicate some of the discussion we have so far had around threat impacting evaluation: Those who are in a positive affect are in an environment that feels comfortable and safe. Therefore, they can use mental shortcuts because they do not have any reason to be suspicious or skeptical (Bless and Fiedler 2012, 75–76). Those in a positive mood may be more likely to trust. Studies do indeed support this; positive affect—specifically a positive mood-state, as opposed to a temporary positive emotion—can cause people to be more trusting, more prone to confirmation and other biases, and therefore potentially more gullible (Forgas 2019). Very little research, if any, has focused on how affective moods influence conspiracy ideation, but some scholarship on QAnon specifically notes that it is "filled with positive affective experiences" because of the shared group values and experiences (Bessarabova and Banas 2023, 88). Once a conspiracy theorist has found an in-group with which they feel comfortable, that comfort and trust may promote credulity within the social space.

Negative affect can promote distrust, causing people to be more skeptical (Forgas and East 2008; Forgas 2019). They trust less. What starts as a negative affect, a feeling like threat or anxiety, could motivate that person to seek answers and closure wherever possible. Bessarabova and Banas (2023) write:

> QAnon tells its supporters that even though forces of evil are conspiring against them, these forces have been identified and will be dealt with harshly. These main tenets of QAnon might help restore a sense of order, alleviate anxiety, and provide an illusion of control. (88)

A conspiracy theory can soothe and supplant negative mood states with the positive affective state of now being "in the know." The positive mood states generated by being a part of the group reaffirm the conspiracy adherence, cementing the conspiracy and working against efforts to draw the person away from those beliefs.

That said, those of us who are outside of the conspiracy theory can use the knowledge of affective states to our advantage. Cultivating a positive affective state within the classroom (Greer 2023) or in our conversations can help promote our trustworthiness to others. The more we are trusted and seen as authorities, the more our information evaluation instruction will resonate.

WHO WE CHOOSE TO TRUST: COGNITIVE AND PARASOCIAL AUTHORITIES

When we do not possess enough knowledge on a topic, we decide whether to trust someone or something based on their perceived competence and expertise. For example, most of us have not empirically studied gravity, so we trust the expertise of those who have (Russo et al. 2019). We might evaluate an author or creator based on whether they are qualified to speak on that topic, or we may judge the publishing house or reputation of a brand that confers authority to its content. Where once readers could confer credibility on a source based upon its review processes or long-standing reputation, as in the example of encyclopedias, readers now must assess online information based on very few traditional indicators of a source's authority within a discourse community. Even if an astute reader acknowledges that some authors or creators have more authority than others, it has become harder to rely on traditional heuristics, such as an author's credentials, to signal expertise and competence. Traditional notions of authority are approached as inherent to a thing or an individual; however, another way to think about authority is through the lens of cognitive authority (Wilson 1983).

Cognitive authority is a type of intellectual trust placed in an entity, informed by credibility assessments, and filtered through various contexts. These assessments lead to intuitive and complex processes affiliated with correlated concepts such as believability, trustworthiness, fairness, trustfulness, factuality, completeness, precision, neutrality, objectivity, and informativeness (Rieh 2010). Information found via social media or online platforms often asks readers to judge authority based on content. Readers are left to judge such sources through their epistemologies, using "indirect tests" to assess a source's authoritativeness or trustworthiness (Rieh 2010, 1340).

Authority is thus dynamic and depends greatly on us and our feelings over time and in different contexts. An assessment of cognitive authority may be influenced more by emotional reactions or ideology than any rigorous cognitive evaluation (Bluemle 2018). For example, we recognize the expertise and competence of those in our daily lives: friends, family, colleagues, doctors, and other professionals, and the nature of this trust is dynamic.

No matter our vocation, we all acquire limited knowledge through direct observation and experience; we learn the rest through secondhand knowledge derived from external sources. New online information systems challenge the notions of traditional authority by creating a false equivalency between information creators and formats in social media feeds or search results. For example, scholar Bill Badke has referred to this era as one of "the wisdom of crowds and a diminished appreciation of expertise" (Badke 2015, 191). Part of his analysis centered on how crowdsourced knowledge, such as Wikipedia or Google's "People Also Ask" section of their search results, has fundamentally changed readers' assessments of authority. Google may confer credibility on a source based on its search results rankings; a social media influencer may confer credibility on a brand or product they promote.

Indeed, the attention economy has birthed what has been termed the "influencer industry" (Hund 2023; Yallop 2021). Much like becoming a devotee of a musician (e.g., a "stan" or "Swiftie"), where followers can feel swept into a cultural movement and track each moment online, readers may also follow social media influencers who opine about cultural flashpoints, brands, products, or lifestyles. Within these realms, a universe of like-minded followers can be found via forums, groups, apps, and various social media platforms. Where cognitive authority revolves around an individual assessment, parasociality (a one-sided relationship a person has with characters, performers, or other figures experienced through media) often occurs through community interactions; in these spaces authority is conferred through the community, and the influencer is judged on similar indirect tests. Such tests may evaluate longevity, reliability, competence, and expertise. In the case of QAnon, followers ascribe authority to Q based on perceived expertise and qualifications according to a conspiratorial worldview in particular community discourse. However, the Q community has struggled to assess reliability, such as when Q's voice or messaging changes, leading followers to wonder if the creator has changed; or when Q "oversteps ... and upsets people," making followers question the validity of their claims (Goldman and Vogt 2018).

When someone opts to follow an influencer, especially their advice, we might discuss this as derivative authority—that is, we give away authority on a particular topic because we think they are accurate about certain things (Swanson 2023, 160). We may also discuss such influence as parasocial interactions or relationships. The first study examining these types of relationships was published in 1956, laying the foundation for an entire field of research (Liebers and Schramm 2019, 4). Significantly, parasocial relationships, like other social relationships, endure beyond a single interaction and "develop into a longterm relationship between a media user and a media character" (Liebers and Schramm 2019, 5). Although the research is broad and varied, some themes have emerged, especially with the advent of social media. Parasocial relationships occur more often in those who are lonely, dissatisfied, and emotionally unstable; they can serve as a substitute for insufficient social contact (Liebers and Schramm 2019, 16–17). Virtual influencers have become increasingly prevalent because of technological advancements, and studies have found that they engage consumers just as effectively as humans, but their artificial identity poses credibility concerns (Lim and Lee 2023). We have observed the dangers of parasocial relationships, especially of virtual influencers, in our research; librarians have told us that more often than not, a patron espouses conspiracy theories because someone they follow online spreads misinformation (Beene and Greer 2023). Library workers' responses to this trust evaluation vary; given that library workers are skilled in information literacy assessment and instruction, many fall back on information literacy models promulgated through the profession.

TRUST AND AFFECT IN INFORMATION LITERACY MODELS

The phrase "information literacy" was conceived by Paul Zurkowski in a 1974 report for the National Commission on Libraries and Information Science. In it, he argued for information literacy as a response to new and expanding modes of publishing, which broadened information access (Zurkowski 1974, 6). Similar reports followed, leading the American Library Association (ALA) to provide a working definition of information literacy in 1989 as "the ability to recognize when information is needed" and effectively find, evaluate, and use information (ACRL 2006). In 2000, a division of librarians within the ALA devoted to academic libraries approved the Association of College and Research Libraries (ACRL) *Information Literacy Competency Standards for Higher Education*, the first codified document dedicated to the instruction and assessment of information literacy within higher education. Eleven years later, a task force was convened to review and update these standards for a new era of online information. The outcome of this work was the *Framework for Information Literacy for Higher Education* (*Framework*), published in 2016 and based partly on the definition and use of threshold concepts developed by economists Jan Meyer and Ray Land. Symbolizing transformative learning, threshold concepts are irreversible, integrative, possibly bounded by the discipline, and likely troublesome (Meyer and Land 2003, 4–5).

The *Framework*'s six threshold concepts (ACRL 2016) ushered in an expanded understanding of information literacy as a "set of integrated abilities encompassing the reflective discovery of information," with attention to how information is produced and disseminated through social, economic, and ethical lenses. Information professional and scholar Rebecca Kuglitsch recommends academic librarians teach the concepts "as a type of teaching for transfer," whereby students learn to apply information literacy concepts to their respective disciplines (Kuglitsch 2015). The new *Framework* thus represented a departure from earlier standards and skillsets assessments. The broadening of how information professionals approached and thought of information literacy was also transformative as they worked to adapt the *Framework* to various disciplines and institutional settings.

Beginning in 2017, a group of University of New Mexico (UNM) library faculty began investigating cognitive and epistemic information evaluation processes related to information evaluation and trust. Realizing the difficulty of assessing online information, Russo et al. turned to genre theory (Miller 1984), theories surrounding cognitive authority (Wilson 1983), fact-checking techniques (Buttry 2014), and the systematic evaluation of the failures of evaluative checklists often used in information literacy instruction across the K-12 and college spheres. Their research highlighted a disconnect between the content and context of information presented online, where information is both what it communicates (content) and how it is packaged and distributed through information systems (context). Sometimes, these categories overlap, but it can be helpful to think of them separately because the online information environment often flattens or collapses the two. For example, undergraduate students often have trouble distinguishing between a website, an article, or some other format (Greer and McCann 2018) when viewed online. Authority and context indicators relied upon in the analog world may be stripped altogether online, which may contribute to the spread of misinformation (Cooke 2017). The UNM library faculty's article, "Strategic Source Evaluation: Addressing the Container Conundrum," developed an evaluation strategy for use with information sources, predominantly online, to help students decide whether to trust (and subsequently use) an information source. The article contributes a unique strategic approach grounded in two information literacy threshold concepts: authority (to help make an accessible judgment of intellectual trust) and format (to help make more informed decisions about the content they find in a browser). Follow-up research that investigates how undergraduate students make information sources to trust is ongoing and important themes are emerging, including an over-reliance on bits and pieces of webpages (e.g., links and menus) and whether they feel a website is "professional," whether the students ever leave the page to verify information, and how affective reactions inform trust (Russo et al. 2019).

To date, information professionals' predominant guiding philosophy has been the 2016 *Framework*, accompanied by disciplinary companion documents in analogous literacies (e.g., visual literacy, data literacy, etc.). As authors of the companion document *Framework for Visual Literacy in Higher Education*, we ascribe to the knowledge practices (i.e., instruction outcomes) and dispositions (i.e., mindsets) outlined in these documents. Even though the *Framework* accounts for some affective components, we argue it does not go far enough, which we expand on in chapter 13.

At the forefront of this research, Troy Swanson published his tome *Knowledge as a Feeling: How Neuroscience and Psychology Impact Human Information Behavior*, continuing his long-standing interest in the overlap between affect and information evaluation (Swanson 2023; Swanson 2006). Through a systematic reckoning with the gaps within library and information science resources and literature, Swanson examines other fields' findings on the role of emotions and intuitions in information behavior. One of the breakthroughs of this critical work is his argument that the cognitive and affective dimensions inform and build upon each other; indeed, the mind-gut connection is genuine when it comes to "feelings of knowing." This fact has been largely overlooked in the library literature and is thus poorly understood. A better understanding of how the mind parcels content, sifts it for essential bits, and connects information to emotional reactions would better prepare information professionals to teach library patrons and students to slow down and evaluate their feelings and thinking before assessing or using a source.

A newer information literacy model has emerged to encourage students to pause and verify an information source's truth claims. The SIFT model, initiated by Mike Caulfield (Caulfield 2017)[1] addresses the fact that students spend far too much time trying to evaluate the content of online information and far too little evaluating an author or their claims through strategies such as lateral reading. SIFT stands for Stop; Investigate the source; Find trusted coverage; and Trace claims, quotes, and media back to their original context (Baer and Kipnis 2023). SIFT asks readers to pause first and verify information before trusting and using a source. However, since it doesn't account for the complexities of cognitive authority or how online emerging formats can easily deceive our intuitions, that "feeling of knowing," SIFT still relies on traditional heuristics when it asks readers to "find trusted coverage." Without a thorough inventory of how and when we trust, we are left to the same ideologies, biases, and personal epistemologies to guide us through misinformation, misleading claims, and disinformation.

A recent study attempts to rectify this situation, examining the impacts of emotional reactions and cognitive and parasocial authority figures on students' source evaluation, especially in the likelihood of one's probability of disseminating misinformation (Abdeljawad 2023, 190–94). One remarkable finding was the study's accounting of how social media platforms confer authority on certain users (e.g., the blue checkmark on X, formerly known as Twitter) or social media influencers' roles on a student's trust evaluation. Part of the appeal of new and emerging social media platforms is the ability for readers to contribute easily to a conversation, share information, and become meta-influencers among their own followers. While students expressed skepticism about a source's accuracy, very few demonstrated critical analysis, thus leading to misinformation dissemination (Abdeljawad 2023, 194–95).

New technologies and affordances, wrought by ChatGPT and other AI, have likewise challenged the library and information science field, especially in how users interpret and construct authority, how they come to trust information, and whether they will use or share the information generated. The field is beginning to grapple with such technologies, calling for a broader appreciation of large language models and algorithmic realities (see chapter 12). Information professionals have thus far fallen back on SIFT and other source evaluation checklists (Blechinger 2023) with little regard for the metacognitive, affective, and social dimensions of online information creation and dissemination.

TRUST AND AFFECT IN THE METALITERACY MODEL

The metaliteracy model engages four domains, or areas, of learning, as derived from the works of Benjamin Bloom[2] and John Dewey,[3] as well as the revision of Bloom's *Taxonomy* by Anderson and Krathwohl: cognitive, metacognitive, affective and behavioral (Bloom 1984; Dewey 2010; Anderson et al. 2000). Table 5.1 provides a brief overview of the four learning domains of metaliteracy; for this section, we will focus on the metacognitive and affective domains relevant to trust.

The metaliteracy model engages the affective and metacognitive domains through learning objectives such as "Reflect on how you feel about information or an information environment to *consider multiple perspectives* [emphasis added]" (Jacobson et al. 2018). For learners, this objective requires trust. First, they must trust themselves to parse their feelings to honestly and objectively understand how their affective states affect their evaluation. In the AIM model mentioned above, Forgas (2002) describes:

Table 5.1. Metaliteracy's Four Learning Domains

Domain	Concepts	In Practice
Affective	• Affective states: moods, emotions, physical feelings • Internal and external expressions • Often instantaneous—affective response can occur before the cognitive	• Analyze personal biases • Consider the impact of emotions on responses to information • Practice slowly responding so that the affective response can be tempered by the cognitive
Behavioral	• Individual behavior and actions • Application of knowledge • Behavioral responses within a social learning setting	• Physical application of knowledge—being able to utilize and manipulate technological tools • Learning choices made in response to learned behaviors
Cognitive	• Thinking and knowing • Logic, reasoning • Information processing	• Think through information, using prior knowledge and additional resources to verify or challenge • Organize information for later access and retrieval
Metacognitive	• Thinking about one's thinking and learning • Monitor other domains of learning	• Journaling • Pausing to consider and parse affective, cognitive, and/or behavioral responses

The combination of the two processing dimensions of quantity (i.e., effort) and quality (i.e., openness and constructiveness) produces four distinct processing styles: direct access processing (i.e., low effort, closed, not constructive), motivated processing (i.e., high effort, closed, not constructive), heuristic processing (i.e., low effort, open, constructive), and substantive processing (i.e., high effort, open, constructive). According to the model, affect infusion is most likely when a constructive processing strategy is used, such as substantive or heuristic processing. In contrast, affect should not influence the outcome of closed, merely reconstructive tasks involving motivated or direct access processing. (8)

Metaliteracy objectives encourage either heuristic or substantive processing. Although using affect as a mental heuristic is a low-effort process (thus more likely when in a positive affective state), it still requires the conscious consideration of "how do I feel" to use that feeling as an evaluative shortcut. Substantive processing, conversely, "requires individuals to select, encode, and interpret novel information and relate this information to their pre-existing memory-based knowledge to produce a response" (Forgas 2002, 8). Substantive processing is high effort and involves the metacognitive domain of learning. In the last chapter, we explained the "Dunning-Kruger effect," in which people vastly overestimate their own cognitive abilities; importantly, Kruger and Dunning wrote that "people who lack the knowledge or wisdom to perform well are often unaware of this fact. We attribute this lack of awareness to a deficit in metacognitive skill" (Kruger and Dunning 1999, 1126). We trust ourselves exactly when we should not. Trusting oneself can be tricky, and can lead to overconfidence in one's abilities, but by using critical metacognition, we can more effectively evaluate information and make decisions.

Secondly, there must be trust in others. The metaliteracy characteristic of openness, present in this objective, invokes "being open to new ideas, insights, and perspectives [to allow] individuals to think beyond their own biases that might limit their learning experiences" (Mackey and Jacobson 2019, 20). To be open to new ideas and new experiences involves trust that in doing so, one will not lose oneself. Consider, for example, the identity threat discussed in chapter 2: When identity threat is engaged, people are less open to new ideas. Their negative affective states shut down the openness and trust that would allow them to engage with new ideas and broaden their horizons. The metaliterate model, emphasizing information in a multimodal and social environment, moves beyond the individualism of previous literacy models. In this age, information is social—and we must approach it with this in mind.

NOTES

1. SIFT was further updated in the "Check, Please! Starter Course," available at https://checkpleasecc.notion.site/checkpleasecc/Check-Please-Starter-Course.
2. Benjamin S. Bloom, *Taxonomy of Educational Objectives, Handbook 1: Cognitive Domain*, 2nd ed. (London: Addison-Wesley Longman, 1984).
3. John Dewey, *How We Think* (Boston, MA: D.C. Heath, 2010).

6

Strategic Conversations: Tactics to Build Trust

Stephanie was preparing for a family gathering when she found herself in an awkward conversation with her brother-in-law's then-girlfriend (let's call her Agatha). The COVID-19 pandemic was just kicking off. Agatha began talking about how hospitals were receiving funding based on the number of deaths that occurred there—and how mainstream media wasn't reporting it. There were so many questions and protests Stephanie felt at that moment; instead, she took a deep breath, wanting to end the conversation as quickly as possible. She knew fact-checking would be pointless. Katie and Stephanie were just beginning their research into QAnon and related conspiracy ideation, and this event served as one of the catalysts for them to explore tips and techniques for navigating tricky conversations such as this one.

We often find ourselves in conversations and interactions leading to emotional overwhelm and a flurry of possible choices and reactions. Many of us, as Stephanie did, choose to avoid such topics in conversations. This is normal. However, there are strategies and tactics that we can utilize during such difficult conversations: Metacognition, curiosity, empathy, and humility are just some examples. We can learn how to model care, mindfulness, and presence in these situations.

Some of the more challenging interactions, as illustrated by the example above, are with someone one cares about but who believes in a conspiracy theory. Full-blown conspiracy ideation is a disease of loneliness and isolation, and social connections with friends and family can ameliorate it. A sense of belonging is so crucial to human experience that Maslow included it as one of his five motivational needs (Maslow 1943). Conspiracy theories such as QAnon thrive precisely because they "provide a social identity that is unfulfilled in other areas of life" (Allen et al. 2023, 181). Among conspiracy theorists, anecdotal evidence makes clear that human connections function as both a motivating factor and also, importantly, a way out (Beene and Greer 2023). How can we break through and create those human connections? Is it even possible to build trust in this age of mistrust?

STRATEGIES FOR BETTER INTERACTIONS

Two essential concepts at the root of successful interactions and conversations, whether with friends, family, colleagues, patrons, or students, are *cultural humility* and *intellectual humility*. Both concepts have a fair amount of scholarship across multiple fields and rely on the notion of empathy. Traits of empathy include experiencing another person's point of view, the ability to put yourself in someone else's shoes, and developing intrinsically motivated prosocial behaviors. Empathy enables collaboration, relationship building, and morality; cultivating empathy takes time and usually begins during childhood. Researchers have found that people can progress in their empathy skills and that those who spend more time with individuals different from them are more likely to be successful in their endeavors. Other research suggests that reading about others unlike oneself and meditation or mindfulness can encourage empathy (Psychology Today 2023).

To that end, scholars have suggested that developing empathy training for service professionals leads to a stronger community and better service. Mathieu Lajante et al. (2023) enumerate four empathetic competencies they believe could be cultivated in other service professions: communication, relationship building, emotional resilience, and counseling skills. In their pragmatic suggestions for implementation, they suggest considering the service environment and whether interactions with customers/clients/patrons will be predominantly in-person or mediated via technology. Nonverbal cues like facial expressions and body language are crucial for communicating empathy in face-to-face interactions, whereas technology-mediated interactions require more work to communicate empathy if the interactions do not involve videoconferencing. Moreover, they discover and distinguish a difference between *affective* empathy (i.e., emotion-sharing) and *cognitive* empathy (perspective-taking), which are highly dependent on whether the interaction takes place over email, text message, or some other asynchronous technology versus in-person interactions or those via synchronous videoconference or webinar. Scholars have pointed toward a third dimension of empathy beyond affective and cognitive—*somatic* empathy is the ability to sense another's experience in an embodied way (Sofer and Goldstein 2018, 103). Finally, the length of the interaction matters. Longer or more frequent interactions with another person, a friend, or a family member take more empathetic effort than brief interactions with strangers.

This last point is important. Scholars, again predominantly in the health field, have discovered that prolonged emphasis on empathetic interactions can lead to "compassion fatigue" and burnout, two unfortunate possibilities for anyone working in a service position. Mahmut Evli (2023) discusses this phenomenon in the nursing profession, and a growing number of librarians have studied its occurrence within librarianship (Ettarh, 2018; Geary and Hickey 2016; Martin 2009). Our research has corroborated this challenge within the library profession. Librarians in our 2023 survey commented directly on burnout and compassion fatigue, such as one who lamented, "I have totally lost my compassion for [conspiracy theorists]." Constant effort to draw on a deep well of empathy eventually leads to neglect of the self and feelings of burnout. How we discuss service, our expectations of those in the field, and subsequent training should be examined with the goal of alleviating these feelings.

The global pandemic has led to a renewed emphasis on self-care, metacognition, and a pedagogy of care. Several interventions have shown promise in these efforts. An emphasis on empathetic, dialogic interactions with students during classroom discourse, building upon the tenets of critical pedagogy, has been shown to increase classroom community and lead to more empathetic classroom dialogue (hooks 2003; Patel 2023). Another intervention has demonstrated a direct link between fostering reflection and empathy through mindful writing assignments (Howard 2023, 3–6).

However, because empathy takes effort to develop and maintain, and studies have shown that we are more likely to empathize with others like us, its practice remains challenging. Like a muscle, empathy can be flexed and worked on, and it's honed over time. In particular, the more that people can develop relationships with those outside their community, or with those of different socioeconomic statuses or racial, ethnic, gender, or religious identities, the better. Sometimes, our efforts to be empathetic can cause harm. Empathy may inspire us to leap to the defenses of someone else when they may not want or need our help, for example, or could be motivated by our own selfish desires (Psychology Today 2023).

Because empathy has its limitations or even deleterious effects, a growing body of scholarship has focused instead on developing cultural humility and/or intellectual humility. The concept of humility within popular culture varies quite a bit, ranging from associations with "being humbled," a reference to learning a profound lesson about one's place in the world, to "humbling yourself" before an authority. Although both concepts draw upon notions of humility, this is not exactly what cultural humility or intellectual humility entails. As David Hurley et al. explain, cultural humility embodies the concept that "my norms aren't the only norms, and unfamiliar norms aren't necessarily wrong" (Hurley, Kostelecky, and Townsend 2019, 549). These authors advocate for developing cultural humility in place of cultural competence, especially in place of diversity training within librarianship. For example, instead of assuming that one understands the cultures and identities that inform patrons' attitudes, worldviews, or mindsets, cultural humility asks us to check those impulses and assume a humble stance (e.g., "I don't know what I don't know"). To that effect, they state:

> We may not know or understand the cultures of the person we are serving, but we can be open to the knowledge that cultural factors are present. We can recognize what identities we are bringing to the interaction. We can follow the patron's lead as to which of their cultural identities are relevant to a situation. We can recognize cultural and power issues that are introduced by the library context itself and commit to addressing structural issues which interfere in the interaction or with our service outcomes. (Hurley, Kostelecky, and Townsend 2019, 553).

They are joined by a widening group of library workers integrating cultural humility into their daily work (Andrews, Kim, and Watanabe 2018; Hodge 2018).

An analogous concept is intellectual humility, framed as a fundamental component of building understanding and empathy in conversations. Intellectual humility can be defined as "intellectual flexibility, security in one's own viewpoints, and openness to and respect for others' views" (Huynh and Bayles, 2022, Abstract). Intellectual humility encourages sensitivity to our biases that may inform our perspectives, as well as attending to any gaps that might exist in our expertise and experiences. Church and Samuelson apply this concept to "persistent, intractable disagreements" where each party believes they are the accurate one (2016, 274). Indeed, they argue that being open to where the evidence might lead is an epistemic virtue, and not without its challenges, especially when the disagreement pertains to deeply held positions or beliefs (e.g., religious, political, moral) (273–80).

Intellectual humility has been examined within the context of conspiracy ideation and disbelief in science, which can exhibit similar traits of intractability (Huynh and Bayles 2022; Plohl and Musil 2023). In light of conspiracy theorists' dogmatic commitment to their beliefs, scholars have suggested that intellectual humility can be an antidote to conspiracy ideation. The more an individual associates intellectual prowess with their identity, the harder it will be to change their minds about their beliefs; they may feel threatened when they are challenged because their convictions are so integrated into their notions of self-worth. Those who exhibit intellectual humility, however, are "able calmly to consider ideas that contradict, oppose, or refute their own beliefs because the individual is secure in themselves and in their own ideas" (Huynh and Bayles 2022, 563). Likewise, Nejc Plohl and Bojan Musil found that openness to revising one's viewpoint positively correlated to trust in science (Plohl and Musil 2023).

The resounding takeaway from this discourse is that beliefs are hard to change but can be modified with time, patience, and effort. It is also important to cultivate an awareness of, and openness to, others' worldviews and truth perceptions because each person has come to their beliefs through a particular epistemology and life experiences. Because beliefs can be so intractable, Church and Samuelson argue for indirectly influencing belief formation when they are particularly problematic; within oneself, one can track the accuracy of beliefs in light of current evidence, reflect and systematically check in with our positions, and learn new ways of thinking about our convictions (2016, 282). One way to systematically check in is through naming our and others' emotions, which helps the logical part of our brains process complex and nuanced feelings (Lindquist et al. 2012; Mlodinow 2023). This labeling of emotions can act much like tapping the brakes when encountering traffic, lowering heightened emotional states, and is key to an empathic response. "Wow, you sound frustrated" or "That must have been frustrating" can go a long way toward stemming the tide of emotional overwhelm. Scientists have discovered that if we can identify our emotions when we're feeling them (Barrett 2006), we may be able to better regulate them (Morie et al. 2022)—and have studied MRIs of our brains before, during, and after labeling emotions (UCLA 2007). Our brains return to baseline more quickly if we can name the emotions we are feeling.

NAVIGATING HARD CONVERSATIONS: TIPS AND TECHNIQUES

Grenny et al. (2021) define "crucial conversations" as those high-impact conversations where opinions vary and emotions are elevated; examples can include a breakup, asking a friend to repay a loan, or critiquing a colleague's work. Importantly, they link their research to long-term health, much like the research on emotional regulation; avoiding such crucial conversations only serves to prolong and repress emotions that could bubble over later, while handling such conversations poorly can be equally detrimental. We all have avoided hard conversations or handled them poorly at one point. The biological underpinnings of a threatening or high-arousal situation have been well-studied—and these types of conversations arouse those same biological mechanisms (commonly referred to as "fight, flight, or freeze" physiological reactions, where the body prepares to flee or fight, or becomes paralyzed in the moment). During a high-stakes conversation, body language or raised voices can trigger such responses.

So, what are some tactics they suggest we use when anticipating, or finding ourselves in, such conversations? The following tips are synthesized from Greeny et al. (2021), Stone, Patton, and Heen (2023):

1. **Enter crucial conversations with clear motives for a resolution.** What do you want out of the conversation? What would be the preferred outcome? What relationship do you have with the others involved, and what

relationship would you like once a resolution has been reached? Try to vocalize such goals during the conversation; doing so may establish a common purpose with other parties involved and minimize conflict.

2. **Monitor your emotions and behaviors.** We will all slip up, and becoming self-aware is a lifelong process. However, avoiding such things as eye-rolling, finger-pointing, or raising your voice can go a long way in our message being heard. Moreover, by stopping yourself in your tracks when you do notice these behaviors, you may also avoid a fight-flight-freeze reaction in yourself and others, leading to a better outcome from the conversation. By monitoring your physiological reactions and taking a deep breath or a break, these overwhelming emotions may subside so that you might again tap into the more rational and logical part of your brain. A situation in which both parties are affectively aroused is like an impending traffic collision; are there steps you can take to avoid it?

3. **Avoid binary positions or options** (right vs. wrong, good vs. bad, plan A vs. plan B). This can be as simple as assigning blame or as complex as lodging yourself into the mentality of the "best" or "correct" plan. Binary positions may be self-defeating and lead to defensiveness in the other person. Could the truth be somewhere in the middle, or could an outcome embrace multiple positions or outcomes?

4. **Do tell your story as you understand it, but ask others for their understanding of the facts.** Difficult conversations are rarely about getting the facts right; they are about conflicting perceptions, interpretations, and values.

5. **Be careful about assuming intention in the other person.** We often assume we understand the motivations or intentions of another person, but we are often wrong in our assumptions. It is better to ask others what their intention or motivation behind a line of reasoning or their actions might be (these are the "why" and "how" questions explored in the "Socratic Questioning" section below).

6. **Avoid assigning blame.** Much like trying to determine an objective "truth," this is subject to our perceptions and values and is often self-defeating. More often, all people involved in a disagreement contributed to the misunderstanding in some way.

7. **Adopt a learning stance**. We will discuss this more in the curiosity section below. Stone et al. argue that this stance can lead to better problem-solving, involving all parties in the disagreement (Stone, Patton, and Heen 2023).

Some conversations are so polarizing or intractable that implementing such techniques can be challenging. One such area involves deeply held convictions or identities (e.g., religious or ideological positions). There will be elements we cannot change, but being transparent will make a conversation go more smoothly. Even if we cannot change certain elements, we *can* change how we respond.

As has been discussed previously in this book, conspiracy theories and misinformation thrive when there are gaps or ambiguities in knowledge, which proliferate during times of war or catastrophe. For example, the eruption of conflict in the Middle East in the fall of 2023 has galvanized communities worldwide, often leading to opposing, sometimes violent, stances. It has led to a range of complex emotions that hinge on deeply held convictions and personal beliefs. Universities are navigating these conversations with varying levels of success.

In these conversations, fact-checking will only get you so far. And much like engaging around belief in a conspiracy theory, it can often backfire. Two recent think pieces are helpful when approaching such polarizing conversations. Public health scholar and professor Sandro Galea (2023) encourages us to examine the lens and biases that we bring to such discussions, including our ideologies and beliefs, as well as where and how we are getting our information. Social media rewards rapid engagement, and mis- and disinformation can proliferate within minutes. Like so many others, he implores that all parties think about their desired outcomes and take a moment—a ten-second pause, to be exact—before responding to a social media post or comment that feels particularly wrong, hurtful, or anger-inducing. *New York Times* columnist and professor Frank Bruni (2023) likewise calls for his readers and students to moderate their impulses and avoid adopting a "prefabricated compass, a pre-formulated message that you graft onto everything, no matter how awkward the fit . . . taking your cues from a political or ideological tribe and making sure that you utter the lines it seems to want you to say." Instead, he argues for a constructive, "earnest, honest examination of the situation at hand" through the type of moderation that Galea advocates.

REMAINING MINDFULLY CURIOUS

Sofer and Goldstein (2018) outline several key principles to remaining mindful when practicing "nonviolent communication": practicing mindful speech and presence in conversation, understanding how words can shape reality, and focusing on creating dialogue that feels as safe as possible for all parties involved. The authors describe how, especially in times of great change, the opportunities for misunderstanding and even violent dialogue are great. Therefore, we must practice mindfulness and presence, which they define as "embodied awareness of our direct sensory, mental, and emotional experience"; they argue that practicing presence is easy for most of us momentarily, but practicing it continually, even during emotionally heightened moments, takes training (16–17). We tend to focus our attention outward, toward the other person, and in reality, we must stay present and attend to the entire situation, including our own minds and bodies. Mindfulness is "being aware of what's happening in the present moment in a balanced and nonreactive way" (25), which requires presence. Given the complexity of communication, transforming our responses "occurs most readily through small shifts over time" (21).

Sofer and Goldstein (2018) connect mindfulness and presence in conversations to curiosity and care. Curiosity, as they define it, means we are interested in learning, and learning requires humility; it also requires enduring patience and a willingness to understand (78). These authors argue that to pay attention to something, we must care—whether about someone else, a topic, our values, or resolving conflict. The quality of care matters, which they argue includes warmth, vulnerability, and flexibility (79).

During difficult conversations, heightened physiological reactions can lead to emotional flooding, an affective condition that affects our ability to take in new information and calmly evaluate it (Orbach et al. 2003). In our previously mentioned survey, emotional flooding was evident in various interactions, and it occurred in library workers' responses, as well as patrons' responses, depending on the content and context of the interaction (Beene and Greer 2023). Being aware of our emotions and practicing care through active and empathetic listening allow us to choose how to show up in a conversation. To this end, Sofer and Goldstein outline two guiding principles: The more we take responsibility for our emotions, connecting them to our needs and desires rather than to others' actions, the easier it will be for others to hear us; likewise, the more we hear others' feelings as a reflection of their needs, the easier it will be to understand them without hearing blame, needing to agree, or feeling responsible for their emotions (Sofer and Goldstein 2018, 152). There are some techniques we can readily employ: remaining mindful and present, observing without evaluating, suspending judgment, and leading with curiosity. Additionally, practicing translating others' judgments and reactions into observations of their stated or unstated needs can yield valuable information on how to move a conversation forward. We can deactivate our own emotional flooding by focusing on our breathing and physiological responses or noticing things in our environment. When we feel more calm and able to observe without judgment, we may gently direct the conversation back to solving a problem or promoting understanding.

Remaining curious is one of the most essential tactics in difficult interactions. Interpersonal curiosity (Litman and Pezzo 2012) is the desire for new information about people, including details about others' life experiences and their internalized thoughts, feelings, and motives. Interpersonal curiosity is a propensity to notice items like photos or knick-knacks when visiting others' houses, scrolling through social media posts, or being curious about others' hobbies, interests, thoughts, feelings, and motivations. Epistemic curiosity (Litman 2012), on the other hand, is very familiar to those working in librarianship and education: It is the desire to obtain new knowledge, the desire for knowledge in its own right, exploring new ideas, or mastering a topic or project. Finally, perceptual curiosity drives someone to "learn something to solve an immediate problem, like finding food, combating bad breath or trying to remember the name of the wonderful actor in that otherwise awful horror movie" (Aberman 2021). All three types of curiosity could be triggered by situations, interactions, or conversations (Gilligan and Eddy 2021; Deitering and Rempel 2017). As educators, we can embody curiosity by encouraging questions in our students, designing activities and assignments that allow them to actively seek out new knowledge to fill information gaps, and welcoming novel or unpredictable situations (Erickson and Noonan 2023). Encourage curiosity by exploring new and various sources with others, modeling flexibility, adaptability, excitement, and interest as we learn new things about a topic; likewise, we can model self-reflection and metacognition as we guide the search and evaluation process (Dietering and Rempel 2017).

Curiosity requires us to remain open-minded and maintain a desire to understand another person. A method for systemic change in organizations, appreciative inquiry, can also serve on the individual level to help guide challenging conversations. Appreciative inquiry, much like curiosity, requires you to consciously consider the positive traits of the person with whom you are talking. What are this person's strengths, or what underlying values do you share? What is it they are doing well? Lastly, and perhaps most importantly for these kinds of conversations, appreciative inquiry involves reframing problems into possibilities (Armstrong, Holmes, and Henning 2020).

SOCRATIC QUESTIONING: GETTING TO THE "WHY" AND "HOW"

Conversations that encourage critical thinking and logic using the Socratic method can help frame difficult conversations. In Socratic dialogue, the librarian or educator uses questioning to help learners parse their assumptions and the evidence they rely on for their ideas. The seminar, or learner-centered Socratic method, requires a subversion of one's typical authoritative guidance regarding information; instead, the authority becomes a companion to the learner's quest. By not directly challenging the conspiracy theorist but instead gently questioning with an open curiosity, conversation can occur.

There is no set, defined method for Socratic questioning, as our knowledge of Socrates's methods is all secondhand (Fischer 2021). One common method, illustrated in sources like Plato's *Republic*, is to question the terms being used; in the words and spirit of Inigo Montoya, "You keep saying that word. I do not think it means what you think it means" (Reiner 1987). Because words and their connotations are fluid and contextual, helping a person critically examine how and why they use particular language can lead to deeper questions. The point in these exercises is not to cause perplexity for its own sake but to arouse curiosity about what is untrue, to help others realize that they have to seek new knowledge (Katsara and De Witte 2019, 112).

The aporia, or puzzlement, engendered by Socratic questioning throws one's state of equilibrium into flux, provoking the learner to re-engage with their knowledge to reach stability again. At the same time, because this destabilizing occurs within a dialogue, the learner is not left alone in their aporia; rather, Socratic questioning allows for "empowerment, encouragement, empathy, and extended engagement" (Robinson 2017).

One strategy is to use the "awkward pause," or silence of ten to fifteen seconds, to help think through what has been said and consider what should be asked next. As with any new skill, the Socratic method will take time to develop (Thinknetic, n.d.).

The steps of the Socratic method can be summarized as follows ("Socratic Dialog Method" 2022; Sutton 2020):

- First, clarify. Ask the person to explain their belief or understanding in their own words.
- After pausing to take in the information, repeat what they have said in your own words to demonstrate that you are starting on the same page.
- Use questioning to investigate the evidence used to support their propositions. What evidence is there? Why do they trust that evidence?
- During the questioning phase, there will be points of opportunity to challenge the evidence or the assumptions. Is there evidence proving the opposing point of view? This should not be done aggressively but with open curiosity to keep the person engaged and not defensive. Encourage the person to restate any beliefs with any new insights or clarifications that have occurred as a result of the dialogue.
- Repeat this process as necessary to engage critical thinking further or help the person see other points of view.

This method encourages trust and relationship-building through empowerment, encouragement, and empathy. Implementing this strategy can trigger the incremental process of someone withdrawing from deeply held (mis) beliefs. Another way to do that is with "the nudge."

NUDGING AND OTHER STRATEGIES

Nudge by Richard H. Thaler and Cass R. Sunstein (2009) argues for a revolutionary way to approach choices or to provide "choice architecture" through design or during interactions with others. Their theory has been built upon by many other researchers, who have discussed "nudging" in everyday decision-making (Johnson 2021), interactions over social media (Horne, Gruppi, and Adali 2019; Alsaleh 2022), discussions with conspiracy theorists or science skeptics (Beene and Greer 2023), or even in public health contexts (Kim 2020). The idea behind "nudging" is pretty simple: We all have the ability to make better decisions, given the right circumstances; it might take "nudging" from another person or technology to move us in an optimal direction.

In our article "Library Workers on the Front Lines," we found that library workers were using nudging, but only after a relationship had been established (Beene and Greer 2023). In our first article, "A Call to Action," we detail how that relationship might take shape—and the discussion aligns with strategies for difficult conversations (Beene and Greer 2021). During the first interaction with a patron, a librarian might probe their critical thinking and worldview; if they appear defensive, defiant, or entrenched, it is a pretty good indication that they are not willing to engage an alternative viewpoint yet (Basu 2020). Establishing common ground by finding something to agree on allows for mutual goals and interests, similar to the "pool of shared meaning" strategy outlined by Grenny et al (2021). Over time, patrons might be willing to offer a little more information that librarians can use to assess their stance and openness to new information. Nudging patrons toward critical thinking and reflection occurs over time through small interactions. These techniques have been demonstrated to be useful in healthcare interactions, for example, when nudging patients toward accepting an intervention they might otherwise be against (Kim 2020).

A complementary framework is offered by McIntyre (2021), who argues for humanizing the science denier. In discussions where facts have been mis-interpreted or misunderstood, or where information has been gathered from social media, McIntyre argues for a noncombative stance. Like Thaler and Sun-stein, he advocates for longer conversations with climate change skeptics, con-spiracy theorists, and so-called science deniers to insert reflection and critical thinking. Before nudging someone toward these skills, McIntyre asserts that an understanding of some basic principles undergirding disbelief in science is necessary. For example, trying to understand how and where someone is cherry-picking their evidence might lead to an opening to discuss information habits or sources. Attempting to understand someone's underlying beliefs in what science can achieve or tell us about the world, their respect for authorities and experts, and who their cognitive authorities might be could lead to a better conversational outcome because it begins with listening to understand rather than to argue. Finally, over time, logical fallacies may present themselves, and these, too, could be highlighted for correction. In part 3 of this book, we will delve more into what scientists have termed "debunking" and "prebunking" to correct such fallacies. For now, it is enough to say that these conversations will be smoother if some sort of relationship has been established, and if there is mutual respect in the other person's fallible humanity.

Outside of library interactions and conversations, we might also think of the ways in which educators nudge their students. Whether by encouraging students to integrate different viewpoints or prompting them to read and use specific sources, nudging can occur through formal instruction, meetings with students in groups or one-on-one, or by thoughtfully scaffolding assignments. Instructors might also prompt students to broaden or sharpen their research questions or hypotheses. Each of these scenarios considers a burgeoning relationship between teacher and student, the topic being explored, and insertions of critical thinking and alternative viewpoints along the way.

STRATEGIES FOR ONLINE INTERACTIONS

As Emerick and Dea (forthcoming) succinctly summarize, "Knowing when and what to say within the public square is often messy and complicated." Those who have spent time on social media or the comments section of any website may despair of any productive conversations occurring in the online environment. And yet they do happen, with one of the most powerful examples being that of Megan Phelps-Roper. She grew up in the Westboro Baptist Church, the infamous organization that protests at military funerals, and speaks of being five years old the first time she held up a "God Hates Gays" sign. Megan became one of the church's most erudite and vocal proponents, going on various national media to discuss their beliefs and engaging on social media. It was the latter that showed her the way out: "The end of my antigay picketing career and life as I knew it [was] triggered in part by strangers on Twitter who showed me the power of engaging the other" (Phelps-Roger 2017). Out of the cacophony of emotional flooding on her Twitter feed came those who approached her with civility. That led to conversations, both on Twitter and offline. The seeds of doubt were planted through these conversations.

When considering Megan's situation, there are a few salient points that can be drawn out. First, effective conversations occurred when others approached her with openness and curiosity. They did not do so by jeopardizing their own values but rather engaged her in a polite, civil dialogue. Second, listening is important; they first strove to hear and acknowledge her point of view before respectfully offering their own. Third, these conversations took time—a single tweet did not cause her to shift her entire life that same day. And lastly, hearkening back to the discussions above, the people who engaged Megan on Twitter saw her as a human being, despite what they considered to be her horrific views.

Conflict can be productive; "ideological arguments are essential to deliberative democracy" (Baughan et al. 2021, 2). Online arguments often turn toxic or useless, however, as the parties involved resort to ad hominem attacks, bullying, or other toxic behaviors. The mediation of the screen separates us from our humanity. Deciding when and where to engage and voice opposition is fraught with moral and philosophical considerations; while some see not engaging as a "silent assent" that only affirms toxic views, others acknowledge that sometimes silence is the safer or saner choice (Saul 2021). We explore neutrality and non-engagement in chapter 11.

The choice of platform and its design makes a difference for online dialogue (Gurgun et al. 2023; Binnquist et al. 2022). A dedicated forum for civil conversation around heated topics, Reddit's "Change My View" (https://www.reddit.com/r/changemyview/), for instance, provides an excellent example of social media conversations that are engaging and productive, by design. Users post their reasoning for opinions on topics that range from the banal ("shaved cold meats are superior to thin/thick cut meats") to real societal problems ("There's a lot of thinly veiled anti-semitism in the African American community the Hamas attack has brought to the surface"), inviting the community to engage with them and think through the issues (Jhaver, Vora, and Bruckman 2017). Users are motivated to comment on posts that pique their interests, and the tone of civility within the forum encourages them to model that behavior, along with moderators that actively enforce the group's rules (7–8). Importantly, the moderators follow rules put in place by the users themselves, not enacted as a top-down, unilateral approach to what they consider correct. There is a fine, but crucial, line between enabling civility and censorship—"moderation, and especially moderation that is unexplained or viewed as biased, hurts open dialogue" (Baughan et al. 2021, 13). The tenets of the "Change My View" community are validated by research studies that "suggest that it is not mere exposure to the outgroup that produces change, but rather the quality of that exposure including factors such as a cooperative environment, common goals, equal status, and norms endorsing contact" (Stray, Iyer, and Puig Larrauri 2023).

Studies are teasing out strategies and technological innovations to encourage initiating or maintaining productive discussions online (Gurgun et al. 2023). For example, in an analysis of what facilitates hard conversations online, Amanda Baughan and her coauthors (2021) found that image- or video-centered platforms have fewer arguments; utilizing such media when having conversations might help to break up any tension and could serve to reinforce points. Numerous studies have found that, when difficult conversations do occur, users prefer to take them into more private spaces where they can be more focused, such as chat or private messaging; platforms that include these services will be able to promote better dialogue (2).

METALITERACY AND ONLINE CONVERSATIONS

Although the mediation of the screen often makes things worse, there are unique affordances that can produce more productive conversations than what might happen in person. The asynchronous nature of online communication, for example, forces a pause between a comment and its response, although this disruption can also be frustrating (Baughan et al. 2021, 9). By developing the metaliteracy habits of reflective metacognition and lifelong learning (remaining open to new ideas), we can train ourselves to approach the online space as a place of potential dialogue rather than a cesspit of negativity.

For those structuring learning environments to facilitate discussion, the asynchronicity of the online medium can be leveraged to encourage metacognition. Interpersonal mindfulness (defined in Masrani et al. 2023 as "nonjudgmental acceptance and nonreactivity") interventions such as "*speed bumps*: a mandatory waiting period before users can send (potentially harmful) messages during online conflict" (5) can force the issue.

Utilizing reflective questions can help others think metacognitively. In one study, reflective questions encouraged deeper reflection, more prosocial behavior, and a greater determination to learn. Reflective questions that are personalized and encourage more cognitive processing of information, rather than emotional processing, were also found to be more effective (Lee et al. 2023). Much of this can be framed using metaliteracy's Goal 4: "Develop learning strategies to meet lifelong personal and professional goals" (Jacobson et al. 2018). This goal and its related objectives encourage the learner to appreciate that learning is an ongoing process and that different perspectives can enrich one's own knowledge.

Alison Hosier (2019) engages metaliteracy to encourage students to be open and receptive to different perspectives and new information by engaging "models of wrongness" to illustrate that fallibility is human. In her teaching, Hosier focuses on metaliteracy objective 4.1: "Recognize that learning is a process and that reflecting on errors or mistakes leads to new insights and discoveries." Centering our own potential "wrongness" as a construct in our thinking and responses forces us to ensure that we do not reply out-of-hand, instead crafting thoughtful, considered responses that rely on evidence and reflection instead of emotion. Metaliteracy Goal 4 and its objectives overlap with those of a "growth mindset," allowing for errors to "become opportunities to reflect on a different way forward" (Mackey and Jacobson 2022).

The social online space is difficult, to say the least. Philosophers Emerick and Dea, quoted from their forthcoming publication earlier, acknowledge that "human and technological realities are far from ideal," noting that many times engaging in conflict online has deleterious or opposite effects from that which we intend. They propose a "disposition that can help us when we are torn between opposing oppression and contributing to a flame war." Their proposed disposition centers on "being human," which calls back to many of the tenets discussed above that led to Megan Phelps-Roper breaking from Westboro Baptist. To be human is to resist the polarity and the hero/villain duality that social media engagement can often engender: "We need to remind ourselves that we belong in the "just-right" Goldilocks space between those two extremes." React less, they are saying, and look for a middle ground. Center humanity—both in oneself and others. They caution, however, that this does not mean giving ground to extremists; there instead needs to be a careful deliberation and thoughtful response "recentering on the others we wish to support, the values we wish to enact, and the likely outcomes of our response." In this, they remind us that responses do not need to happen in the space in which they originated. Sometimes, we can more effectively promote change by choosing to engage, instead, in person, through volunteering for nonprofit organizations or organizing or attending events that support our viewpoints.

Part III

How Conspiracy Theories Exploit Distrust in a Post-Truth America

7

Historical and Religious Foundations of American Conspiracies

Stop me if you have heard this before. A vast network of satanic pedophiles has infiltrated our country. Our children are in danger like never before. Secret tunnels, midnight rituals, the drinking of their blood, and the violation of their innocence are occurring in every city and every town.

No, this is not QAnon. Rather, this is the "Satanic Panic" of the 1980s, which saw daycare workers, parents, and others accused of heinous crimes. Some were convicted based on children's testimony that was often wildly fantastic and obtained under dubiously ethical means. Most accusations were later proven false, but not before lives were ruined. During this time, though, the media and local gossip convinced most of the country that it was all real, that our children were in danger, and that this particular conspiracy was not just a runaway theory.

QAnon adherents may feel they are privy to a shocking revelation about a global cabal that is trafficking children and illuminating the nightmare that is our current society—but they are only the latest in a long list of people who have fallen for conspiracy theory tropes repeated over centuries. Many compare QAnon to the Satanic Panic of the 1980s, and indeed, a genealogy of conspiracism connects the two, with numerous overlaps—but the roots go much deeper.

QAnon both overtly and covertly references antisemitic conspiracy theories, with Mike Rothschild (2023, xiv) prefacing his book *Jewish Space Lasers: The Rothschilds and 200 Years of Conspiracy Theories* with the comment: "Almost all conspiracy theories are rooted in antisemitism, and almost all antisemitism is rooted in conspiracy theories." QAnon, with its ability to integrate any conspiracy theory, no matter how outlandish or contradictory to its narrative, started with antisemitism and then generously seasoned it with additional forms of prejudice. To know better is to do better, we hope. In this chapter, we explore the foundational elements of antisemitic, religious, and misogynistic themes that have shaped the superconspiracy of today.

FROM POISONED WELLS TO BIG PHARMA

In the fourteenth century in Western Europe, public wells became the main source of drinking water for urban populations. This vital resource also presented a vulnerability: Corrupted water could efficiently strike large numbers of people very quickly (as was demonstrated by the famous study of cholera contagion in the nineteenth century; see Johnson 2007). Concurrent with this new dependence on public water sources was a curious rise in poison accusations, poison treatises by medical authors, and a growing generalized anxiety over the risk of being poisoned.

Historian Tzafrir Barzilay (2022) has traced the first well poisoning accusations to 1321 in France, and at first, the marginalized group under suspicion was not Jews but lepers. They were accused of conspiring to poison wells to spread leprosy so that, among other nefarious plots, all would suffer their pain and ostracization. Barzilay connects allegations against the lepers to a concerted effort to persecute them "in a protracted process of segregation and attempts at the appropriation of lepers' holdings" (61). The first accusations of well-poisoning eventually included Jews, who allegedly hired the lepers to poison the wells.

By the middle of the century, however, the Black Death raged, and well-poisoning accusations had shifted from lepers to other outcasts. Although well-poisoning accusations have, in popular historical imagination, been connected exclusively to antisemitism, Barzilay (2022, 3–5) reconsiders this narrative, noting that people of all faiths were accused of this crime. Notably, the allegations were nearly always concocted by authorities to fit a particular narrative for "political or economic benefits"; in the depths of the plague, the already-persecuted Jews were often the chosen group to scapegoat: "That medieval decision-makers made the effort to implicate the Jews shows that they were convinced that Jews were hated enough for the accusations to be believed" (193). The example of Tidericus and the traveling priests with whom he was burned because of their alleged subservience to a Jewish plot illustrates the extreme consequence of this hatred.

Well-poisoning accusations were the fad of the fourteenth century and died out after about 1422 (Barzilay 2022). Fast forward roughly six hundred years, however, and a new plague, COVID-19, spread like wildfire and caused millions of deaths (WHO 2024). Conspiracy theorists and authorities would similarly seek blame, starting with the Chinese in general or the Wuhan labs in particular, but eventually coming around to implicate the Jews as part of, you guessed it, a long-running plot to take over the world and make its populations subservient. In China and elsewhere, publications based on the *Protocols* fueled conspiracy theories that Jews were to blame (Rothschild 2023, 213, 217). In QAnon circles, the Rothschild family (more on them below) were accused of having patented the virus several years prior to the pandemic; Jewish billionaire and philanthropist George Soros was named as one of their accomplices (244–45). The development of the vaccine provided a small but critical shift in the conspiratorial mindset: Now the poison was not the virus, but its preventative, with George Soros being among the many accused of "paying to use the vaccine as a vector for either global genocide or implanting tracking microchips in people" (264). The technology and contexts may have shifted from water to pharmaceuticals, but the fears have not.

THE JEWISH OTHER

In 1350, the people of the city of Visby in Gotland, an island off the eastern coast of Sweden, burned Tidericus the Organist to death (Cole 2020). Plague had come to the island, and the townspeople agreed that the source was a Jewish conspiracy to poison their wells with the illness. Tidericus was not a Jew. In fact, there were no Jews on the tiny island. But he was an outsider, either a traveling musician or an immigrant to the area, and he, along with traveling priests and others, was convicted of having conspired with Jewish contacts to spread the plague. In his exploration of Tidericus's fate, Richard Cole (2020) found that this narrative was not unique:

> This is a classic motif in the accusations made by Hanseatic administrators to explain plague outbreaks elsewhere. Indeed, chains of employment, with a supposed commissioner allegedly paying others to distribute poison, who sometimes in turn commissioned their own subordinate poisoners, were common in several medieval plague fantasies. (42)

The Gotlanders' acceptance of this trope reflects the ease with which bureaucracy and conspiracies mix, as mentioned in chapter 5. During this period the urban center, Visby, had connections to the Hanseatic League (its trading ships being the most probable actual cause of the plague), with the residents there being mostly German settlers, as opposed to the native Gotlanders who resided in the more rural areas of the island. The tension between the two groups may have sealed Tidericus's and the others' fates; uprisings against Hansard populations in other areas were increasingly common, so to protect their own, the Visbyers may have sought a scapegoat (Cole 2020, 70–74).

Tidericus's death was just one of many examples in the late medieval period of Jewish individuals, or in his case, Jewish proxies, executed for allegedly poisoning water sources. Conspiracy theories require a group of conspirators, and in the Christian hegemony of Western Europe (and, later, North

America), the marginalized Jew presented the perfect victim. Anti-Judaism laws often physically disenfranchised Jews, confining them to ghettos, requiring them to wear badges (often yellow triangles, as opposed to the Nazi's use of the Star of David), and restricting their occupations. Fortunately and unfortunately, banking and other financial management were open to them, and as Mike Rothschild (2023, 8) points out, Jewish culture has placed a heavy emphasis on literacy and learning, leading to medieval and early modern Jews being among the rare few who could read and understand contracts, keep records, and do the math necessary to exchange currencies or calculate interest. Many ended up in positions of power, as "court Jews" who managed the finances of rulers, lawyers, or bankers. As a result of these relatively few successes, and the jealousies they aroused, the enduring symbol of the miserly, greedy, gold- and power-hungry Jew was born.

The Jews have also been ascribed secret occult knowledge, magical abilities, and otherworldly powers. Consider, for example, the legend of the Golem of Prague (Oreck 2024) or celebrities in the 1990s extolling the mystical Kabbalah while sporting red string bracelets. Envy has bred appropriations alongside denunciations of Jewish culture. For example, in the superconspiracy QAnon, gematria has been appropriated, a Hebraic numerology system from the Kabbalah that we first mentioned in chapter 4. QAnon adherents use gematria to "decode" increasingly unhinged secret messages everywhere (Fox 2022).

THE SECRET CABAL THAT RULES THE WORLD

The Illuminati. The Hidden Hand. The Committee of 300. Going by many names throughout the past few hundred years, the various theories that a secret globalist cabal is working behind the scenes to plunge society into chaos and enact a New World Order in its stead, one that will enslave and decimate the populace, are legion. While the Illuminati were originally a real eighteenth-century secret society in Bavaria, their charter purposes were more benign, focusing on rendering "unto man the importance of the perfection of reason and his moral character," fighting injustice, and championing "knowing and science" (Brotherton 2017, 27). The founder was raised a Jesuit Catholic, not Jewish, and his less-than-charming personality led to the group's banishment within a decade. But that hasn't stopped conspiracy theorists from building on the group's history, ascribing to them ever-more-fantastic activities and goals and ignoring their dissolution. Instead, they surmise that the group is obviously an underground Jewish cabal.

The early twentieth century saw the creation of a new supposed cabal, one that would gain such currency and work its insidious way into so many minds that it provides a direct genealogical link to the Russian pogroms, the rising antisemitic movement throughout the world, and, chillingly, the Holocaust.

Even those who have never heard of the *Protocols of the Elders of Zion* have seen its themes repeated in the words of politicians, celebrities, and crank scholars. Written (or, really, mostly plagiarized) by the Russian secret police in the last years of the nineteenth century to blame the country's troubles on the Jews, the *Protocols* purports to be a record of the secret meetings of the "Elders of Zion," a Zionist cabal that plans to install a "Super-Government" that will "be of such colossal dimensions that it cannot fail to subdue all the nations of the world" (Bronner 2003, 7). The document "reflects in theory the practical transition of a primarily religious prejudice that later became a social sentiment into a new political worldview" (35). Just for good measure, the Jesuits and the Freemasons are mentioned as either controlled by or allied with the Elders, connecting all of the most vilified groups under one conspiratorial umbrella. Furthermore, all progressive movements, such as "Darwinism, Marxism, Nietzsche-ism" were proposed to be sown by the Elders; they were "the first to cry among the masses of the people the words "Liberty, Equality, Fraternity," all to [put] an end everywhere to peace, quiet, solidarity, and destroying the foundations of the *goya* states" (12–13). The focus on progress as an enemy that destroys the aristocratic class and governmental authorities around the world illustrates how "[antisemitism] is grounded within an antimodern and antidemocratic worldview" (3).

To say that the global cabal that QAnoners believe Trump is going to take down is Jewish is not a stretch; original Q drops contained direct references to the Rothschilds, and a general dog whistle for antisemitism (Rothschild 2023, 240–41). Positioning Trump as a hero working to reveal the cabal and its workings is not unique; when Russia first raided Ukraine in 2022, sycophants referred to him doing just that, with Fox News contributor Lara Logan writing, "He's the man who is standing between us and this New World Order" (Dickinson 2022).

ADRENOCHROME, OR BLOOD LIBEL REBORN

Despite the ban on consuming blood in Judaism, Jewish communities began to be accused in the twelfth century onward of murdering children for their blood, to be used in arcane rituals or baked into their Passover matzo. Magda Teter (2020, 5) has written of the most-discussed blood libel stories in academic literature—the disappearance of William of Norwich in 1144 and the death of toddler Simon of Trent in 1475—as "bookends of the medieval accusations against Jews." Numerous authors have sensitively and thoroughly explored the historical records and underlying contexts for blood libel and its spread (Teter, 2020; Arieti 2016; Dundes 1991), but for our purposes, we will focus on the importance of the information landscape of the times and how it shaped the legend and legacy of this extremely harmful canard.

The beginnings of blood libel did not even begin with an acknowledged crime. Twelve-year-old William of Norwich's body was found in the forest on Good Friday of 1144. The nascent Jewish community in that area, who had settled alongside Norman colonizers, were never formally accused of the death, although the child's uncle implicated the Jews (McCulloh 1997, 701). And yet, as outsiders in the area, they were natural suspects—and the few mentions of rumors in the historical record seem to confirm that suspicion surrounded them (Teter 2020, 18–23). Not until Thomas of Monmouth wrote his *Life and Passion of William of Norwich* several decades later, however, did the accusations coalesce into a full-fledged mythology, making the victim "a stand-in for all Christians, indeed, for Christ himself, whom Jews killed out of hatred" (Teter 2020, 18). Thomas's account served a hagiographic purpose, attempting to make a case for the boy locally revered as a saint to be formally canonized despite numerous evidentiary and theological gaps in the case (McCulloh 1997, 702; Teter 2020, 18–23). Despite the work having probably "little impact" (Teter 2020) on the spread of the blood libel trope, the *Life and Passion* presents the first example of blood libel presented in print through the lens of Christian symbolism and passion imagery. Thomas was able to spin the story of William's death as a direct echo of each stage of Christ's passion: He is mocked, he is tortured, and he is crucified. An allegedly winter-blooming rose bush over William's grave, alluding to Marian iconology, connected the child-saint to the growing cult of the Virgin during this period (Teter 2020, 18). From this time forward, illustrations of blood libel accompanying texts would explicitly connect victims to the suffering of Christ through iconography, reaffirming and solidifying the justification in the medieval Christian mind between alleged Jewish guilt for Christ's death. As we have explored in previous chapters, visuals are strong cognitive influences.

It is in the case of Simon of Trent, however, that the power of media can be felt most strongly. Simon was a toddler in 1475 when he disappeared one day, arousing fear that he had fallen into a local canal. This was proven correct when his body was found in the part of the canal that ran under the house of a local Jewish family. Rather than mourning the obvious drowning death of the boy as a horrific tragedy, the local ecclesiastical authority viewed it as a prime opportunity to create a local saint. Teter refers to the campaign wrought by Bishop Johannes Hinderbach as "a fight over records and memory" (2020, 44), with him "[deploying] a sophisticated multimedia propaganda campaign in the aftermath of the death [. . .], exploiting the new printing technology (see chapter 1) to disseminate the story far and wide" (377). Hinderbach chose witnesses and evidence to utilize or suppress, crafting a careful narrative to promote his version of events in the trial of the Jew Samuel and his family, and then, as the published version of the story was incorporated into various chronicles throughout Europe. The results of his disinformation campaign, much like the conspiracy propaganda promulgated today through social media,

Figure 7.1 "Jews Sacrificing a Christian Child" from *Schedel's Chronicarum,* reprinted in George Woodberry, *A History of Wood Engraving* (1883), p. 58. Note the crucifixion-like pose, the "doubting Thomas" figure sticking an implement into the child's side, and the basin to collect his blood. The figures in the room are denoted for the medieval Christian audience as Jewish through the use of the pointy hat in the back left (the pileus) and their animalistic, grotesque features.

had far-reaching consequences; the case of Simon saw, among other things, the "shift in papal policy of protecting Jews against blood accusations" (44).

Jews would continue to be accused of ritual murders throughout the twentieth century. With Jewish immigrants settling themselves in America came the baggage of blood libel:

> In September 1928, 4-year-old Barbara Griffiths went missing in Massena, New York. A rumor that Jews had kidnapped and killed her as part of a religious ritual gained traction, leading police to question local Jewish leaders and the town's rabbi about her disappearance. (Bloom and Moskaleno 2021, 31)

Today, QAnon has taken the foundational aspects of blood libel and mixed them with post-Enlightenment knowledge to craft a bit of macabre pseudo-science. Followers now believe that the satanic pedophiles who are trafficking children are torturing them, provoking a terror response so that they can harvest the chemical adrenochrome from their blood. Adrenochrome is a real substance. Its actual uses are mundane, as are its sources, as it can be lab-created. But conspiracy theorists believe that adrenochrome is harvested from the blood of traumatized children to create an immortality elixir for the elite, including Hollywood celebrities and political notables (Hitt 2020). Rumors (and doctored clips) abound of a "Frazzledrip" video purporting to document the ritualistic sacrifice of a child by Hillary Clinton and her aide Huma Abedin (Emery 2018). *The Passion of the Christ* star Jim Caviezel has now become known less for his acting than for his numerous, teary-eyed appearances railing against "adrenochroming" and the dangers our children face from the global cabal (Feeld 2022). This portion of the QAnon mythology, tacked on after it spread from the chans to social media, is a "direct echo" (Rothschild 2023, 127) of blood libel.

FINANCIAL CONSPIRACIES

Although the stereotypical miserly, money-grubbing Jew has existed through-out history, the success of a banking family from Frankfurt starting in the eighteenth century gave that stereotype a name: Rothschild. The five sons of patriarch Mayer Amschel Rothschild would go on to establish banking and financial dynasties throughout Europe, leading to them becoming one of the wealthiest families in the world by the mid-nineteenth century (Rothschild Archive, n.d.). The Rothschilds' reputation for financial success and philan-thropy made them household names. Art, literature, and theater carry their images and their stories, including the play *Fiddler on the Roof*, which still retains the original song title "If I Were a Rothschild" (instead of "If I Were a Rich Man") in its Hebrew production (Rothschild 2023, 189). The family's wealth and success made them simultaneously adored and championed by Jews who saw in them exemplars of success without sacrificing one's faith. It also made them reviled by conspiracy theorists who would go on to accuse them of profit-ing from and controlling all wars, creating and controlling the Federal Reserve of the United States, funding the Holocaust, using space lasers to advance a climate change agenda, and on and on and on. Mike Rothschild (not related) wrote of the family and the elaborate and bizarre multitude of conspiracy theo-ries surrounding them: "Who besides the Rothschilds could simultaneously be accused of funding the works of both Ayn Rand and Karl Marx?" (2023, 156)

In the beginning, Q drops referenced the Rothschilds, and the conspiracy community gleefully built on the various legends surrounding the family. Connected to references to the coming financial portion of the storm are constant refrains about the evil Rothschilds and their control of global financial systems—they are the cabal, or at least part of the cabal, that Trump is working to overthrow. As QAnon has shifted and its mythology has morphed, financial conspiracy theories such as Nesara/Gesara, in which all debts will be expunged and a universal income (just don't refer to it as that) will be implemented (Griffin and Sardarizadeh 2021), have been integrated into the narrative, along with the United States re-implementing the gold standard that the Rothschilds, allegedly, moved us away from. The death of Lord Jacob Rothschild, the most prominent of the family's heirs and a dedicated philanthropist and patron of the arts, was announced as this chapter was in progress (Cowall 2024). Conspiracy forums and news reports on the event were full of commenters wishing him a good time in hell.

QANON AND RELIGION

The QAnon movement has always had Christian overtones, with many describing it as a religion unto itself. Amarasingam et al. (2023) analyzed QAnon through the framework of a new religious movement that borrows heavily from popular culture to shape meaning and belief, describing it as having many of the characteristics of these movements. Journalist Jeff Sharlet (2023) attended multiple Trump rallies to explore the intersections of religion and conspiracy. He interviewed several attendees, many of whom were clergymen. These believers in God and Trump made comments that borrowed themes from the prosperity gospel movement, an outgrowth of the Christian Right that "emphasizes a heavenly reward for righteousness," promising "'amazing results' you can measure and count" (49–50). Those ideas resurface in the Nesara/Gesara promises discussed above.

QAnon utilizes fundamentalist Christian beliefs in its main worldview. The Armageddon-like narrative of Trump overthrowing the cabal and ushering in one thousand years of peace and prosperity reflects the biblical apocalypse, or the "dispensational pre-millennialism" (Bernstein 2021, 19) of evangelical Christianity. In these stories, the temple of Jerusalem will be rebuilt, sacrifices will resume, the Jews will enter into league with the Antichrist, and a cataclysmic war will ensue over seven years. Christians will be Raptured into heaven, and only the Jews who convert will survive (18–19). Bernstein (2021) writes of this mythic drama:

> The current polarization of American society cannot be fully understood without a working knowledge of the above dispensationalist narrative, which strikes the majority of well-educated citizens with a secular orientation as bizarre. In contrast, for a significant minority of Americans, this sequence of prophesized events is as familiar as *Romeo and Juliet* or *The Godfather*, and the appeal of televangelists such as Jerry Falwell,

Jim Bakker, and Jimmy Swaggart rest solidly on their dispensationalist credentials. (19–20)

Unsurprisingly, pastors are spreading this message. Those Sharlet (2023, 116–17) interviewed professed belief that there are "secret murders everywhere," "pedophiles and evil," and that "God has chosen Trump." QAnon influencers interweave this rhetoric with literalist interpretations of the Bible via online forums and social media platforms. As we wrote in an article exploring QAnon influencers and their religious rhetoric:

> The battle between good and evil is Biblical; God is an American. [QAnon social media posts] state things such as "The season of dancing in the streets is upon us as the TRUMP [*sic*] is sounding and the time of Presidential occupation is here." Here, the Biblical trumpet of Revelation has been conflated with former president Trump, who, in other posts and comments, has been declared "a decedent [*sic*] of King David's line of Judah." (Greer and Beene 2024).

For the acolytes of Q, then, their fight is not just to "Save the Children" but to save *souls*. Faith is a powerful motivator, and the nature of belief fuels uncritical credulity. In our networked information landscape, QAnon influencers use their popularity to proselytize and peddle various political conspiracy theories that have become associated with QAnon, including those surrounding "groomers"—linked to saving the children. QAnon influencers perpetuate such threats through their promotion of the "groomer" rhetoric and affiliated conspiracy theories, even challenging followers to take action through school board and city council meetings (Gatehouse 2022). The term "groomer" in QAnon ideology reflects historical and contemporary threats to LGBTQ+-affiliated communities (Martiny and Lawrence 2023; Mogul, Ritchie, and Whitlock 2012).

MISOGYNY AND WHITE SUPREMACY

The Satanic Panic of the 1980s provides an example of a constructed and manipulated narrative. In his book *We Believe the Children: A Moral Panic in the 1980s*, Richard Beck (2015) details the gross misinterpretation of physical evidence and the bullying nature of interviews, which led very young children to confess abuse where none had happened. The epistemology of the adults, convinced that crimes had occurred, was flawed from the beginning, and it shaped their interpretations and the case information released to the media. Many were also acting on flawed, outdated, or poorly constructed scientific information; the field of child abuse investigations was new and, at this time, a bit of a Wild West. Beck has connected these unfounded fears to the seismic shift in

American society that was occurring in the 1980s, in which more households became two-income families or divorced mothers were single parenting:

> [Fear of pedophiles] was used to justify the punishment of women who were looking for work, women who were at work, or women who simply thought that she and her child might both benefit from the child being allowed some time to play on his own—in other words, women whose failure to devote every moment to their role as mothers was viewed as literally criminal. (Beck 2015, 264)

Notably, the fathers of the children in the daycare cases during the Satanic Panic were not implicated as the mothers were. The blatant misogyny and inequity of the secondhand blame for children being harmed have roots in Christian traditionalist notions of the family and the prescribed gender roles prevalent in orthodox religions. QAnon freely draws on these traditions, as well as a right-wing populism that has subverted feminism into an embrace of traditional gender norms, Othering those who do not conform (Bracewell 2022). Sharlet's (2023) "men's rights group" interviewees elucidated components of the "great replacement theory," which posits that coming demographic shifts in the population will cause Whites (specifically, White men) to be in the minority.

QAnon's adoption of such anxieties turns this theory into one where elites are masterminding these demographic shifts worldwide—but especially in the United States. Whether through immigration policies, educational systems, or government reforms, these societal changes are deemed to be orchestrated and nefarious, with their ultimate aim to remove power from the White race. Such conspiracy ideation is linked to extremist violence, xenophobia, misogynoir, and neo-Naziism (Topor 2022; Bailey 2021; Lovelace 2022). QAnon influencers sometimes link biblical passages to White supremacist themes, such as urging followers to "keep bloodlines pure," an overt reference to fascism. For instance, Conner (2023) ties QAnon to "fascist movements dating back to the Nazis," which "have a long history of co-opting popular cultural movements in order to gain membership, draw widespread attention, and to normalize talking about ideas couched in racist ideology (i.e., questions and debates over who really controls society are little more than anti-Semitic dog whistling)." Others have analyzed the use of Mein Kampf in influential right-wing donor circles, Trump's "Big Lie" rhetoric, and the xenophobic, racist rightward push in U.S. politics (Neely and Montañez 2022).

Indeed, Jones asserted that QAnon promoted violent activism and support for right-wing politicians to bring about "The Storm" (a moral and legal reckoning) and "The Great Awakening" (unavoidable reality to the masses) (C. Jones 2023). Unsurprisingly, QAnon's use of such mantras has attracted and absorbed adherents whose views align with White supremacists, extrajudicial violence, and policies that target marginalized communities.

IMPLICATIONS FOR TODAY

To offer up a well-worn yet applicable Winston Churchill quote from an address to the House of Commons in 1948, as the world still reeled from the violent and horrific Jewish genocide of the Holocaust: "Those that fail to learn from history are doomed to repeat it." The repetition of conspiracy theories and their roots in hatred and Othering results more often than not from ignorance and inexperience with those who are different, or from fear of change as the world marches on through time. These historical echoes continue to reverberate today, with politicians continuing to put their feet in their mouths, such as Marjorie Taylor Greene's screed about space lasers partly controlled by the Rothschild family causing California wildfires (Beauchamp 2021) or West Virginia state senator Mike Azinger, a Baptist, commenting incorrectly on Jewish doctrine to justify his beliefs on abortion (Mehta 2024). Unfortunately, antisemitism is on the rise, and it is not just confined to idiotic comments; a 2018 mass shooting at the Tree of Life Synagogue in Pittsburgh, Pennsylvania, killed eleven people and was motivated by conspiracy theories (Coaston 2018).

As educators, we are change agents. By familiarizing ourselves with history, we can help our society do better. We can provide learning opportunities. We can advocate for inclusion. Much of the social justice work needed to push back against these ancient prejudices can feel antithetical to the hallowed notion of the neutral librarian—but it needs to be done (and that neutrality is explored further in chapter 11). For those who are not sure where to start, the following organizations provide resources and tools for fighting antisemitism and hatred:

- Anti-Defamation League, https://www.adl.org/
- Hillel International Campus Climate Project, https://www.hillel.org/confronting-antisemitism/
- Southern Poverty Law Center, https://www.splcenter.org/
- UNESCO's "Addressing antisemitism through education," https://www.unesco.org/en/education-addressing-antisemitism

8

When Everyone Becomes a Participant

CONSPIRACY THEORIES ON SOCIAL MEDIA

It was 2021, and a young White girl had just gone missing; her name was Gabby Petito, a vlogger and influencer. Her disappearance captured considerable mainstream social media attention. Suddenly, it seemed, everyone was a detective. Social media users scrutinized the tiniest details from her last days of filming her travels with her boyfriend. Influencers and casual amateur sleuths brainstormed all the possible theories for what had happened to her. The QAnon community also participated, calling Petito a "crisis actor" in what was surely a false flag, or staged crisis.

How did social media contribute to such an interest in this one girl's life? What role does conspiracy ideation play in this process of online sleuthing? And, how does visual media, in particular, aid in what amounts to a participatory game with very real-life consequences?

Throughout this book, we have explored how the affordances of the Information Age and social media lend themselves to the promulgation and proliferation of information disorder and conspiracy theories. Online communities, however, garner more than just passive adherents. Those who join see themselves as active digital champions and contributors to the group's body of knowledge and mythology. In the QAnon community, adherents follow "breadcrumbs," or clues, to decipher "comms," secret communications addressed only to those in the know. Everything becomes a clue: the color of the tie that Donald Trump wears, the items in the background of a video, the position of a flag. Consider, for example, the early "pizzagate" event mentioned in chapter 3, wherein John Podesta's emails planning a pizza order were deciphered by conspiracy theorists as secretly referring to child pornography.

The rise of social media and the types of media shared on it have encouraged conspiracy ideation to become a participatory game. This chapter explores the role and importance of visual media in proliferating mis- and disinformation, the rise of amateur sleuths, and how specific interest groups on social media serve as feeder communities to QAnon and other conspiracies.

VISUAL MEDIA'S ROLE IN PROLIFERATING CONSPIRACY THEORIES

Visual media are pivotal in today's rapidly changing information environment. It has become more common for the everyday consumer of news and social media to question the authenticity of images, texts, and videos—and to take it upon themselves to figure out "the real story." In online communities, much of the shared content consists of visual media.

Among the reasons the human mind processes and creates meaning from visuals quicker than text (T. Palmer 2019) is a cognitive process called "the picture superiority effect." The idiom "a picture is worth a thousand words" captures this idea; a basic application would be the visual signage for transportation. Marotta (2023) explores how images engage and disengage cognitive processes, applying a neurophenomenological perspective to visuals' role in information saturation. Like in Kahneman's (2013) *Thinking, Fast and Slow*, Marotta and other scholars describe how visual media can short-circuit our brains to bypass slower cognition by accessing emotions quickly and viscerally (e.g., the "gut reaction"). Journalism professor Thomas Palmer (2019) encapsulated this by saying that the image is "the juggernaut in the perceptual process" (123).

Besides still images, scholars have explored how a dynamic picture superiority effect occurs with multimodal visuals such as videos (Buratto, Matthews, and Lamberts 2009). Palmer analyzed this common practice of reusing images, videos, or screenshots outside their original contexts to reshape a narrative, a phenomenon he termed the "intersemiotic contextual misrepresentation of photojournalism" (T. Palmer 2019, 104). Indeed, multimodal media can present an even greater challenge when trying to assess the veracity of visual media because the multiple channels of information can lend credibility to what otherwise could be doubted if the information was shared purely through one mode (e.g., image, text, audio, etc.) (Serafini 2013, 2022). In chapter 12, we will delve more into how new technologies like generative artificial intelligence are affecting image use and reuse and their role in perpetuating misinformation.

For now, we will explore how visuals in our daily lives transform us from consumers to participants. Anyone with a smartphone is now a photographer. Whenever we share or disseminate information, we reshape the visual narrative. Without healthy ingrained habits for evaluating shared visual media, it becomes all too easy to perpetuate mis- and disinformation, and we are all susceptible. For example, although Katie and Stephanie are both highly skilled in visual media evaluation and research its role in spreading false information, they have fallen into the trap of sharing something via social media without double-checking its accuracy. In the early days of the pandemic, Katie remembers believing and sharing a popular meme circulating on social media: an image of animals in the Venice canals, with the message that they had returned because humans were no longer interrupting their natural environment. This image was debunked shortly after as a fabricated narrative.

In both cases, we felt sheepish, given our background and research. But this innate trust in visual information is a common human fallibility. To see is to believe, especially when one wants to believe it is true. Hodges (2023, 129) summarized in 2023 that "present-day conspiracy narratives spread in large part through the networked circulation of decontextualized digital images, which accrue new narrative significance as they enter new contexts and arrangements, traveling further from their authentic sources and meanings over time." With each new edit and share, the visual material takes on additional meanings and wilder interpretations. Our participation enables this spread of faulty information; we only hope we can catch ourselves in time, or learn to pause and evaluate appropriately before sharing.

A PARTICIPATORY ONLINE GAME: THE RISE OF AMATEUR SLEUTHS

With the rise of the social web, amateur sleuthing has risen alongside influencer culture. Especially as more people turned to online spaces during and after the pandemic, online armchair detectives have been given a platform to opine about everything and anything. One only needs to open TikTok or YouTube to view amateur sleuths reporting on stories and their investigations. However, these are more akin to interpretations than rigorously fact-checked reports from traditional journalism (B. Jones 2022). While some social media companies attempt to flag or remove misinformation, creators are often protected under freedom of speech and freedom of expression, and our current online climate has fostered a motivation to create the next viral post or top-charting podcast (Blair 2023).

The power of visual media to capture users' attention and emotions enables breathtaking and exhilarating participation in solving mysteries online. Nowhere is this more evident than in true crime circles (Aguilar et al. 2021; Mathiesen 2022). Law enforcement and journalism sometimes rely on these crowdsourced investigations for tips and clues. This recruitment of the public to crowdsource expertise is not new (Badke 2015). It was only natural that open-sourced investigations would follow in mainstream and social media outlets. The Columbia School of Journalism discussed the potential benefits and pitfalls of crowdsourcing evidence when the topic was of urgent interest to the public (e.g., wars, diseases, etc.). In their interview with Alexa Koenig, director of the Investigations Lab at the University of Berkeley, they concluded that open-source investigations have "made it possible for reporters to challenge official accounts" and "uncover stories that they could not have told otherwise"; however, a "reliance on this kind of analysis has also fueled misinformation by lending a false sense of certainty to claims based on impartial and, often, unverified material" (Golding 2023).

Indeed, as the trust in institutions and expertise has fallen, people often turn to their online communities for crowdsourced advice (Pew, 19 September 2023). This decline in trust has extended to traditional authorities, from libraries to higher education, banks, healthcare professionals, and teachers. While there may always have been affinity groups that coalesced around their distrust of authority, the internet has made it easier for anyone to find their community. For instance, during the pandemic, social media communities often spread mis- and disinformation, making doctors' lives harder as patients earnestly quoted wild theories to them, or became unwilling to prevent or treat maladies due to seeing or reading something online (Baker and Maddox 2022; Yasmin and Spencer 2020).

In QAnon community groups, screenshots, videos, photojournalism or government documents, and other images are shared, usually out of context, for community members to ascertain "the truth" (Heřmanová 2022). Two recent conspiracy theories associated with the QAnon community illustrate this phenomenon.

In 2021, when a large shipping container got stuck in the Suez Canal (Gladstone and Specia 2021), QAnon conspiracy theorists analyzed every aspect of the ship. Evergreen, the Taiwanese company that operated the ship, was emblazoned with massive letters on the side of the ship and linked by conspiracy theorists to Hillary Clinton's codename "Evergreen" that she would supposedly use with her Secret Service agents (Gatehouse 2022). They also analyzed the ship's call sign, a unique identifier used for ships and boats, which in this case was H3RC, seemingly confirming the linkage to Clinton, whose initials are HRC. In the conspiracist worldview, there is always more to the story than what appears in mainstream media. In this case, they believed the disaster confirmed that the Clintons and the Clinton Foundation were at the heart of a global cabal, with the cargo ship full of children being trafficked by Clinton and her allies. It never occurred to the community members that they were committing logical fallacies and jumping to conclusions. The conspiracy theory was just that—a theory, a bit of nonsense. (When the ship was dislodged and unloaded its cargo, it included vast amounts of spoiled fruit and a giant model dinosaur for a golf course, among other things.) This episode illustrates the participatory nature of deciphering clues from mainstream media and imagery, fitting pieces of a large conspiracy puzzle together to fit a preconceived conclusion.

The case of the stuck ship also illustrates an all-too-common problem within conspiracy communities. Users must understand the ever-growing and ever-sophisticated information systems built to populate the internet with content, many of them multimodal. Crowdsourcing a mystery is not only fun, but it also gives outsized agency to every actor in the story. Deciphering clues gives users a sense of importance, envisioning themselves as digital citizens searching for the truth and bucking the authorities.

Several observers have linked this idea of online puzzles and games to the QAnon movement. Even Q seems to endorse this mindset. When Q returned in June 2022, whomever it was posted, "Shall we play a game once more?" Some scholars have indeed likened conspiracy theories that proliferate online to vast participatory games. For example, Quinn (2023) traces other online participatory trends dating back to the 1990s and 2000s that elevated personal epistemologies above traditional expertise, laying the groundwork for the conspiracism surrounding the COVID-19 pandemic. Quinn investigates how "the denigration of traditional expertise" and the promotion of personal health tracking were "co-opted by social media platforms that had already corporatized participatory culture, allowing political groups to mobilize around the suspicion, if not assumption, that medical expertise could be questioned and eventually replaced" (1). He concludes that because platforms like Facebook prioritized emotional engagement over veracity, conspiracy cultures that promoted the overthrow of traditional hierarchies of expertise and prioritized personal autonomy became enmeshed with political movements that emphasized participation—online and offline (13).

Similarly, BBC correspondent Gabriel Gatehouse (2022) analyzes the rise and mainstreaming of QAnon in his podcast, *The Coming Storm*, where he opines that what started as a game perpetrated by one user (Q) on the chan boards grew in its participatory nature as social media influencers platformed it: "[F]ollowers build upon a shape-shifting narrative, connecting the dots between seemingly random events; together, they form a sort of crowdsourced folklore, an overarching super narrative that helps explain a bewildering world." By crowdsourcing folklore, conspiracy theorists concoct a much simpler narrative than reality presents, full of villains and heroes battling it out toward some endgame. As QAnon migrated to popular social media that monetized interactions, many followers no longer realized that they were (perhaps unwittingly) participating in a live-action role-play (LARP) game whose plot was being rewritten.

Likewise, game designers, philosophers, and political analysts have noticed the overlap between a gamified, participatory culture and QAnon. In his podcast episode "A Philosophy of Games That Is Really a Philosophy of Life," *New York Times* correspondent and political analyst Ezra Klein (2022) interviewed C. Thi Nguyen, a philosopher, about approaching our twenty-first-century milieu as a high-stakes game that we do not realize we're playing. During their conversation, they discussed Berkowitz's (2020) treatise, "A Game Designer's Analysis of QAnon." Nguyen and Klein discuss the merits of Berkowitz's positionality as an alternate reality and LARP game designer, with his unique insight that misinformation and conspiracy culture, especially QAnon, are games that play *people*, with built-in gaming and reward mechanisms (Bortnick 2023). The early days of the internet and chan boards, as covered in chapter 3, turned the popular tabletop and LARP games into online, evolving scripts constructed by the players. What makes QAnon different is its centering on *apophenia*, or the human tendency to perceive a connection or meaningful pattern between unrelated and random things; the plot endlessly evolves because there is no oversight or conclusions (Berkowitz 2020). Like Berkowitz, Bortnick is also an alternate reality game designer and scholar who argues that even though core QAnon members may have recognized its origins on the chan boards, the game morphed into a political movement through its platforming on social and mainstream media networks. By encouraging a distrust toward social standards and a reliance on an internal world, QAnon fosters a community that increasingly relies on circular reasoning: "I know Q is right because I did the research, and I did the research because I felt Q was right." The QAnon community rewards people for seeking the truth and wanting to be identified as an expert or a "true patriot." When adherents find others that affirm these beliefs and desires, they feel they have "come home."

SOCIAL IDENTITY AND CONSPIRACY BELONGING

Our selves and identities are performative and constantly evolving (Butler 1990; Lindemann 2014); we construct our narratives, choosing the bits and pieces we wish to project to the world. A person becomes a performer online, where our "real" identities are hidden or mediated by a screen and video filters. Cover (2012) explored the disparate performances that occur online in profile identity management and friend/follower management. The affordances of social media allow for the discourse of self to be carefully curated through one's profile:

> The establishment and maintenance of a profile is not a representation or biography but performative acts, which constitute the self and stabilise it over time as the effect of those choices. Written, selected and revised, this is a performance that requires carefully chosen responses that present an intelligible self with integrity, unification and recognisable coherence. (Cover 2012, 181)

Similarly, who one "friends" or follows on social media, or in some cases, who one decides to block, also serves to bolster the construction of the online self. Cover (2012) wrote of this process that "it can be argued that the act of coherent and intelligible identity performances are not only to maintain norms for social participation but are done in the context of those in our circle of friends who—often unwittingly but within disciplinary society—surveil" (183). Through the curation of a friends list, and privacy settings, the social media user selects who will be allowed to view the performance, which serves to further construct and reinforce the profile identity performance. Consider, for example, those who have "work," "family," and "friend" social media identities—separate behaviors or separate accounts, even, that allow them to engage in a variety of discourses that keep their various identities separate and salient for each selected group. The affordances of different platforms often enable these separate identity behaviors; Kaskazi found, for example, that study subjects tended to be more expressive of their whole selves on Twitter while more selective on Facebook (Kaskazi 2014). While not all go to the trouble of having numerous social media accounts, many can identify with a moment of reflection—what will my mother/friend/coworker think of this?—before posting.

Social motives for conspiracy ideation were mentioned briefly in chapter 4; belonging to a conspiracy theory group can ease feelings of isolation and loneliness. Taking this further, Sternisko, Cichocka, and Bavel (2020, 2) observed that "[p]eople are prone to form social identities in which group membership becomes part of the self." The authors further explored how various motivations connect to conspiracism and identity, positing that "social identity motives draw people foremost to the *content* of a conspiracy theory while uniqueness motives draw people foremost to the *qualities* of a conspiracy theory [emphasis added]." If one identifies as a Republican and a strong patriot, for example, the narratives of the "Big Lie" conspiracy of Trump winning the 2020 election may be more appealing. With Qanon, especially, the conspiracy theory has become, for many followers, intertwined with their personal and political identities.

To add to this tangled web, political identity may not be the initial driver of conspiracy ideation. Enders et al. (2022b) suggest that political content may not attract followers, as has been posited elsewhere, but rather a "dark triad" of antisocial personality traits (i.e., psychopathy, Machiavellianism, and narcissism) alongside a generally non-normative or contrarian disposition. Their findings suggested that

> while self-identified partisan/ideological extremity may factor into QAnon support, it seems that the type of extremity that undergirds such support has less to do with traditional, left/right political concerns and more to do with extreme, antisocial psychological orientations and behavioral patterns. (1846)

In the case of those who exhibit the "dark triad," the *qualities* of a conspiracy theory may be more salient than the thematic content itself. A conspiracy theory that provides secret knowledge that others do not have or that makes the follower more unique motivates those who exhibit particular personality traits.

The affordances of social media have allowed conspiracy theories to grow, spread, and evolve. While a case could be made for the influencers exhibiting the dark triad of personality traits, the followers appear to be more motivated by belonging to the communities (Greer and Beene 2024). Affective states, such as emotions, seem more salient in their discourse; they are motivated by the excitement of the conspiracy theory, their trust in the parasocial relationship with the influencer, and the epistemic closure that the conspiracies provide. In these communities, there is a substantial overlap with religious identity, and the focus of the conspiracies has shifted to center on what benefits there are to the individual follower.

GATEWAYS TO QANON: RELIGION AND ALTERNATIVE HEALTH

With the interconnected nature of social media, it is increasingly likely that a person with interests from outside a conspiratorial narrative will find themselves in communities that effectively function as channels into QAnon or other conspiracies. More than just an accident of algorithmic entropy, as interest groups develop and become further and further entrenched in their own ideals, information disorder can "enter the building," so to speak, and begin to coalesce with the group's initial motivations. Two major identities that have notable overlap with conspiracism include religious groups online (specifically, evangelical Christians) and alternative health and wellness spaces.

RELIGION AND CONSPIRACISM

As explored in other chapters, much of the QAnon worldview borrows from evangelical Christianity, serving as a powerful motivator for those who are faithful to follow the movement. The QAnon dualism of "good vs. evil" and "us vs. them" satisfies an inherent need for order and cohesion in a world that feels full of chaos, something that traditional religion historically supplied but that has been increasingly replaced by the individualistic, choose-your-own-influencer style of modern evangelical movements. Gatehouse, for example, muses that QAnon might draw adherents who view it as a story told in parables, much like the Bible, rather than a literal reality (Gatehouse 2020).

QAnon, though not within a recognized denominational scheme, pulls on religious themes, decontextualized scripture Q-drops, and other elements resulting in a bricolage that fits, or at least speaks to, a certain pocket of the population that is dissatisfied with the social and political landscape today. That emotion of grievance and resentment, that people with different beliefs and different lifestyles (some of which violate deeply held beliefs, such as drag queens) are living just as happily and fulfilled, are channeled into persecution-complex narratives. (Lundskow and Mac-Millen 2024, 145)

QAnon social media influencers illustrate a combination of right-wing nationalism, prosperity gospel, and the conspiratorial worldview (Sharlet 2023). In the rhetoric of these new social media communities, participants speak incessantly of "God's plan," with bountiful riches and rewards that are imminent for true believers. Posts also illustrate the superconspiracy nature of QAnon, as its mythology becomes increasingly complicated and credulous. Conspiracy theories revolving around the "Flat Earth," vaccine and Big Pharma industries, and the financial Nesara/Gesara conspiracies are all tied neatly into God's plan for humanity (mostly America), as well as Trump as a modern King David—imperfect but called on by God to save his people. Inherent contradictions abound as the mythology evolves. The intersection of the conspiracy with religious fervor leads to a circular reasoning that justifies every small detail as prophetic or affirming, with Argentino describing that "QAnon conspiracy theories are reinterpreted through the Bible. In turn, QAnon conspiracy theories serve as a lens to interpret the Bible itself" (Argentino 2020, para. 4).

For those external to conspiracy communities, the intertwining of religiosity with QAnon should not be dismissed. Religious identity is an extremely strong component of one's personal identity, and often, adherents have firm values tied to right and wrong, truth and fiction. Thus, when attempting to nudge a person from such a worldview, one must disentangle a search for truth from a trust evaluation with respect for the core values of the person espousing conspiracism.

CONSPIRACISM, ALTERNATIVE HEALTH, AND WELLNESS

The overlap between fitness and wellness industries, alternative health, and conspiracy theories has been well-documented in both news media and scholarly literature. So, while this coalescence may seem new, it is more likely that QAnon infiltrated an area already ripe with conspiracism (CBS News 2021). Influencers might thread posts about child trafficking, for example, or use a hashtag associated with QAnon (e.g., #thegreatawakening) alongside promotional posts about their businesses, products, or philosophies. Indeed, the idea of an "awakening" can be deployed for New Age spirituality just as readily as it can for Christianity (Meltzer 2021). Such infiltration has not gone unnoticed in fitness circles; for instance, CrossFit distanced itself from congressional representative Marjorie Taylor Greene, a CrossFit practitioner and evangelist for QAnon (Brooks and Jamieson 2021). Yoga instructors likewise began speaking out about the QAnon influence overtaking their classes and online spaces

(Roose 2020a). A casual user of social media, dabbling in New Ageism, yoga, or alternative health, may very well receive targeted advertising or see pretty Instagram posts promoting QAnon and other conspiracy theories (Baker 2022; Chang 2021).

Influencers can provide a gateway for followers to learn about QAnon and other conspiracy theories because they provide community spaces already well-networked around similar values, hobbies, and motivations. Much of the recent scholarly attention has focused on how the QAnon worldview has unified those who may harbor legitimate suspicions about vaccinations or the capitalist inclinations of the pharmaceutical industry with a broader conspiracist mindset. Public health scholarship has long devoted a branch of its research to combating vaccine hesitancy, including how misinformation and conspiracy theories can hinder public health outcomes (Larson 2020; Farhart et al. 2022). A few sources have explicitly discussed the commingling of the QAnon and anti-vaccination movements, highlighting that the ideologies behind both movements emphasize fighting against big institutions (Dickinson 2021; Inform 2023). Elevating an individualized stance to healthcare can "act as an affective epistemological hinge for other forms of conspiratorial thought" (Fitzgerald 2022). Lewandowsky, Gignac and Oberauer (2013) explored this overlap, finding that conspiracist ideation predicts a broader rejection of science.

While researching alternative health influencers for another research project, Stephanie zeroed in on the QAnon influencer IET, a certified chiropractor and CrossFit enthusiast. Like the so-called QAnon Shaman, IET effortlessly blends New Ageism with Christianity, QAnon conspiracy theories with anti-vaccination rhetoric, and distrust of the government with loyalty to former president Trump. Observing IET's social media behavior served as a testament to the power of multimodal information in spreading conspiracist ideologies. Influencers like IET often turn to multiple social media platforms. In addition to posting his own content, he also shares multimodal misinformation (e.g., TikTok videos), which the Pew Research Institute has recently shown to be a dominant information practice for about a third of Americans over thirty years old (Matsa 2023). While he was already an influencer in alternative health circles, after being a featured speaker at a 2021 QAnon conference (Unknown 2021), he skyrocketed in popularity. His posting about QAnon increased through 2022, which coincides with the QAnon community's celebration of Q's return (Kaplan 2022).

Like other influencers whose motivations remain murky, it is unclear how much IET profits from sponsorships and other perks. How much of his behavior serves a financial purpose, how much is a "participatory game" between him and his followers, and how much does he truly believe in? Regardless of his motivations, community members often are there for personal reasons, ranging from affirmation to seeking friends and confidantes. As a result, it is essential that anyone looking to subvert mis- and disinformation among users of these forums and platforms first must focus on relationship-building and empathy.

BREAKING OUT OF THE SOCIAL MEDIA CYCLE

Because of the proliferation of conspiracy theories and the engagement that conspiracy theorists find therein, anyone hoping to break someone out of their epistemic bubble must encourage them to spend less time on social media. Anecdotal accounts often mention time away from doomscrolling being imperative to breaking away (Klepper 2024); for example, a daughter drew her mother away from QAnon by spending more time with her and introducing her to the game Wordle, which filled up time that her mother could have been spending on social media consuming conspiracy content (Gilbert 2022). Libraries can offer more programming that speaks to the gamified experience of QAnon and other conspiracist communities that require staying updated and closely analyzing clues—puzzle games, escape rooms, and mystery games all come to mind.

Our understanding of social media and well-being is still evolving (Parry et al. 2022), given that social media itself is so new in the timeline of technological history. Our relationship with social media has been problematized using different metaphors, each with its affordances for understanding and potential treatments. Vanden Abeele, Halfmann, and Lee (2022, 4–5) summarized this in their paper as "drug, demon, or donut":

> The drug metaphor is directly relevant to users who have severe and persistent problems controlling their social media use—sometimes to the extent that they require a clinical intervention. [. . .] The demon metaphor helps to explore how users can reduce or overcome such social media temptations in their daily lives, using technical and non-technological solutions that impact on impulse-response behavior. Finally, the donut metaphor provides an even broader picture of challenges that social media users face by taking into account the personal nature and situatedness of social media use and overuse. (4–5).

Resources abound to help someone digitally "detox," including hundreds of apps or browser extensions (Lyngs et al. 2019). Trine Syvertsen (2020), in the book *Digital Detox: The Politics of Disconnecting*, noted that, like any self-regulatory or self-improvement behavior, consciously going offline will require work on the part of the individual (and in our neoliberal society, it is up to the individual). She identified six strategies for disconnecting: going offline for set periods of time, developing time management skills, creating screen-free zones, deleting apps and platforms, muting and blocking notifications, or "going analogue or retro" (77–92). While each strategy has success stories, Syvertsen cautions that "for others, it becomes a life-long struggle like a constant cycle of dieting and gaining weight, with no final solution" (94). A systematic review of studies looking at social media abstinence, for example, found mixed support for the method: There were "promising effects on usage itself and on depression symptoms," but other metrics, such as mood, sleep, and cognitive and physical performance, had varied and sometimes even contradictory results (Radtke et al. 2021).

Much like other movements for self-improvement, the root cause of the problem must be addressed. If conspiracy theorists have turned to social media and conspiracy ideation because of isolation or anxiety, for example, then they also need support for those etiologies. Chapter 6 explored how to build trusting relationships with those who exhibit conspiracy ideation; those relationships can be leveraged to suggest resources to help with mental and physical health needs, financial needs, or programs that provide social opportunities.

Social media has become more complex, shaping our narratives even if we are not participating in various platforms. Information on social media is often reported in mainstream news, for example. Events stirred by mis- and disinformation spread via social media can disrupt our "real" lives. We must begin to realize these cultural shifts occurring in real time so that we can intervene in our own media habits, as well as work with others to build insight.

9

When Conspiracism and Real Life Collide

THREATS TO A DEMOCRATIC SOCIETY

Misinformation today spreads like wildfire, made worse by mal-information like doxing, swatting, and malignant hoaxes, spread by social media users who may not know that the information they are sharing is false. These types of information disorder, while not new, have accelerated with the rise of the social web, with sometimes devastating consequences. Stephanie remembers a winter night in 2022, just as her university was preparing for a "post-pandemic normalcy," during which an active shooter hoax was spreading on social media. It turned a typical study night in the library into one of terror. The rumor of an "active shooter in the library" trended on social media while the protocol for active shooter situations was quickly activated. A twenty-minute building sweep occurred with guards and police, disrupting and terrifying students. One patron described trying to leave the building but immediately coming back in, saying, "There's cops outside pointing guns at the building telling me to stay inside." Once an all-clear was issued, stating that it was a false alarm, students and employees were escorted to the parking lot if they felt unsafe. How is this our new normal?

As social consensus erodes, it's as if Americans are watching completely different movies; the same characters are present, but completely different plot lines develop along separate trajectories. The loss of a shared reality is deeply entwined with a crumbling of social trust. The data show that the corroding of the American social fabric has been occurring for decades (Pew 2023). Virtually every U.S. institution has been subjected to this erosion of trust (e.g., various facets of government, elections, academia, law enforcement, journalism), and even though longitudinal data demonstrate an ebb and flow of trust from roughly the 1950s through the 2000s, a sharp decline is evident after 2000 (Brennan Jones 2024), and especially after 2020. Heinberg (2020) states:

When consensus fractures into two directly competing narratives, some people may seek to resolve cognitive dissonance by claiming that the two narratives are equally valid. But this is a difficult stance to maintain, as the narratives are usually mutually exclusive.

In this vacuum, conspiracy theories abound. Are QAnon and other conspiracy theories just a symptom of this fragmented society where reality is not shared, facts are relative, and opposing sides demonize each other? Perhaps 2020 stands out as the year of complete fragmentation because, as the COVID-19 pandemic raged, people were stuck in various levels of lockdown, confined to their echo chambers and seeking epistemic closure through social media and online forums. Decisions around masking, for example, became a way to signal group identity and political ideology. Indeed, one consequence of our current information age that we have explored extensively in this book is that information saturation has led to competing camps, truths, and narratives. Researching something can feel like drinking from a firehose—the sheer amount of information overwhelms, especially when grappling with polarizing politics, a scary new disease, or an uncertain future. It is only natural that we seek to prioritize the influx of information to a more manageable amount. Our natural inclination to form tribes of like-minded people, combined with the necessity to limit the information onslaught, has allowed a greater spillover of conspiracism into society, connecting everyone with similar narratives and worldviews through an internet connection and the desire to connect.

Most of the country watched in alarm on January 6, 2021, as protestors swarmed the front of the Capitol building, eventually breaking in and running riot throughout offices and chambers. The "Big Lie" conspiracy, which claims that Donald Trump's win in the 2020 election was stolen from him through collusion, had gone from vitriolic debates in the media to citizens attempting to take the law into their own hands, and the effects were horrifying. Analyzing that day a few years later in the *Washington Post*, Dan Balz and Clara Ence Morse (2023) opined that the events were a long time coming due to a confluence of forces. They rightly noted that the founders of our government preferred power to be held by the elite class and "sought to create structural protections against [the masses]," including, as examples, the uneven distribution of House and Senate members, the Electoral College system, and the lifetime appointments of Supreme Court justices. These structures, which function to inhibit a true majority rule, combined with a deepening polarization in our political and social landscapes, ignited the proverbial powder keg in the wake of the 2020 election.

ASCENDANT AMERICAN AUTHORITARIANISM

The biggest threat to American democracy, arguably, is political extremism, with one current exemplar being Trump and his followers. A divided media exacerbates this extremism: Dan Pfeiffer writes of the current news climate: "Political communication has transitioned from public relations to information warfare" (Pfeiffer 2022, 19). During a January 2024 interview with cult specialist Dr. Steven Hassan (2024), Alva Johnson described her integral role in the campaign to get Trump elected in 2016 and how the campaign utilized the fragmentation of American media to target specific groups of people down to their careers, income, race, ethnicity, and gender. For example, veterans and military members are targeted by a specific subset of media; when the January 6, 2021, attack on the U.S. Capitol united so many military members and veterans with militia groups and fringe groups, many people wondered how it could be that America's military had become so radicalized. She asserts that we must understand the people identifying as MAGA and the mechanisms by which they were radicalized through their news feeds. To this end, Pfeiffer (2022) points out that

> [l]arge portions of the country never heard any negative information about Trump. And if some of that information slipped through, Americans already surrounded by Trump-supporting peers were conditioned to dismiss it out of hand. They were living in a hermetically sealed information bubble. (xv)

Linking Trump and his followers to the "end of democracy," Johnson argues, "The people who have helped [Trump] accomplish all of this are still a part of his circle" (Hassan 2024). And, we might add, so is the media ecosystem, as it repackages and reframes Trump's lies to make them more palatable while fragmented right-wing media expounds on conspiracy theories.

Correlated to the increase in authoritarianism is the mainstreaming of ideologies that used to be fringe, such as QAnon. Meanwhile, an article by McKay and Tenove (2021) connects disinformation to a decline in democracy. Taking a systematic approach to analyzing whether disinformation is worsened by our online social media environment, the authors conclude that deliberative democracy is threatened through a number of mechanisms, including tactics such as the denigration of "facts and logic, moral respect, and democratic inclusion" to undermine "a polity's capacity to engage in communication" (abstract). Recent research has highlighted the rise in violence, and threats of violence, in our highly polarized moment (Kleinfeld 2023). For instance, Brooks (2024) writes, "According to the Uppsala Conflict Data Program, state- and nonstate violence was higher in 2022 than it was a decade before." The increasing trajectory of violence should be alarming, especially when these cases are correlated with extreme political ideology and media consumption. Indeed, a 2019 FBI bulletin warned of "conspiracy-driven domestic extremists," including QAnon adherents, adding that the current information ecosystem allows such groups to "carry out criminal and violent acts" (Legum 2020).

This designation did not stop its infiltration into American culture and politics; in 2020, Americans' awareness of QAnon more than doubled, from 23 percent to 47 percent (Pew 2020), and by 2021, roughly 25 percent believed in one of the core tenets of QAnon, including that "the government, media, and financial worlds are controlled by Satan-worshipping pedophiles," who will be persecuted under the coming "Storm," and "that violence may be necessary to save the country" (PRRI 2021). One article analyzed how mis- and disinformation, such as the infiltration of QAnon tropes into mainstream media, threatens the epistemic integrity of democracy (Lewandowsky et al. 2023). Their premise began with the democratic ideal of a shared body of knowledge from which to operationalize the levers of democracy; without these, democratic endeavors falter or fail. Mis- and disinformation campaigns, especially those that target elections, threaten shared knowledge and thus the epistemic integrity of democracy. Analyzing data, they argued that the "toxic effects on democracy of misinformation . . . call for corrective political action" (4).

Salient to our purposes is the "Big Lie" itself. Scholars who research how harmful tropes recur throughout time emphasize that the Big Lie is a reiteration of past propaganda like Hitler's *Mein Kampf*, with devastating consequences (Neely 2022, 13, note 6). The overlap between QAnon conspiracism and fascism cannot be ignored; for instance, Conner ties QAnon to "fascist movements dating back to the Nazis," which "have a long history of co-opting popular cultural movements to gain membership, draw widespread attention, and to normalize talking about ideas couched in racist ideology (i.e., questions and debates over who really controls society are little more than anti-Semitic dog whistling)" (Conner 2023). Scholars have examined the effects of the Big Lie, noting that disinformation campaigns (i.e., disinformation that is targeted, widespread, and repeated over time) are particularly effective at sowing distrust in elections (Mauk and Grömping 2023; Pillai, Kim and Fazio 2023). As explored in chapter 7, America has a long history of intermingling politics, conspiracism, and White supremacy. QAnon, as a new superconspiracy, has provided a proverbial "fresh coat of paint" to these old, dangerous tropes. Anxiety over demographic shifts and world events drives interest in the conspiracies, and their very narratives echo and distort White fears into hidden boogeymen that are working behind the scenes to take power away from the [White, hegemonic] people (Taub and Leatherby 2024). For example, as we mentioned earlier in discussing Sharlet (2023), "men's rights activists" speak openly about the "great replacement" and other racist and sexist fears. These fears reached their apex in Kamala Harris, a Black and South Asian woman whose rise to power as the U.S. vice president embodied anxieties about changing demographics. Targeted malinformation spread among social media, amplifying those fears:

> In the run-up to the election, a photo mosaic of Harris's face, purportedly made up of photos of "All the Black Men She Locked Up and Kept in

Prison Past Their Release Date for Jail Labor," went viral. The image was a fraud. Upon closer examination, the meme appeared to have used the same few images over and over. (Pfeiffer 2022, 42).

The use of all Black men in this instance was not just an aesthetic choice to reflect the vice president's skin tone; instead, the message to angry White men would have been, "If she does this to her own people, what will she do to *you* when she has more power?" Fear and anger have become the most salient driving forces in the ontologies of White authoritarian males, which in turn drives potential violence and extremism (Topor 2022; Bailey 2021; Rousis, Richard, and Wang 2022; Gonzalez 2022; Hernandez Aguilar 2023).

Indigenous scholar and activist Julian Brave NoiseCat made parallels between QAnon rhetoric and White colonizers' oppression of Indigenous peoples: In the fears of the QAnon worldview, actual historical actions have been internalized, mirrored onto the Other, and projected outwards (Remski and Brave NoiseCat 2023).

In a comment following his initial Twitter post, Brave NoiseCat further opined, "It's all so Freudian. The fear that it will happen to them stems from an implicit admission that they did it to others" (https://twitter.com/jnoisecat/status/1526289791821783046). As QAnon subsumes more overt antisemitic, xenophobic, and misogynistic conspiracy themes into its larger story, fed by a polarized public, American authoritarianism enters into a new age.

While there has been an uptick of authoritarianism globally (Fisher 2022b), the United States could be viewed through the prism of extreme

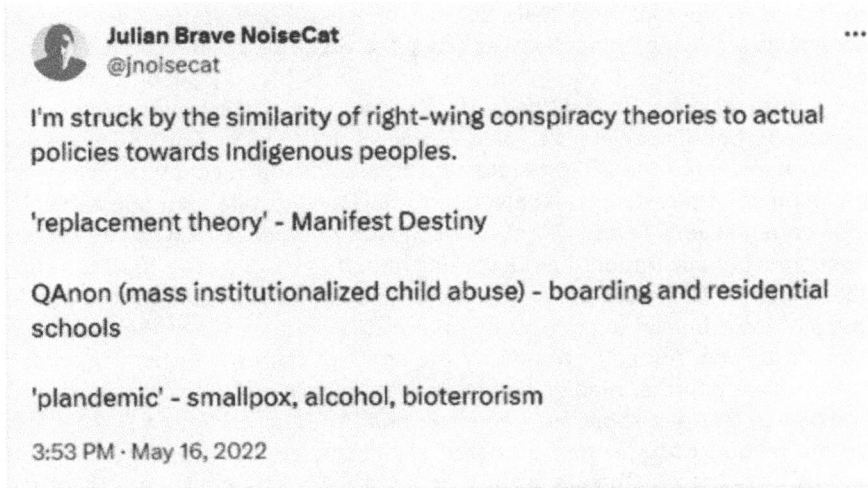

> **Julian Brave NoiseCat**
> @jnoisecat   •••
>
> I'm struck by the similarity of right-wing conspiracy theories to actual policies towards Indigenous peoples.
>
> 'replacement theory' - Manifest Destiny
>
> QAnon (mass institutionalized child abuse) - boarding and residential schools
>
> 'plandemic' - smallpox, alcohol, bioterrorism
>
> 3:53 PM · May 16, 2022

Figure 9.1 Screenshot of Twitter post from Julian Brave NoiseCat [@jnoisecat], May 16, 2022.

individualism, the notion of civil liberties, and the idolization of the "self-made" person. Recent attention has turned toward Texas (Legum 2024; Khardori 2024) and the American West (D'Angelo 2024) (among other states and regions), which have squared off with the federal government in what could be framed as a continuation of the patchwork of state policies and approaches to the COVID-19 pandemic. D'Angelo (2024), in her interview with author Betsy Gaines Quammen, traces the roots of hotbed extremist movements in the West to the Bundys, religious sects, and even cults that have blazed a trail of defiance, sometimes culminating in violent standoffs with the federal government. Viewed through the lens of sovereignty and the fascination with the ethos of the American cowboy, these disparate movements start to look more similar than they are different. One offshoot of this libertarian ideology is the Sovereign Citizens Movement, which dovetails with conspiracy ideation by avoiding anything with a whiff of "Big Brother Government," including legal documents, licenses, and state boundaries. In previous research, we discovered that adherents of the Sovereign Citizens Movement were patronizing libraries, especially law libraries, causing confusion and consternation for library workers. Members of this fringe group claim to be independent from laws, statutes, and proceedings unless they consent. In one interaction, a patron explained that "we don't have to pay taxes, [and that the] right to travel means the right to drive without licenses or registration" (Beene and Greer 2023).

These seemingly niche ideologies proliferate online, mainstreaming their reverence for individual autonomy in ways that manifest in offline actions, including threats to government officials and appointees. The blind adherence to individual liberties also fuels distrust of federal and state governments, serving as a rallying cry for smaller groups to organize against them. QAnon, of course, welcomes these groups as well, as its broadly suspicious mindset already assumes that a "deep state" is working against everyday heroes looking to root out social evils.

The events of the 2020 pandemic and presidential election led to a preponderance of threats against elected officials at the state and federal levels. One potent example was Dr. Anthony Fauci, an immunologist who had served under four administrations before seeking retirement. During the 2020 COVID-19 pandemic, Dr. Fauci, serving under President Trump, became the public voice of the administration, updating the media on the state of the pandemic and lockdowns. Already agitated by the limits of the lockdowns, conspiracy theorists were further riled up by the video *Plandemic*, which promoted several conspiracy theories about the pandemic and Dr. Fauci (Neuman 2020). The disinformation documentary garnered significant attention on social media and led to numerous threats against Dr. Fauci's life from conspiracy theorists (Bennett and Perez 2020; Stracqualursi 2022). Some of the wilder theories hypothesized that Dr. Fauci was actually a body double, while the "real" Dr.

Fauci was locked up in Guantanamo (along with other "deep state" politicians) because Trump was secretly rounding them up in preparation for "The Storm."

There has also been mobilization against state governors and poll workers, in addition to entire bodies of the federal government, such as the Federal Bureau of Investigation and the Department of Justice. Michigan governor Gretchen Whitmer, who had promoted lockdowns and social distancing during the pandemic, was the target of a kidnapping plot in late 2020 from local militia members who planned to overthrow the state government and ignite a civil war (Egan and Baldas 2020). Individual congressional members, secretaries of state, school board officials, and more have had to worry about their and their families' safety. For many, it has led to early retirement from the government.

Potent forms of malinformation have been weaponized against public officials, including against everyday people and volunteers. Doxing, or publicly exposing personally identifiable information, like addresses and phone numbers, usually online, is a particularly harmful problem affecting elected officials and activists. As is swatting, or criminally harassing someone by deceiving law enforcement and emergency services into responding, even sending SWAT teams to someone's home address, usually after a doxing incident. These incidents have surged over the last five years (Ellison, Sanchez, and Marley 2024). Unfortunately, swatting involves hoaxes and can affect public institutions like libraries, K-12 schools, government buildings, and more. Hoaxes like the one described in the vignette opening this chapter are also malinformation perpetrated by internet users with an agenda to sow chaos. The increase in these criminal acts is troubling. We must consider why they have surged since the 2020 election and what ideologies and beliefs may be fueling the increase. The broader picture of how conspiracy theories are infiltrating our "regular" lives will help us understand the true scope of the problem and its long-ranging implications.

Thanks to social media, many groups and ideologies that would have remained fringe are now openly organizing—and their contests for power are covered by mainstream, alternative, and social media platforms. For example, Moms for Liberty, a group that began in Florida, quickly orchestrated book challenges nationwide, appearing at school boards and libraries, reading aloud from books they deemed "indoctrination" of liberal ideologies. We will next examine these challenges, bans, and other actions directly affecting American libraries and educational institutions and how their underlying motivations and beliefs nest within the larger QAnon movement.

RISE IN COORDINATED BOOK BANS AND OTHER THREATS TO LIBRARIES

Libraries are no strangers to book bans and challenges; the American Library Association (ALA) keeps an updated list of banned books over time. However, the unprecedented number of book challenges in 2023 (ALA, n.d.) was largely due to coordinated efforts propagated by groups like Moms for Liberty. In his investigation of how QAnon infiltrated the American public, Gabriel Gatehouse (2022) opines, "This wasn't the first time in American history that school books had become a cultural flashpoint, but now there was the Internet." Over 2022, the word "groomer" (connoting a pedophile) became a catchphrase used to denigrate anybody or anything that promotes allyship with LGBTQIA+-identifying people (Gatehouse 2022); similarly the term Critical Race Theory (Crenshaw et al. 2019), the rather niche theory employed in law and graduate schools to describe intersectionality and its effects on employment discrimination, began being used as a negative reference to liberals and liberal policies. During the pandemic, kids and parents were isolated at home, with virtual schooling invading the living rooms of countless Americans. As a result, some parents who may never have paid close attention to what their kids were being asked to read before the pandemic were distressed to find they ideologically disagreed with what their kids were being taught. At the same time, millions turned to the internet, finding like-minded others who inflamed and confirmed their views. Alongside the soaring internet use was the steady decline in local news coverage (Sullivan 2021), making anything newsworthy, even at the local level, a potential national news item (Joseph 2024) As the pandemic receded and lockdowns lifted, groups of parents organized online to confront schools and libraries under the guise of "parents' rights." Moms for Liberty has been the most famous example, but there were others. Their rallying cry was against what they called the "indoctrination" of America's youth—especially around the concepts of intersectionality and systemic racism, or gender affirmation for LGBTQIA+ people. This "indoctrination" fit right into the QAnon playbook, with its suspicions about the "deep state" and a "cabal" of sex traffickers working to instill a "New World Order," unbeknownst to a public who was largely "asleep" (i.e., oblivious) to malicious machinations. While not everyone who stormed school board, city council, and library board meetings were QAnon adherents, a good many were—and, as always, QAnon beckoned with open arms to those who already displayed a conspiratorial mindset (Gatehouse 2022).

Libraries and educational institutions have also rallied, alarmed at the unprecedented increase in book challenges. Where libraries and schools already had statements and policies upholding academic freedom and a commitment to diversity, equity, and inclusion, as well as collections and reconsideration policies (Jones 2009), they now scrambled to update them, anticipating that members of the public might appear at meetings, looking to censor constitutional protections like freedom of speech or freedom of expression (Natanson 2024; Salman 2024; Legum 2024). Indeed, organizations like PEN America have sounded the alert on censorship, as they observed that even mundane items like dictionaries have been removed from school shelves

(McDaniel and Natanson 2024). Even those who promote book bans have limits, however, as former *Fox News* anchor Bill O'Reilly discovered when his books were challenged. After this rather predictable consequence, he decided that a Florida book challenge law that he initially championed had gone too far (Soule 2024).

Books that are challenged may not always be removed; there are a host of responses schools and libraries are taking, including quarantining books or denying the banning of books. Both librarians and educational institutions can review their policies to keep them current, make sure each frontline worker is aware of the policies, and furnish a copy of them to any patron. They can also utilize listservs to ask that library and school supporters attend board meetings to defend the books in question. These tactics have been used with success. In chapter 11, we examine the default notion of neutrality and how it is being wielded by activists and patrons exhibiting conspiracy ideation; though many library collections and reconsideration policies hew closely to the concept of neutrality, it can be a trap.

Citizen activism and citizen journalism, consisting of non-professionals documenting what occurs in public spaces, have been used to give voice to those who have none and to unveil what are all-too-often ubiquitous violations of law and equal rights. Recently, however, attention has centered on what now occurs under the pseudo-official-sounding "First Amendment audits," in which people enter public buildings and announce their intention to film as part of their First Amendment rights. These setups are typically intended to be confrontational, increasingly taking place at school board meetings, public libraries, and other sites of contested experiences to expose the supposed nefarious public officials who are bad actors. Leavey (2022) explored the history of such public activism as a legitimate method of social justice critique within the public sphere, cautioning that such tactics are increasingly being utilized by one side of the political spectrum.

> The broad appeal of First Amendment auditing is an expression of shared American political cultural values. However, given that libertarianism and constitutional conservatism are prominent among First Amendment auditors, the community contributes to the seepage of reactionary right-wing populism into their own practices and the larger mediated public sphere, particularly as related to conspiracism. Such positions have the potential to metastasize among some users into identity-driven right-wing populisms and forms of fascism. (82)

While passively recording in the public sphere connotes openness and fairness in gathering evidence, some utilize their recordings to sow malinformation. Perhaps one of the most infamous of these is Project Veritas, a conservative group that, in 2015, doctored videos they secretly filmed at Planned Parenthood locations to make it appear that the healthcare organization was illegally selling fetal tissue (Tavernise 2019). While such tactics are extreme, it behooves us to remember when confronted with these citizen journalists that some are more dedicated and will go further to ensure their agenda is supported than others. There are also financial motivations; because of the potential for "going viral," many of these interactions also make money for the instigators (Brown and Mulligan 2022).

As sites of book and other challenges, public libraries face increasing "audits" of this kind (Balzer 2022). Due to patron privacy and other considerations, libraries can enact policies and place limits on these behaviors, restricting to certain areas or banning these audits altogether (Caldwell-Stone 2019). One of our survey participants (Beene and Greer 2023) described a citizen journalist moment, where the patron was convinced the government and the library were out to get them; this led to them taking pictures and filming people in the library without their consent, because they were convinced such people were "cyber stalker[s] and was going to submit [the material] to the FBI." In consternation, the library worker expressed that they were "caught off guard" and that they "understand a customer talking to us about this conspiracy theory, but just taking pictures of random people . . . made this [interaction] extra odd." This patron was known for their conspiracy ideation, but this public activism surprised the librarian. Whenever these events occur, as with any interaction with someone who may be agitated or showing signs of extremism, remaining calm and professional will always be the best approach.

ADDRESSING THE CRISIS

Scholars and theorists have proposed solutions to this crisis of polarization, disinformation, and ascendant authoritarianism. Some highlight the regulations the European Union (EU) has implemented, especially regarding social media companies, data privacy, and election integrity (Lewandowsky et al. 2023). Others have suggested specific methods for tech companies to depolarize platform users (Stray 2022). Institutions like Freedom House release reports tracking the state of democracy, with a 2023 report stating that the decline in deliberative democracy did not start with Trump and did not end after he was out of office; instead, "[d]isturbing problems that predated his administration—legislative dysfunction, partisan gerrymandering, the excessive influence of special interests in politics, ongoing racial discrimination, and the spread of polarization and disinformation in the media environment— remain unaddressed" (Rapucci 2023). One of the more troubling trends has been the acceptance of "extreme actors" and what is considered "acceptable behavior" in systems of governance. It is thus essential for each of us, especially elected officials who have sworn an oath to uphold the U.S. Constitution, to address this systemic decline.

Librarians and educators are uniquely poised to prepare learners for a lifetime of critical thinking, analytical reasoning, and information literacy. The core values for the U.S. librarian profession, as promulgated by the ALA, include the promotion of social justice and democracy, which "presupposes an informed citizenry." John Dewey, one of the founders of the ALA, argued that a core component of the educational endeavor is to promote democracy (Haber 2020). Today, the ALA and the Association of College and Research Libraries (ACRL) continue to produce information literacy standards and frameworks that advocate for cultivating discerning citizens and lifelong learners; however, as we have explored in this book, the pervasiveness of misinformation and disinformation presents a distinct challenge to frameworks, checklists, and praxes centered around information literacy. As Barbara Fister (2017) surmises in her essay, "Practicing Freedom for the Post-Trust Era," we encourage students to "read widely [and] think critically" because we're preparing them for an ambiguous and complex world that involves weighing evidence and equipping learners to "engage with the world as citizens and perhaps change it for the better." Rapidly changing information landscapes demand a new approach to teaching, recognizing, and countering the kind of conspiratorial disinformation that intentionally exploits group polarization. It is a challenge, but one that libraries especially need to address as sites of both ideological conflict and potential resolution. Nancy Kranich, in her 2020 article, "Libraries and Democracy Revisited," argues that libraries should capitalize on this tumultuous democratic moment to "catalyze the shift from merely informing citizens to engaging them . . . reclaiming our "essential role as cornerstones of democracy" (abstract).

When QAnon eventually fades, a new superconspiracy will undoubtedly rise to take its place, as conspiracy theories have been a feature of American society since its foundation (Uscinski and Parent 2014; Walker 2013). Each of us is responsible for becoming more familiar with information systems, their role in propagating misinformation and disinformation, the mechanisms by which conspiracy theories spread, and tips and techniques we can implement in our professional and personal lives.

10

Strategies for Preventing and Countering Conspiracy Ideation

Katie's family enjoys cooking and eating dishes from many different cultures. Her daughter loves chicken tikka masala, so with excitement, Katie found a new, rather elaborate recipe that promised to be "just as good as a restaurant's." Katie's husband has been doing most of the cooking lately, but for this one he created the marinade and Katie did the rest. It was delicious. Leftovers were parsed out to local family members, and when they called to compliment it, Katie mentioned that she had been in the kitchen for about two hours working on it, "forgetting" the work her husband did. "He said you would say that!" her grandmother jokingly chided her. "When he dropped it off, he warned me that you would take all the credit, but he contributed." It was humbling for Katie to realize that her husband had used the misinformation debunking formula perfectly ... on her.

Anyone wishing to correct conspiracy ideation potentially is in for a long struggle that may have little reward. As we have explored previously, the psychological drivers of conspiracy ideation are strong. That said, doing nothing will accomplish nothing, so in this section, we examine the research on potential methods to both prevent and address conspiracy ideation. Unlike nudging, which should be used within the context of a relationship, as discussed in chapter 6, these techniques can be utilized in briefer encounters or broader applications, such as a general-audience social media post.

THE SPECTRUM OF CONSPIRACY IDEATION

Thankfully, not everyone who gets sucked into online rabbit holes will end up storming a government building over election results. Sometimes, people may start to question the narrative about moon landings or the JFK assassination—and it ends there. Sometimes we can catch ourselves feeling sucked into conspiracy ideation, linking disparate events together to form a pattern or narrative, leading us to question what has been readily accepted by society. By recognizing that we, as humans, are prone to this type of thinking, we can start from a place of empathy when encountering those voicing conspiracy ideation, rather than dismissing them as hopelessly gullible, or worse, stupid. As librarians and educators, we may be more prone to empathize and listen to patrons and students before concluding that reasoning with a conspiracist is hopeless. Quickly being able to assess where someone falls on the spectrum of conspiracy belief can save a lot of time, energy, and consternation, as it allows us to quickly understand what might be possible in terms of nudging people out of the rabbit hole or helping them from falling any further into it. When we think of "falling down a rabbit hole," it might be helpful to think of a spectrum or stages of beliefs and actions that can lead to a wholesale endorsement of a conspiracy theory. For example, Franks et al. (2017, 6–9) developed a model of conspiracy ideation based on interviews with a wide range of people who voiced belief in one or more conspiracy theories; their typology ranges from Type or Stage 1, in which people start to ask questions, to Type 5, when they embrace "belief in improbable and frankly supernatural explanations for events" (Pierre 2020). Pierre, while noting that Franks et al.'s typology is a good start, problematizes it as having "blurry borders and unclear pragmatic distinctions between types" (Pierre 2023, 25). He proposed instead a model that has five levels: nonbelievers, fence-sitters, true believers, activists, and apostates (25–26). Strategies to counter misinformation will depend on where one falls in this model—a true believer or an activist, for example, will be harder to "nudge," whereas a fence-sitter will most likely be more open to discussion.

The spectrum of conspiracy ideation was illustrated in the survey we conducted of librarians in the United States who had encountered conspiracy theorists (Beene and Greer 2023). One participant described how the same question prompted different reactions from people, depending on their level of belief:

> There were 2 interactions with the same question about if the United States was a corporation. [In] the first ... [t]he patron wanted information and was satisfied when I explained that it referred to the incorporation of Washington, D.C., and not the U.S. as a corporation. The 2nd person was a bit more into the [conspiracy] theory, but I shared the same info.

In this case, the librarian assessed the spectrum by how the patron reacted. If this interaction were to continue, they could use this information to inform further engagement with the patron. The first patron, for example, may not require further assistance, or they might return with more contextual questions to research (e.g., when and how Washington, DC, was incorporated). For the second patron, the librarian is now armed with the knowledge that the patron may not have believed their explanation and could anticipate more or similar inquiries.

ASSESSING IN-PERSON

In our first article (Beene and Greer 2020), we recommended several strategies for engaging with conspiracy theorists during in-person interactions, with an emphasis on the role of empathy and neutral language. Librarians and educators often already possess these skills; a concerted mental check-in during these engagements can help us center ourselves and be better prepared for patrons anywhere on the spectrum of conspiracy ideation.

We can begin by self-monitoring during our interactions with patrons and learners, attending to the subtle cues we may send to them via our body language, facial expressions, tone of voice, and language. Some questions to ask might be: Am I tensed up anywhere? What is my body language possibly conveying? Does my facial expression convey openness and empathy? In addition to body language and facial cues, spoken language also has significant effects. We can monitor our tone of voice during these kinds of interactions to avoid escalating or shutting down a conversation, particularly if we are inadvertently perceived as harsh, argumentative, or judgmental (Rohlinger 2020). Additional self-monitoring questions could include, "What types of language am I using, and could it be more inclusive of diverse experiences and perspectives?" As with any argument, centering ourselves in a conversation, including our perceptions and arguments, can de-escalate the other person—using "I" instead of "you" statements and being careful to include questions that open up the conversation to their perspectives. This positioning reduces the emotional burden on the other person, allowing for more open engagement. Therapists and others have also flagged the use of "but" (which can be replaced with "and"), "should," and "ought" as terms that can instantly throw up barriers to productive conversations (Klipfel and Cook 2017; Scavnicky-Yaekle 2015). In our article, we provided the following example of how language can be adjusted: instead of "You may think that sentient reptiles control the world in a secret shadow government, but there is no evidence of that," try, "I understand that is a terrifying thought, and you want to get as much information as possible. Let's try and look critically at what we can find together." Another useful method is to lean into our training for reference interactions, expressing curiosity about how the patron became interested in this topic, or what else they have discovered, where they have looked for information so far, and if the patron is just curious or seeking information for a particular purpose, such as a research project, assignment, etc.

ASSESSING IN ONLINE SPACES

Much of conspiracy ideation in our current information landscape derives from engagement in online spaces; social media algorithms can introduce content, or it can be shared from social connections. The rabbit hole dive proceeds from there. However, a person who has only watched a few videos is in a very different place mentally and emotionally than someone who is heavily invested, following conspiracy influencers and engaging with others who share their beliefs. While it can be hard to assess those with whom we do not already have relationships, clues can be found in the information sources they share and how they utilize questionable sources in arguments –where do those fall on the dis/information spectrum? How do they respond when their sources or ideas are questioned?

CURRENT RESEARCH ON ADDRESSING CONSPIRACY IDEATION

"Prebunking" and the Inoculation Method

First proposed by William J. McGuire (1964), inoculation theory derives its foundational ideas from the medical procedure of inoculation, in which the body's immune system is exposed to a weakened form of a pathogen to train it to resist the pathogen when and if it is encountered in the wild. McGuire extended this as a metaphor for mental resistance against persuasion (201). The basic idea that McGuire developed, that by exposing a person to a potential persuasive attack, that person will be less likely to fall for similar attacks in the future, has found merit in the work of other scholars who have expanded its scope. Scholarship on the use of inoculation theory has increased since the beginning of the twenty-first century, concurrent with the rise of networked information since, as Lewandowski and van der Linden (2021, 357) aptly observe, "[T]he propagation of misinformation through online social networks closely resembles the spread of a virus."

Because of the ebb and flow of interest in this theory, research and understanding of the mechanisms of inoculation theory have been slightly uneven. Banas and Rains (2010) conducted a meta-analysis of forty-three inoculation theory studies. The utility of inoculation theory was confirmed, although the authors noted several areas still lacking in the research: the mechanism by which inoculation confers resistance to varied attacks, and the relationship between time and inoculation effectiveness. Maertens et al. (2021) tackled the issue of long-term effectiveness, finding that the longevity of inoculation can be extended through regular "boosters" that recall and reaffirm misinformation defenses; thus, when utilizing inoculation methods, repetition over time needs to be considered as part of the overall strategy. Similar to how staying updated with vaccination boosters reduces our susceptibility to a virus, even as it evolves, we may need to be "boosted" periodically against mis- and disinformation—and our patrons and students could use these "boosters" as well. There is misinformation, and there are conspiracy theories—and conspiracy adherents can be notoriously stubborn about their beliefs. Banas and Miller (2013) tested inoculation theory using an actual conspiracy theory message, the 9/11 "truther" film *Loose Change: Final Cut*, concluding that "the preemptive nature of inoculation may be the key to preventing conspiracy theory influence" (198). In an important note that reinforces the importance of relationships and establishing cognitive authority, as explored earlier in this volume, studies have also demonstrated that "the more positive perceptions a recipient has of the source of the inoculation, the more effective the inoculation process" (Compton et al. 2021, 8).

The COVID-19 pandemic provided numerous test cases for this theory (Van Bavel et al. 2020; Van der Linden et al. 2021), with research indicating that utilizing inoculation theory to prebunk misinformation can "not only help people to identify fake news easily, but it could also change their attitudes and behavior to rely on more trusted information in the public health area" (Kassen 2023, 647). A recent study extended these results, examining how inoculation worked against different misinformation types on social media, with similarly positive findings (McPhedran et al. 2023).

The affective role of threat in placing the reader on guard and more effectively engaging the persuasion-immune response seems to be an essential component that needs to be considered when implementing this strategy (Barbati et al. 2021; Banas and Miller 2013; Banas and Rains 2010). Typically, a threat in inoculation messaging includes a forewarning and/or a refutational preemption. Forewarning serves to put the recipient of the message on alert that there will be attempts to persuade their beliefs. Refutational preemption serves to provide explicit examples of what the persuasive attempt may be, along with a counterargument (Clear et al. 2021). Compton (2021) weighed in with a review of threats in inoculation theory literature, finding that threat in the research has been neglected. Therefore, understanding its mechanisms remains a bit murky, acknowledging that "we might be using the wrong affect constructs to understand the threat as it functions in inoculation theory" (4294). Indeed, two types of affective conceptualizations of threat appear to induce negative emotions in the other person, such as fear or apprehension, or motivate them to defend themselves. Banas and Richards (2017) critique the traditional conception of threat within inoculation theory research, measured on a scale that utilized words connoting fearfulness. They posited: "Perhaps the problem [with research showing threat does not correlate to resistance] is that the traditional threat variable focuses on concepts related to physical safety rather than on motivation to defend one's attitudes (166). The authors proposed that "[c]onceptualizing threat as motivation to defend one's attitudes (hereafter labeled motivational threat) is more consistent with the theoretical role of threat in inoculation theory" (169); their research shows that motivational threat "is more strongly related to resistance than the traditional threat variable" (174). Critically, "motivational threat, to the exclusion of traditional, apprehension-based threat, functioned as the mechanism by which inoculation-conferred [sic] resistance" (175), highlighting the importance of getting threat "right" when attempting to inoculate learners against disingenuous persuasion (Compton et al. 2021).

Inoculation theory can be utilized both to convey resistance and to debunk already-internalized mis/disinformation (Wood 2007). Inoculation messages can also protect against other inoculation messages in a process known as "metainoculation" (Banas and Miller 2013). As one study has found, inoculation theory provides benefits that other forms of counteractive persuasion do not, suggesting that "unlike other forms of scientific messaging [. . .], inoculation does not seem to elicit boomerang effects (or psychological reactance) in the context of contested scientific issues" (Compton et al. 2021, 8). The "boomerang effect" is when a person exposed to a message decides instead to believe the opposite of that message, which tends to be a defensive response if someone feels threatened (Ma and Hmielowski 2022). Another obstacle is the "continued influence effect (CIE)," in which previously accepted misinformation is still treated as truth even after having been corrected; CIE has been modeled as a "cognitive effect, with social and affective underpinnings" (Ecker et al. 2022). CIE's cognitive component has been theorized as a memory integration problem or a selective retrieval problem; essentially, our brains pick and choose which information to store in working memory, and which information to retrieve when confronted with misinformation. Repetition, as mentioned above, or more detailed refutations of misinformation could help in these instances. These cognitive biases present important challenges when considering how best to educate others to avoid information pitfalls. Understanding how the boomerang effect or CIE manifests in affective responses cannot be stressed enough. Ecker et al. noted that CIE also hinges on motivational factors: how much the source of correct information is trusted if the correction poses a threat to the person's ingrained worldview and identity and if the correction makes the person feel uncomfortable (Ecker et al. 2022; Susman and Wegener 2021). Thus, it bears repeating: Pay attention to *how* and *what* you communicate. Conveying empathy and respect and using non-threatening postures and language are as important as the message.

STORYTELLING AND GAMIFIED INOCULATION

Studies have shown some evidence for utilizing a narrative or storytelling approach with the inoculation method (Biddlestone, Roozenbeek, and van der Linden 2023). Although the evidence for this is mixed (Ecker, Butler, and Hamby 2020), utilizing the story to make the misinformation correction more compelling is worth considering as you structure inoculations. Examining how others use narrative is also critical. Kate McDowell (2024) contributes an excellent study of how COVID-19 misinformation utilized storytelling to spread bad information. She suggests that storytelling analysis and understanding narrative structure can help create more effective communications, noting, "Efforts to address complex social issues require understandings of storytelling and retelling as a fundamental process of everyday information circulation." The use of storytelling may prove helpful in inoculation treatments, as discussed in chapter 8. Perhaps more importantly, an understanding of the tropes, narrative structures, and mechanisms of conspiracy theorizing, like those discussed in chapters 7 and 8, will help us recognize and resist those recurring themes in the future.

As we write, new research is examining the utility of "counterfactual thinking" as a prebunking strategy (Bertolotti and Catellani 2023). Counterfactual thinking functions as a sort of psychological storytelling, as people create scenarios around events to explore alternative explanations and causal factors, "conditional 'if only' thinking to stimulate what could or might have been" (Schlechter, Hoppen, and Morina 2023). Researchers have known for some time that conspiracy theorists utilize counterfactual thinking to "effectively insulate their beliefs from reality, uphold their opinions, and even justify subsequent behaviors, such as spreading them to other people" (Bertolotti and Catellani 2023). Intriguingly, Bertolotti and Catellani explored whether encouraging counterfactual thinking as a prebunking strategy would encourage more critical evaluation of information. After reading information on COVID-19 research and then a message with counterfactual thoughts, study participants were encouraged to envision their own "what if" scenarios relevant to the issue. They were then given a series of headlines to evaluate as true or false. This initial study has important implications for the future trajectory of research on prebunking, as it

> showed that individuals with a high conspiracy mentality are less likely to find plausible a fake headline when they are pre-emptively exposed to counterfactual messages proposing claims on the same issue as "What if . . ." scenarios. These participants also showed less reactance towards prebunking messages than when they were exposed to more direct forewarning. (Bertolotti and Catellani 2023, 8)

As we think about strategies for encouraging critical thinking, we might engage in "what if" counterfactual thinking and storytelling scenarios. These thought experiments can serve as a necessary "neutral ground" exercise to avoid engaging defensive mechanisms, and may help encourage critical inquiry and evaluation.

Additionally, scholars have attempted to gamify inoculation and prebunking, popular examples being the *Bad News Game* (https://www.getbadnews .com), and *Cranky Uncle* (https://crankyuncle.com). The University of Cambridge, in partnership with DROG and Gusmanson Design, has developed several games designed to debunk specific misinformation categories, notably *Harmony Square* (https://harmonysquare.game/en), with more planned (https://inoculation.science/inoculation-games); they also offer a series of videos that address specific manipulative techniques (https://inoculation.

science/inoculation-videos/). The games and videos can be easily integrated and utilized in various educational settings and purposes.

Although research has shown these gamified interventions can reduce susceptibility to misinformation (Roozenbeek and van der Linden 2020; Basol, Roozenbeek, and van der Linden, 2020; Cook 2021), recent studies also suggest that the inoculations can reduce belief in valid information, too, so they should be used with care (Graham et al. 2023; Modirrousta-Galian and Higham 2023). Global skepticism can lead students to believe that all sources have an agenda, leading to distrust of expert sources. It is incumbent upon educators to help students evaluate the authority of a variety of sources without engendering global skepticism. The role-playing mechanism that many of the games use, in which the player is the "bad actor" spreading misinformation, can still be a valuable tool for bringing awareness of the various manipulative techniques used in spreading misinformation. Learners may need help contextualizing these types of games to draw a distinction between misinformation and reputable, reliable information.

Ultimately, using a narrative approach or online games should be considered just one piece of a multi-level strategy; think of these techniques as conversation starters, initiating what will hopefully be deeper and more meaningful opportunities for questioning and connecting.

DEBUNKING

Sometimes, it is too late for inoculation, and misinformation has already taken hold. Research on the "stickiness" of conspiracy theories such as climate change or the various theories associated with the COVID-19 pandemic provides strategies for how we might nudge people away from deeply held beliefs (including the nudging technique discussed in chapter 6). Debunking is a method that has been studied to good effect, although research on this is ongoing. The *Debunking Handbook* by Lewandowsky et al. (2020) proposed a more robust formula than fact-checking to debunk climate change myths:

1. Start with a fact
2. Warn that a myth is coming
3. Explain how the myth misleads
4. Repeat the fact

The debunking formula can be adapted to fit any mis- or disinformation. The authors cautioned that this will not be a one-time process; as such, again, having an established relationship with the conspiracy theorist will be most helpful. The second step of the debunking process—"warn that a myth is coming"—draws on inoculation theory. The third and fourth steps, explaining how the myth misleads and then repeating the facts, are both measures indicated in subverting CIE.

Petrov (2021) conducted mathematical modeling of inoculation and debunking, noting that inoculation studies have focused on the effectiveness of inoculation with individuals and not on an epidemiological level; his conclusion that inoculation and debunking have serious flaws is sobering but must be considered as we look to find solutions. Inoculation, affecting as it does single individuals, cannot keep up with the fast spread of misinformation on social media. It is not contagious. Petrov did find that "debunking is tardy but relatively effective in long-term perspective" (4) because debunking methods can be spread, unlike inoculation.

One of the authors of the *Debunking Handbook*, John Cook, maintains a "Skeptical Science" YouTube channel, which includes videos on the debunking method, making science "sticky," and more (https://www.youtube.com/ @SkepticalScience). The Skeptical Science website has examples of the fact-myth-fallacy formula for several climate change statements, as developed for their MOOC "Denial101x" on climate change denialism (https:// skepticalscience.com/denial101x-videos-and-references.html); an example is provided in Figure 10.1.

Because the research on these techniques is still evolving, it can feel overwhelming to try implementing them in person. Thankfully, several excellent resources provide help; in this section, we include those resources and other tips that we have gathered, starting with the excellent "Toolbox of Interventions against Online Misinformation" (https://interventionstoolbox .mpib-berlin.mpg.de/index.html). In this resource, a consortium of scholars reviews current research on various methods with examples. The Rand Corporation also maintains a list of "Tools That fight Disinformation Online" at (https://www.rand.org/research/projects/truth-decay/fighting-disinformation/search.html).

FRICTION AND THE ROLE OF METALITERACY

Introducing friction, or an intentional pause to think about information, into evaluative practices can help stop the spread of misinformation. Two recent studies have demonstrated that the simple question of "Why do you think this is true or false?" when examining a news headline reduces the impetus to share false information (Fazio 2020; Pillai and Fazio 2023).

This forced pause allows people to reflect on their affective and cognitive responses to information. It demonstrates the metacognitive domain of learning in the metaliteracy model, reflected in learning objectives such

WE'RE CAUSING GLOBAL WARMING

FACT	MYTH	FALLACY
For thousands of years, our atmosphere has been in balance. Humans have upset the balance.	"Human CO2 emissions are tiny compared to natural CO2 emissions so our influence is negligible."	**Over-simplification:** considers only natural CO2 emissions and ignores natural CO2 sinks.
Human emissions are responsible for all of the increase in CO2 in the air over the past two centuries.	"Volcanoes produce more CO2 than humans."	**Jumping to conclusions:** volcanoes do produce CO2, but over recent centuries the amounts are too small to account for the observed changes in the air.
If we stopped emitting CO2, it would take thousands of years for the atmosphere to return to pre-industrial levels.	"CO2 has a residence time of only 4 years so CO2 levels would fall quickly if we stopped emitting."	**Red herring:** how quickly a CO2 molecule moves around the climate system is different to how long it takes CO2 level to return back to normal.
Greenhouse gases are like a blanket. They trap heat, sending it back down to Earth where we measure it.	"Greenhouse effect violates the 2nd law of thermodynamics."	**Misrepresentation:** 2nd law talks about net flow of energy and doesn't forbid some flow from cool to hot.
Emitting more CO2 means more heat is being trapped high up in the atmosphere where the air is thinner.	"The greenhouse effect is saturated so adding more CO2 won't affect it."	**Over-simplification:** considers atmosphere as a single layer when it's multiple layers.
Ice cores tell us warming causes the ocean to emit more CO2. Combined with greenhouse effect, this is a reinforcing feedback.	"CO2 lagging temperature means greenhouse effect is minimal."	**False dichotomy:** it's not one or the other but both. CO2 causes warming and warming causes CO2 to rise.
One human fingerprint is a cooling upper atmosphere with a warming lower atmosphere. Satellites have measured this pattern.	"One fingerprint of human-caused global warming is the tropospheric hot spot which hasn't been observed."	**Red herring:** hot spot is irrelevant to greenhouse warming.
Satellites measure the warming effect from CO2 - the increased greenhouse effect is an observed reality.	"CO2 is a trace gas so it's warming effect is minimal."	**Red herring:** trace amounts of substances can have a strong effect and this is irrelevant to the warming potential of CO2.
Changing patterns in the yearly and daily cycle confirm human-caused global warming, rule out the sun.	"The sun is causing global warming."	**Cherry picking:** ignores human fingerprints and recent period where sun and climate move in opposite directions.

Figure 10.1. Denial101x lectures adhering to Fact-Myth-Fallacy structure. Denial101x, CC BY-ND.

as, "Examine how you feel about the information presented and how this impacts your response." A response could include a gut reaction to information, a choice to trust or distrust a source, or to share the information with others. Learning to pause and evaluate one's mental state and reaction to the information before re-posting or sharing information can greatly reduce the spread of false information.

Compton (2019, 75) has argued that "one of the most important features of inoculation is how it can enable a proactive approach to metaliterate learning—preparation for deliberation and dialogue." In his exploration of the connections between inoculation theory and metaliteracy, he suggests they are "complementary," with inoculation explicitly supporting the metaliterate behavioral, cognitive, affective, and metacognitive learning domains. He argued that "one of the most important features of inoculation is how it can enable a proactive approach to metaliterate learning—preparation for deliberation and dialogue" (75). One can strengthen the other by considering metaliteracy goals and objectives when constructing inoculation messages.

The techniques described in this chapter represent the most recent research on potentially effective methods for preventing the spread of faulty information, including conspiracy theories. With all this, however, there are caveats—and a big one is the QAnon worldview. Banas and Bessarabova (2023, 263), writing specifically about QAnon, noted that the superconspiracy poses unique challenges: It is tied to a political (social) identity, so it is more salient to a person's worldview and therefore more resistant to change—even more so if the QAnon worldview has become enmeshed with one's religious beliefs, as explored in chapter 8. QAnon is constantly evolving and shifting to absorb other conspiracy theories, "making it a particularly persistent problem" (and more challenging to anticipate and keep up with). Lastly, "unlike many other conspiracy theories, many of QAnon's ideas (e.g., the stolen election) receive a great deal of support from right-wing media." Helping patrons and learners better understand the information ecosystem, particularly how social media and news media feed into each other, could help combat any "authenticity" readers feel conspiracy theories gain by being platformed via major news outlets.

Part IV

Emerging Issues and Strategies

11

Problematizing Digital Citizenry and the Librarian

Your mindset is elitist [sic] and you are dismissing that people may not agree with what you think. You want to dismiss people who have different opinions as conspiracy theorist [sic]. One of your major flaws is that you are alienating stakeholders and people who actually fund libraries.—survey respondent

Librarian and educator are both service-oriented professions; we hold positions of trust and responsibility within our professional roles. We are drawn to these roles because of our desire to serve, to help answer questions, to inspire a love of knowledge, to promote equitable access to information. For librarians, the American Library Association's Code of Ethics codifies our professional passions, reminding us that we must work to uphold such important societal values as intellectual freedom, privacy, and respect. Similarly, the American Association of University Professors (AAUP) advocates and defends academic and intellectual freedom (AAUP 2024). While this chapter will briefly examine the debate surrounding library neutrality, the dilemmas are not unique to librarianship.

NEUTRALITY AND THE LIBRARIAN

The divisive digital age poses problems for us all as we work to navigate, and help patrons and learners navigate, the digital landscape full of disinformation. What is our role when people ask for, or assert knowledge of, problematic information? Is it even our role to distinguish "problematic" information? Is it better, as one survey respondent seems to suggest, to provide all information available, even if one knows it is "stupid stuff"?

I'm pretty good humored and am happy to help the friendly conspiracy nuts in the way that they want. I order the stupid stuff (Flat Earther's books, Urine

Therapy books) but typically keep a healthy amount of factual books to balance the collection.

In our 2023 survey, which is quoted throughout this chapter, we noticed that many participants leaned on notions of neutrality, or the idea that librarians can remain professionally impartial and without biases, such as the participant who opined that "librarians are supposed to be free of bias and personal beliefs," or the participant who stated, "[It's] not my business to straighten them out." Participants mentioned buying books, holding events and programs, and trying to appease patrons by representing "both sides." They were not correcting patrons who came in with disinformation because "it's not a librarian's place to."

Neutrality has long been hallowed within the librarian profession, although, as Dani Scott and Laura Saunders (2021, 153) noted, "[T]he American Library Association (ALA) does not include the word 'neutrality' in its standards or values statements, and thus offers no direct guidance on the role of neutrality in the profession." The International Federation of Library Associations and Institutions (IFLA, 2012), *does* include "[n]eutrality, personal integrity and professional skills" for "collection, access and service" in its Code of Ethics for Librarians and Other Information Workers. This inclusion has not been without its critics, many of whom point out that the principle of neutrality exists in opposition to the social justice work that IFLA itself promulgates (Bačić 2018); in his critique of the document, David Lankes (2012) illuminated its inherent contradictions:

> This very document screams bias. It shows a clear bias towards open access . . . hardly universal. It shows a clear bias towards transparency, and equitable access. . . . Just because we agree with them doesn't make them neutral. Librarians are heavily biased towards access and equity.

Lankes's comments illustrate the very real reality that our work and our values are inherently biased, despite the bias being inherently understood as positive and productive to society.

In the United States and Canada, codified ethics and values such as intellectual freedom, service, and access, combined with an aversion to censorship, seem to have been conflated in the profession as a mandate for neutrality. However, even as some fight for neutrality, we seem unable to agree on what exactly that means and how it looks in practice (Scott and Saunders 2021). In a survey of librarians on divisive issues, for example, there was strong agreement with scenarios like, "When a patron asks for your opinion about a political figure you should not comment" (161, figure 5). Things got muddled, however, when participants were asked to weigh in on whether "[l]ibraries should allow white supremacist groups to meet in their community rooms."

Only 10 percent of librarians strongly agreed with this statement, and nearly 50 percent strongly disagreed. Twenty percent neither agreed nor disagreed ... the librarians were neutral on neutrality. Gerolami (2020) exhorts that such positioning is not a neutral choice in itself, as it can be "mobilized to support the status quo" to the exclusion of marginalized groups.

The debate around librarian neutrality has variously centered on collections, exhibits/programming, room rentals to outside groups (Popovich 2021), and services (i.e., reference and research help). And yet, these activities are inherently non-neutral. Lankes opined in his *Atlas of New Librarianship* that "as librarians, the work you do has an impact on the community. As a librarian, you can't believe this and also believe that you are somehow a neutral force in the life of a member" (Lankes 2011, 119). Adhering to supposed neutrality has consequences. When taken to extremes, librarians can be so devoted to the democratic ideals of free access to knowledge that even requests such as information on how to make a bomb have been answered without pause (Hauptman 1976; Dowd 1990), an occurrence that one author described as constituting an "ethical vacuum" (Hauptman 1976).

It is hard to pin down a definition of neutrality for the profession because it has never existed; as one writer commented, "There is no neutral ground on which to stand anywhere in the world" (Jensen 2008). Indeed, the very existence of public libraries, with the impetus to provide information to everyone in pursuit of an educated citizenry, reveals an ontology of motivated intent.

ETHICAL NEUTRALITY

Librarians often point to "neutrality-adjacent" terms and ideas within ALA's Code of Ethics or Core Values of Librarianship to shape their professional identities and practices. Most libraries have carefully structured collection development policies that outline the goals for a collection and what shall and shall not be purchased for patron use, as well as clear policies for when items are challenged. These policies support and justify the important work that libraries do in promoting access to information and fighting against censorship. However, the information-disordered society in which we find ourselves presents unique challenges for the information professional. A democratic approach to information access is a value that needs to be upheld and championed, and so the librarians in the survey who resist providing any hint of personal bias or opinion are not acting in bad faith. This democratic ideal, however, as codified in ALA's Professional Ethics, is woefully contradictory:

> A democracy presupposes an informed citizenry. The First Amendment mandates the right of all persons to free expression, and the corollary right to receive the constitutionally protected expression of others. The

publicly supported library provides free and equal access to information for all people of the community the library serves. (ALA 2021)

Although these statements may seem to support the value of democracy, one must first ask the question, "What does it mean to be an informed citizen?" In our information-disordered society, does "free and equal access to information" necessarily lead to an informed citizen? If we take a teleological approach to ethical librarianship, then "informed citizen" should consider the dismal rates of American adult literacy (Barbara Bush Foundation, n.d.) and reject the use of the word *citizen*, which negates the fact that librarians also serve people who are not U.S. citizens. In addition, patrons are likely to have little to no training in any of the literacies that are necessary for the Information Age. Jack Andersen (2005, 20–21), writing prior to the dominance of social media, exhorted librarians to engage in critical discourse about traditional modes of knowledge organization. His emphasis on bibliographies, cataloging systems, and traditional encyclopedias seems quaint now (although search engines are mentioned briefly as an afterthought). However, his reasons for the need for such critical discourse are still relevant:

> The modern librarian envisioned as an information critic is sorely needed because systems of knowledge organization, in particular with the rise of the Internet, are part of our everyday life and human activities. This means that we are more than ever dependent on such systems, but at the same time *we need critical insight into how such systems work and why* (Andersen 2005, emphasis added).

Librarians are uniquely trained to understand how today's information systems work, and why. An adherence to neutrality subverts our professional expertise and stifles our crucial role in society—a role that goes beyond providing access to information, but also advocating for a critical discourse of ideas central to societal structures. These concerns expand on the core values of "public good" and, perhaps more importantly, discuss education and lifelong learning:

> ALA promotes the creation, maintenance, and enhancement of a learning society, encouraging its members to work with educators, government officials, and organizations in coalitions to initiate and support comprehensive efforts to ensure that school, public, academic, and special libraries in every community cooperate to provide lifelong learning services to all. (ALA 1986)

"Lifelong learning services to all" means that we must do our utmost to engage our communities in information and other literacies, helping learners at any life stage better understand the challenges and affordances of new information production and distribution systems.

THE IDEALISM OF NEUTRALITY

Librarians hold themselves to professional ideals and strive for the improvement of themselves and society, echoing the Idealist philosophy of Plato. And yet, Plato's *Republic* posited that not everyone should have access to all information (Kocergina 2022). These boundaries on information access are contrary to librarians' professional and personal codes of ethics. We are far more likely to encounter librarians espousing a neutral position on information access, even when extremely problematic:

> *They wanted content disputing the "non-existance" [sic] of the Holocaust. It is not my job to dispute patron's theories on content or provide my personal opinions, but rather provide them access to the information they requested. I will always suggest the counter argument resources and then the patron can make up their own minds.*

This librarian's response illustrates an extreme neutral stance, one that does not appear to be aligned with the library community as a whole (LaRue 2018; Enis 2022). Recently, alerted by collection development librarians on listservs and other public forums that popular ebook content providers hoopla and Overdrive had Holocaust denial books and other problematic material, the Library Freedom Project (LFP) and Library Futures (LF) released a joint statement demanding "full accountability" for providing access to misinformation, along with a form letter template for concerned librarians to email the leaders of both companies (Enis 2022). These advocacy groups' actions led to the titles being removed on hoopla and the publisher of a book available for purchase on Overdrive removing that title from its catalog. Fittingly illustrating the ongoing debate regarding this problem was a comment about the removal of the books:

> Is this not censorship? Is this not what librarians and others who tout the ideal that no matter how offensive, we do not pull books off shelves? Are we not all about having anyone find something they want to read, whether it is offensive to someone else or not? The ALA is all upset about the challenges they are receiving on books that have content that is offensive to some parents and challenge the need for the kind of sexual content found in many YA books in school libraries. How is this any different from those things? If you censor one, you will have to censor more. It is a slippery slope here. (Enis, 2018, comment by nanci olsen).

This is not a debate unique to the Information Age, although ebook providers do reflect a change in how users might prefer to access information. In 1999, Drobnicki argued that libraries should purchase and make available material that denies the Holocaust, to shed light on primary source literature that "illustrate[s] firsthand the ugly face of bigotry" (para 7), allowing librarians to place these materials in context with factual scholarship on the Holocaust. The notion is that this sort of action will discourage the conspiracy-theorist patron and guide them to think critically. However, does providing materials from "both sides" necessarily lead to critical thinking? While it is important to preserve these items for scholarly analysis, we would argue that the local public library does not need to have *The Protocols of the Elders of Zion*, for example, on its shelves. The tension between access and preservation bleeds into the digital as well, with the Jim Crow Museum of Racist Memorabilia going against the trend of museums by making digital content available online for public re/use "so as not to enable the creation of bigoted remixes" (McGuire 2024, 16).

Much of libraries' funding depends on donors or voters, which means that libraries often must conform to donors' worldviews and preferences. This fact was terrifyingly illustrated by one survey respondent:

> *I was told by the board not to engage with patrons on any of these topics, as they are deemed "political." Just let the patron spout off and don't argue. I also didn't know enough about what they were talking about to really respond knowledgeably.*

The respondent later elaborated that social media attempts to educate the public in information literacy were similarly shut down by their board. Considering the political, reactionary realities of public library funding and control, some librarians have argued for neutrality to be weaponized, used "proactively and pragmatically to their advantage" (Mathiasson and Jochumsen 2023) as just one of many tools in the librarian's arsenal. For example, Anita Brooks Kirkland (2021, para 12) argues for neutrality as a "radical practice" that utilizes a strict rule deontology to ensure that collections adhere to intellectual freedom without violating the rights of anyone:

> **Libraries** and school districts should have published criteria for the selection of resources, and those criteria should be guided by the rights and freedoms guaranteed in our national constitutions and human rights codes. **Neutrality** means selecting according to these criteria, unbiased by personal beliefs.

John Wenzler (2019) explored several philosophical models of library neutrality and offers a defense of neutrality as a rational position with which to uphold democratic ideals. He advocates that libraries remain neutral, promoting equally the "different conceptions of the good adopted by groups of citizens who are competing for political influence in democratic ways" (60), concluding that "[u]ltimately, radical views that currently reflect minority opinions will more likely get heard if librarians are committed to neutrality than if they are committed to radicalism" (75).

Chapter 11

ON TOLERATION

The example of the Holocaust-denying patron illustrates the "paradox of toler-ance," as imagined by philosopher Karl Popper (1950), an Austrian philosopher of the early twentieth century. His opus *The Open Society and Its Enemies* was a response to World War II and totalitarianism. In a footnote, he described the "paradox of tolerance" as derived from Plato:

> Unlimited tolerance must lead to the disappearance of tolerance. If we extend unlimited tolerance even to those who are intolerant, if we are not prepared to defend a tolerant society against the onslaught of the intoler-ant, then the tolerant will be destroyed, and tolerance with them.... We should therefore claim, in the name of tolerance, the right not to tolerate the intolerant. We should claim that any movement preaching intolerance places itself outside the law, and we should consider incitement to intoler-ance and persecution as criminal, in the same way as we should consider incitement to murder, or to kidnapping, or the revival of the slave trade, as criminal. (546)

Godfrey-Smith and Kerr (2019, 403) provide a sample of how the paradox of tolerance seems to be typically summed up: "If a tolerant society toler-ates intolerance, then tolerance itself will be broken down." These summaries passively and feebly echo the original; they lack the active threat that Pop-per ascribes to the intolerant if they are allowed free reign: "[I]f we are not prepared to defend a tolerant society against the *onslaught* of the intolerant, then the tolerant *will be destroyed*" (1950, 546, emphasis added). While this emphasis on the threat implied by Popper's words may sound alarmist, the cries for book banning in libraries, the demands for "transparent curriculum" in public schools, and the application of "cancel culture" on both the right and left of the political divide are all examples of intolerance that, if unchecked, will overwhelm all other viewpoints and lead to a restricted society for all.

Godfrey-Smith and Kerr (2019) cautioned that tolerance is fraught with various tensions, not the least of which is that "[t]oleration seems to require that a person disapprove of something and yet protect or at least accommo-date its existence" (404). This would seem to echo the approach of some of the librarians in the survey: While not affirming the Holocaust deniers' views, neither do they actively reject them, choosing instead to cling to a "both-sides-ism" that accommodates without fully validating the intolerant viewpoint.

EDUCATION AFTER AUSCHWITZ

Theodor Adorno (1967), a Jewish philosopher who escaped to America during the rise of the Nazi regime, framed an understanding of the role of education in a divided society in his paper "Education after Auschwitz." Adorno's essay, first delivered as a radio address, reflects the unease and pessimism of a society only a single generation out from the horrors of the Holocaust living during the social upheavals of the 1960s. His words chillingly anticipate some of the division, intolerance, anger, and fear that have arisen in our politics and our information landscapes. Adorno's calm assertion, *"The premier demand upon all education is that Auschwitz not happen again"* (1967, 1, emphasis added), speaks to the need for critical literacies and pedagogies that vehemently deny the disinformation that seeks to dismantle historical, scientific, and social knowledge.

Chapter 7 explored how antisemitism and conspiracy ideation are intertwined, with the insidiousness of the one amplifying the other. The danger of the Holocaust is not as distant in history as we may like. Adorno warned specifically about forces such as the rise of nationalism, and the fetishism of technology. His cautions underscore the need for empathy and affective concerns in education: "The inability to identify with others was unquestionably the most important psychological condition for the fact that something like Auschwitz could have occurred in the midst of more or less civilized and innocent people" (Adorno 1967, 8).

To footnote chapter 7, the April 2024 issue of *The Atlantic* led with a cover story exploring the chilling rise of antisemitism in America and the increasing tolerance of intolerance. Among the many examples provided is that of Elon Musk, who "reversed bans that [Twitter's] previous regime had imposed on the vilest anti-Semites. . . . By restoring them to the site, Musk was, in essence, conceding that these words shouldn't have been considered taboo in the first place" (Foer 2024, 32). The increasing comments in the media from politicians, actors, and other public figures should concern us all. If Auschwitz must not happen again, what, then, should we be doing?

ANTI-OPPRESSIVE LITERACIES

The very notion of information literacy is not neutral. The information literacy concept, "Authority is constructed and contextual" (ACRL 2016), for example, acknowledges that what determines an authoritative source of information will change and shift depending on context, while acknowledging traditional authorities and information (thereby positing the existence of questionable, non-authoritative, or untrustworthy information).

Taking the stance that current digital and information literacies are too passive in the face of far-right content on social media, Burnham and Arbeit (2023) proposed an "Anti-Oppressive Social Media Literacy" as an active, oppositional literacy to counteract extremism online. Much of their model depends on understanding the modes of production and dissemination; for example, to know that "engaging with far-right content inputs certain information to an algorithm would inform a user that instead of debunking . . . using a quote tweet [which would count for the algorithm as further engagement], they should take a screenshot" (124).

Social justice and librarians-as-advocates are current trends within the profession (with social justice added to the Code of Ethics in 2019) that do not attempt to espouse neutrality, and in fact regard neutrality in these matters as dangerous and irresponsible. ALA president Emily Drabinski (2018) highlighted this stance as part of a panel on library neutrality:

> If the white supremacists booking your meeting space are not after you, you don't have to know how dangerous they are. Books about reparative therapy for gay people can be simply another view if yours is not the body and mind those authors seek to destroy. To imagine that neutrality could be something we could choose is an intensely privileged position.

Consider the fact that libraries have promoted social justice by creating collections and exhibits or programming that center marginalized voices. Likewise, the issues of net neutrality, reducing the digital divide, open information, and accessibility have all been championed by librarians, among many other issues. None of these are neutral stances.

To be informed is to be critical, and criticality is what is currently lacking, both in skillset and practice. nina de jesus (2014) argued this point in her essay "Locating the Library in Institutional Oppression," in which she situated libraries within their colonialist, capitalist, and White supremacist culture and history, but still saw "emancipatory potential" should they be "[decoupled] from their avowed goal in propping up and strengthening settler democracies." Per de jesus's concerns, it could be argued that the more important stance is not to remain neutral, but rather to ensure that librarianship both models and advocates for social responsibility and criticality of the larger society and its own existence. Popovich (2021) echoed this, writing:

> Liberal intellectual freedom is passive, it waits to be manipulated by charlatans and bigots, and it calls this neutrality. The kind of intellectual freedom I am calling for is active, a commitment to an intellectual life shared by all and lived in common. The decision of a community to de-platform, to violate the liberal principles of free speech where the community considers it necessary, is an integral part of this common intellectual project. (30)

Whether we adhere to neutrality of various "understandings of the good," per Wenzler, or abandon notions of neutrality altogether in the face of our post-truth environment, we must do so actively.

LEAVING NEUTRALITY BEHIND

Lankes (2012) snidely reminded his readers that "[n]eutral has the same root as neuter." The connotations are clear: There is no growth, no future in neutrality. ALA publicly took this stance in 2021 when they approved a "Resolution to Condemn White Supremacy and Fascism as Antithetical to Library Work," which "acknowledges the role of neutrality rhetoric in emboldening and encouraging white supremacy and fascism." The position of this book presupposes that the reader wishes to have a toolkit for challenging or preventing conspiracy ideation, a non-neutral stance, even for a person who perhaps has heretofore championed neutrality. A recent paper, reporting on a "Post-Neutrality Librarianship" symposium, problematized the ongoing, often binary discourse that has been outlined here, concluding that, in the end, what is really needed is reflective practice; librarians need to "strive to make conscious choices in their daily practices and be self-reflexive, critical, and explicit about their choices" (Matthiasson and Jochumsen, 2023, 615). We must champion not neutrality, but reality. We can still afford access to different viewpoints without acknowledging and supporting those that are fantastical, harmful, or otherwise detrimental to society. We can refuse to provide information that, for example, denies the Holocaust, and not sacrifice our professionalism. We must balance our idealism with realism and look to other philosophies to situate and understand the role of information and discourse in our society and in libraries.

12

Artificial Intelligence within a Splintering Information Ecosystem

Guest author: Shawn McCann

We would be remiss if we did not have a chapter discussing artificial intelligence and the ways in which it is reshaping our information landscape, although the technology is changing so quickly that new developments are evolving even as we write. Artificial intelligence (AI) burst onto the public scene in 2022 when OpenAI introduced its chatbot, ChatGPT. The launch of ChatGPT created an arms race among tech companies to get consumer-friendly artificial intelligence products to market as quickly as possible (Weise et al. 2023). With the launch of ChatGPT, concerns about the negative social impacts of AI were outweighed by the market imperative to harness the power of generative artificial intelligence to corporate advantage (Metz et al. 2024). As tech giants threw their development of user-friendly AI tools into overdrive, other sectors of civil society sounded the alarm—the explosion of AI could lead to the use of chatbots capable of sharing conspiracy theories in real time in increasingly persuasive ways (Hsu and Thompson 2023). The presence of conspiracy theories is nothing new, but the speed of the spread of conspiracy theories has been supercharged by internet access and social media, hastening their uptake (Klepper 2024). Now, AI-generated disinformation presents new threats, including the significantly lowered cost of producing and distributing disinformation in support of conspiracy theories, the malicious pursuit of financial gain, political agendas, and the creation of chaos and confusion (Hellinger 2023; Solaiman et al. 2019). Information disorder is impacted by a splintering information ecosystem—information silos expand through myriad apps, websites, and social media. Generative Artificial Intelligence (GAI) is the newest phenomenon shaping this siloed landscape, and our interest here is to examine how it is impacting information disorder.

INFORMATION DISORDER AND AI

Who better to provide a working definition of AI than itself? According to the generative search tool Perplexity.ai:

> Artificial intelligence (AI) refers to the technology that enables computers and machines to simulate human intelligence and problem-solving capabilities. It encompasses various technologies like machine learning and deep learning, allowing AI algorithms to learn from data and make accurate predictions over time. AI can perform tasks that typically require human intelligence or intervention, such as digital assistants, GPS guidance, autonomous vehicles, and generative AI tools like Open AI's Chat GPT. AI is categorized into Weak AI (narrow AI), which focuses on specific tasks like Siri or self-driving vehicles, and Strong AI, which includes artificial general intelligence (AGI) with human-like intelligence. The field of AI has evolved significantly over the years, with applications growing across various industries like healthcare, finance, law, and more.

Perplexity.ai offers prompts below this definition to help users refine the answers to the initial question. As this AI-generated definition of AI demonstrates, chatbots and other GAI tools move beyond providing search results—they answer questions and generate content in a way that mimics human decision-making and conversation. GAI tools can author texts, images, and even sounds (e.g., music, voices), making the critical assessment of information more important than ever (Gozalo-Brizuela and Garrido-Merchán 2023). ChatGPT has fabricated sources (Frosolini et al. 2023), while DALL-E and other image generators continue to train on and amalgamate copyrighted work from creators (Chayka 2023; Chesterman 2023). In November 2022 Meta's GAI Galactica had to be taken down after only three days because it was generating fake research results and attributing fake references to real researchers (Heaven 2022). GAI has impacted virtually every realm, including politics (Jeantet and Savarese 2023), the arts (Velie and Nayyar 2024), music (Veltman 2023), healthcare (Al-Heeti 2013; Passanante et al. 2023), even Pope Francis (Fung 2023).

While GAI cannot *yet* reliably detect other GAI-generated content, its use is being leveraged to create and disseminate content (Aïmeur, Amri, and Brassard 2023). GAI has the capacity to impact information disorder by amplifying the quantity of mis/disinformation (Bell 2023; Zagni and Canetta 2023), the quality of mis/disinformation (Epstein and Hertzmann 2023), and the personalization of mis/disinformation (Zarouali et al. 2022). When assessing the impacts of GAI on information disorder, it may be helpful to use the term *extra-factual information*, which includes both misinformation and disinformation, and other forms of unverifiable information (Greenhill 2019). Using the term extra-factual information helps capture the lived experience of how GAI is impacting information disorder: Misinformation-based rumors can give rise to a disinformation-driven conspiracy theory that has deeper roots in unverifiable myths about a certain group in society (Greenhill 2020). Furthermore, as has been explored in other chapters, human brains do not process misinformation and disinformation differently (Arisoy, Mandal, and Saxena 2022), and (as also discussed earlier in the book) the illusory truth effect causes the frequency with which human beings hear *any* type of information to affect their perception of truth (Hassan and Barber 2021). The sheer capacity of GAI to generate and disseminate fringe views can give them the illusion of a majority-held perspective (DiResta 2020).

In practice, GAI has been used to generate images (Wang, Ling, and Stringhini 2023) as well as data visualizations (Hannah 2021a) to drive specific conspiracy theories online, and the frequency with which these GAI-generated sources are encountered by users facilitates acceptance of them. Furthermore, GAI-generated content is no longer just indistinguishable from human-generated content (Zhou et al. 2023); in some cases it can seem more credible to human users (Kreps, McCain, and Brundage 2022). For example, recalling the "Trump History" Twitter account mentioned in chapter 5, in which President Trump is inserted into images of various historical events using GAI tools, the credibility of the images is often assumed without criticality in Trump- or QAnon-affiliated groups, whereas those who do not support the political extreme right will often take the time to investigate further. This pattern repeats over and over on social media, with QAnon influencers sharing often obvious GAI content to a chorus of "Amen" and "Love this" comments from followers, with skeptics and debunkers trying in vain to point out the content is fake (Greer and Beene 2024).

DEEPFAKES, CHEAP FAKES, AND INTERACTIONAL AND COMPOSITIONAL FUTURES

Interrogating the rise of deep fakes and cheap fakes is a good way to explore the real-world impact of GAI on information disorder. A deepfake refers to the use of GAI and other machine-learning tools to generate a spectrum of fake or misleading audiovisual content, whereas the term *cheap fake* refers to the creation of multimedia with more conventional software such as Photoshop, or in some cases no software at all (Paris and Donovan 2019). The distinction between deepfakes and cheap fakes is being blurred by the accessibility of GAI, and both are intended to manipulate collective public attitudes through the dissemination of disinformation (Myers 2021). In May of 2023, a Trump supporter posted a GAI-generated photo of Donald Trump in military uniform, using the deepfake to imply that Donald Trump has a history of military service (E. Palmer 2023), which had to be immediately debunked because Donald Trump does not have a history of military service. This 2023 deepfake is a part of the same ecosystem of disinformation about Trump's military support, which includes a cheap fake from 2017 of a man claiming to be a Navy SEAL praising Trump for his support of the military. Another recent example of a GAI-generated deepfake is an image of Donald Trump surrounded by Black voters, which was generated with the explicit intent of misleading Black voters (Spring 2024). A recent example of a cheap fake comes from a 2020 viral video of Speaker of the House Nancy Pelosi allegedly slurring her speech. The video, while real, was purposefully slowed down to achieve the effect of slurred speech in an effort to discredit Speaker Pelosi (Elliott 2023). As these examples demonstrate, deepfakes and cheap fakes have similar intended impacts—the manipulation of individuals' opinions to support an agenda undermined by the facts. Donald Trump does not have a record of military service, he is not universally supported by members of the military, Nancy Pelosi's speaking abilities are currently fine, and Donald Trump is not supported by a majority of Black voters. The confusion sown by competing claims can pay dividends for elected officials—researchers have coined this phenomenon "the Liar's Dividend," to capture how politicians benefit from spreading misinformation *about misinformation* to evade accountability (Schiff, Schiff, and Bueno 2024).

Both deepfakes and cheap fakes impact information disorder in similar ways. This can have disastrous impacts, such as those raised by Congresswoman Anna Eshoo (2022) in her letter to the federal Office of Science and Technology Policy, in which she points to GAI models that have produced photos of violently beaten Asian women and pornography featuring real people. The research shows that human beings struggle to detect AI-generated deepfakes (Groh et al. 2022), this struggle does not change when humans are provided information raising awareness of the prevalence of deepfakes (Bray, Johnson, and Kleinberg 2023), and human beings tend to overestimate their abilities to detect deepfakes (Köbis, Doležalová, and Soraperra 2021). The rise of AI-generated "revenge porn," in which explicit images of people are created and shared without consent, has added new layers to an already existing societal problem (Kelleher 2023).

Disconcertingly, the emerging horizon of deepfake technology also includes interactive and compositional deepfakes. Interactional deepfakes mimic human behaviors with realistic GAI-generated behaviors, which are then leveraged to take advantage of multimodal forms of communication. In one of the first headline-grabbing examples of an interactional deepfake from 2019, perpetrators used AI to mimic a CEO's voice in order to demand a fraudulent transfer of $243,000 (Stupp 2019). Interactional deepfakes often combine fraudulent communication via text, video, or email as well convince victims of the authenticity of the communication (de Rancourt-Raymond and Smaili 2023). The combination of AI-generated text, voice, video, and email proves highly effective in cybersecurity attacks (Rahman et al. 2023) with reports of *annual* financial loss to the U.S. economy estimated between $100 billion and $250 billion (House Subcommittee on Cybersecurity 2023; Scherbina and Schlusche 2023). The speculative emergence of compositional deepfakes poses some of the most disconcerting epistemic threats. Compositional deepfakes describe situations in which GAI-generated content could be leveraged as a part of disinformation campaigns over time with observed, expected, and engineered world events layered in with the explicit intent of creating persuasive, fake histories (Horvitz 2022).

As discussed, compositional and interactive deepfake technologies include the threat of GAI-generated text, which means that an important component of evaluating the impact of GAI on information disorder requires evaluating the impacts of text-based GAI-generated content. Some research has contrasted user concerns about deepfake videos with the lack of concern for GAI-generated text-based disinformation (Gamage et al. 2022). Humans do not have the capacity to differentiate between GAI-generated news articles and news articles written by human beings (Kreps, McCain, and Brundage 2022), much like we have not demonstrated the capacity to differentiate between GAI-generated images and real images. Research on the capacity of GAI to generate high-quality misinformation with little human involvement shows that GAI can customize language for specific groups by drawing on stereotypes and racist tropes (Buchanan et al. 2021). GAI-generated text-based misinformation can establish clarity, credibility, and transparency, and even acknowledge its limitations when compared with human-generated text-based misinformation. In some examples, when compared with human-generated misinformation, GAI does a *better job* of enhancing detail, communicating limitations, drawing conclusions, and simulating personal tones (Zhou et al. 2023). Given the capacity of GAI-generated misinformation to comply with the parameters outlined in current information assessment guidelines, it's clear that GAI is creating new challenges for information disorder. Although recent research shows that information literacy interventions still somewhat positively impact an individual's hesitancy to share extra-factual information generated by GAI (Adjin-Tettey 2022), the speed, quality, and scale of the dissemination of harmful content may render individually-focused educational interventions irrelevant.

Given our research, Stephanie began playing around with different generative AI platforms as they were rolled out, with a particular eye toward conspiracy theories. In mid-2023, she attempted to push Bing's ChatGPT, Open AI's ChatGPT, and Google's Bard to disseminate disinformation and conspiracy theories. Of the three, only Open AI would reply that it wasn't trained to have opinions—or it would generate a both-sides message or relay that it is a neutral arbiter of the truth. This is, of course, problematic, as theorists have long highlighted the bias inherent in algorithms and large language and data models (O'Neil 2016; Cheney-Lippold 2017; Yong Jin 2021). Of the three, Bing's ChatGPT was the most problematic, with its responses that walked right up to the line of endorsing debunked conspiracy theories. This experiment, it could be argued, occurred in the early days of ChatGPT—surely these systems have been improved. This experiment is anecdotal too; therefore, her results are not systematic or generalizable. However, it did elucidate the discrepancies between ChatGPT platforms and confirmed her suspicions that, if we're not careful, generative AI could reproduce and disseminate harmful information.

STRATEGIES FOR COMBATING GAI-GENERATED EXTRA-FACTUAL INFORMATION

AI Content Identification and Fact-Checking

Flagging and accurately labeling AI content for users is a starting point for combating AI-generated extra-factual information. Platforms are already beginning to investigate scalable ways to identify AI-generated content. Meta, Facebook's parent company, is working with industry partners to establish standards to mark content that was created using AI tools. These would include invisible flags in the metadata or other similar watermarks on the AI-generated content. The invisible markers would then be detectable by platforms, such as Facebook, which can then label the content as generated by AI tools. This is a step in the right direction, but only if the standards are followed by everyone producing AI tools. Additionally, bad faith actors may be able to strip out markers identifying AI content, or they could use content generated by AI tools that do not generate the markers in the first place (Clegg 2024).

Technology may provide other avenues outside of just labeling for identifying AI-generated content. Deepfake detection tools were developed because of the dissemination of deepfake content, and many tools now exist to detect deepfakes (Tuquero 2024). However, the efficacy of deepfake detection tools doesn't align with the ubiquity of deepfakes themselves. For example, in January of 2024, there was a robocall of President Biden's voice discouraging New Hampshire primary voters from voting (Swenson and Weissert, 2024). Many news organizations concluded the call was a deepfake, and the company Pindrop used their deepfake detection engine to confirm that the call was indeed AI generated (Balasubramaniyan 2024). However, journalists at Politifact tested four other detection tools to see if they could also correctly identify the robocall as a deepfake. The tools tested were Elevenlabs Speech Classifier, AI or Not, Play HT, and Buffalo University's Deep-fake-O-Meter, and the results were mixed, with one tool even concluding the call was likely human (Tuquero 2024).

Automated fact-checking is another way to combat AI-generated extra-factual information. Support for fact-checking has increased dramatically in recent years, particularly in response to the study of extra-factual information in the fields of journalism and archival studies (Graves and Amazeen 2019; LeBeau 2017). However, the pace of fact-checking accomplished by journalists and other professional fact-checkers is incapable of matching the scale of the dissemination of extra-factual information (Sullivan 2019). Natural Language Processing (NLP), a term that refers to a machine-learning technology that enables computer programs to understand human language as it is colloquially used, may be one tool in the AI suite that can be used to automate fact-checking by flagging inconsistencies and claims in text that contradict established facts (Guo, Schlichtkrull, and Vlachos 2022). One fact-checking organization, Full Fact, collects information from live TV, online news, and social media pages, and it uses AI tools to identify, label, and match claims. This use of AI is only part of Full Fact's process, where humans are still heavily involved.

In the future AI may assist with the real-time fact-checking by automating evidence retrieval across text, images, and videos (Singh et al. 2022). It may also be able to perform veracity predictions by comparing the collected evidence with the claims presented to assess the likelihood of certainty for a particular claim (Shu et al. 2020). However, fully automating veracity predictions to remove content can backfire and contribute to human mistrust and even reinforce human belief in false claims (Lewandowsky et al. 2012). This is because the last stage of fact-checking, where the explanation for the justification of action is described in an understandable way, is key to ensuring that human beings accept the outcome. Close evaluation of user experience is thus essential in engaging with AI tools, and the application of NLP for the purpose of fact-checking must produce results that are readable (clear), plausible (compelling/persuasive), and faithful to the intent of the fact-checking reasoning process (Jacovi and Goldberg 2020). There needs to be more incorporation of human needs and experience into GAI fact-checking tools to further refine automated fact-checking. Although model accuracy for fully automated AI fact-checking software has improved with newer datasets, the most recent research indicates that full automation is still not desirable when compared with the better outcomes of hybrid human–AI learning opportunities offered by NLP (Das et al. 2023).

AI PREDICTIONS: TRACKING THE SPREAD OF EXTRA-FACTUAL INFORMATION

As much as AI spreads extra-factual information, AI may also present an opportunity to track and predict the spread of extra-factual information by providing multimodal detection across multiple platforms (Singh, Ghosh, and Sonagara 2021). Sentiment analysis, in which AI is used to determine the relative negativity and intensity of a piece of information, may be useful in tracking and predicting the spread of conspiratorial extra-factual information, which often relies on eliciting strong negative emotions (Alonso et al. 2021). Other helpful tools for predicting the spread of extra-factual information are AI tools that track and categorize emotionally polarizing reactions to shared information. This can also be referred to as "opinion mining," and given that widely divergent opinions about a news story may indicate emotional polarization, it may offer an early detection option for fake news (Santos 2023).

The streaming and consistently inconsistent nature of extra-factual information presents challenges for the use of AI to detect extra-factual information (Choraś et al. 2021). The labels and language used by the individuals and entities that spread extra-factual information are often regularly changed because purveyors of extra-factual information are aware that AI tools can be used to detect them. The use of AI can account for this by considering "concept drift" (Wang, Minku, and Yao 2015), but this requires the foresight of planning into the tool to account for inevitable changes required for tracking (Chen and Liu 2018).

USERS AND REGULATION: MITIGATING NEGATIVE IMPACTS OF AI

The research on the use of AI to combat the spread of extra-factual information is clear: Human-centered approaches in the design, use, and deployment of AI are critical to ensuring that the results are beneficial and effective (Gianluca, Mizzaro, and Spina 2020). Practitioners are urging high levels of human oversight coupled with the use of automated processes; a shift in AI design toward the goal of empowering people instead of emulating people; and consideration of instituting AI governance structures that ensure the reliability and safety of AI tools through certification and oversight (Shneiderman 2022). The debate about appropriate regulatory frameworks is well underway, and one of the main goals of these debates is to curb the unfettered use of new AI tools that may spread extra-factual information (Montasari 2024). Recent international collaboration across academics, government, and industry has recommended six human-centered challenges in developing regulatory oversight of the field of AI: (1) Design for human well-being, (2) socially responsible design, (3) respect for privacy, (4) human-centered design principles, (5) actual accountability to governance and oversight, and (6) capable of human interaction while respecting human cognitive abilities (Garibay et al. 2023). EU-based regulatory attempts include the EU's Artificial Intelligence Act, General Data Protection Regulations, the Electronic Communications Code, and the Cybersecurity Act. The goals of these regulatory regimes are to establish clear criteria for risk-based determinations, and ongoing monitoring of the most high-risk GAI systems while safeguarding human dignity, the right to privacy, democracy, and the rule of law (Almeida et al. 2021). More than thirty countries have developed policy frameworks to evaluate the social and ethical implications of AI; however, these frameworks overwhelmingly prioritize the instrumental value of AI over the ethical considerations of AI development itself (D. Schiff 2022). The plethora of proposed policy responses to AI demonstrates that many institutions are prioritizing regulating these technologies, but the variety of policy responses also impedes the cohesion and effectiveness of institutional responses to AI. For example, in the field of academic publishing alone, a variety of AI-use policies creates confusion instead of control: The use of AI-generated text and images is banned in the journals published by Science (Gu et al. 2022), the journal *Nature* allows AI-generated text but not images or videos (Nature Editors 2023), and *JAMA* allows AI-generated content but requires users to disclose its use and which technologies were used (JAMA Network, n.d.). The variety of responses from reputable academic journals on the use of AI-generated content raises complicated questions about information literacy models that rely primarily on assessing the authority of source information to determine credibility. Will educators use publishers' policies on the use and disclosure of AI content as an important indicator of a given source's credibility? Does this mean that the journal *Science* is a more reliable source of information than *JAMA*? At the very least, this example points to the need for uniform policies across sectors in responding to problems posed by the continued use of AI.

As the national and international policy arena slowly moves toward agreed-upon governance structures capable of responding to new challenges presented by AI, independent fact-checking organizations and institutions that encourage user-driven reporting of suspicious content may play an important role in checking the spreading of extra-factual information (Gradoń et al. 2021). Libraries are key institutions in combating the spread of extra-factual information contributing to information disorder (Glisson 2019), but recent analysis of library practices in reaction to AI shows that most librarians still rely on the reiteration of authority-based source evaluation instead of wrangling with emotionally based reactions that spread quickly in a post-truth world (Revez and Corujo 2021). New Media Literacy practices including civic engagement, development of social media literacy skills, critical information literacy, automated fact-checking, use of GAI-powered fake news–detecting tools, and deep learning supported by neural networks may help curb the spread of extra-factual information (Shahzad and Khan 2022). One of the most effective tools against combating extra-factual information is the maintenance of open-access research that is easily available to students and the public in support of self-learning—elevating access to libraries of public universities as an important resource in combating information disorder (Herrero-Diz and López-Rufino 2021).

It is important to note that current research shows that individual awareness of being fact-checked is not an effective deterrent against the practice of sharing extra-factual information; however, a demonstrably impactful deterrent to the spread of extra-factual information is the threat of social isolation, indicating that policies of freezing and banning accounts are currently the most effective policy interventions to combat the spread of extra-factual information

(Wasike 2023). Given that bots may not reliably respond to something as human as an individual fear-of-isolation, policies that automate the freezing and banning of suspicious accounts may be prudent and could be adopted with the force of statutory oversight accompanied by legal enforcement mechanisms outside of the tech sector. Combining the automation of proven policy interventions (like automatic account-freezing), with the support of human-centered fact-checking institutions to guarantee that the reasoning behind the automated actions is appropriately communicated to users, demonstrates the kind of human-checked automated processes that could slow the spread of GAI-generated extra-factual information. Going forward, a multi-pronged approach including government intervention, user education, and checks and balances built into platforms by requiring user-verification and controlled sharing, and independent information-verification services, may help manage the spread of extra-factual information (Gupta et al. 2022). Practitioners combating information disorder must continue reflecting on educational frameworks and available tools to assess their practical impact and advocate for upstream policy mandates that can mitigate the generation and spread of GAI-generated extra-factual information. The profit motive driving tech companies to quickly capitalize on the power of GAI poses a threat to almost every sector of society, suggesting that one of the possible policy interventions to mitigate the threat of GAI may be to place limits on profit sharing for large tech companies unleashing GAI technologies that have demonstrated negative social outcomes.

OUR FUTURE WITH AI: ENVISIONING GUARDRAILS AND OVERSIGHT

AI is a double-edged sword that presents a clear and present threat to critical information literacy while also offering tools to combat the spread of extra-factual information. Because of the capacity of AI to create an unprecedented flood of credible but erroneous content, and its ability to spread that content at a scale faster and farther than any human being ever could, it is incumbent upon society to use AI as a tool to combat the problems created by AI itself. Effective tools may include uniform labeling of AI-generated content, deepfake detection software, real-time fact-checking, and the use of AI to anticipate and predict the spread of particularly harmful extra-factual information. A both/and approach of collaboration across public and private institutions including the development of user-centered educational tools and enforceable policy mandates must accompany any automated AI interventions to stop extra-factual information. Ethical frameworks for the development of AI, human-centered design and intervention, and legally mandated practices offer some hope that the net societal impact of AI will yield more good than harm. While the use of AI presents as many, if not more, questions than answers in combating information disorder, one thing is clear: Ignorance of AI's use and impact will only impede critical information literacy. Practitioners must engage with AI to understand and combat the information disorder that AI itself is exacerbating.

13

Stemming the Tide and Looking to the Future

Conspiracy theories are the "worst-case" scenario when it comes to information disorder. Librarians took as their purview the formation of information literacy as part of the professional drive to form an educated citizenry (Goldstein 2020), but we need to confront a hard truth, as demonstrated by the growing problems of information disorder: Our current efforts are failing (Wineberg et al. 2016). As this book has hopefully made clear, we are among a growing body of researchers seeking to expand the current frameworks to include a more holistic accounting of affective states; lateral reading and other fact-checking techniques in an increasingly social and digital world; and evolving challenges in the information landscape, including generative artificial intelligence.

To confront the challenges of today's information landscape, we must first critically examine the very term that we use so often: *literacy*. While information literacy was first envisioned in the 1970s as the skills needed to read and use information, how are we conceiving of literacy half a century later in our networked age? As our field becomes crowded with "literacies" of all kinds— visual literacy, media literacy, data literacy, news literacy, and on and on—it can be hard to know where to start, where to end, and what will truly be most effective for our learners (Badke 2019, 55–57). This final chapter examines how the issues of information disorder highlight the need to problematize the current hegemonic models of information literacy and look to new ideas for our information future.

FOUNDATIONS

The pedagogy of information literacy in the United States has been largely built on the strength of two documents, both from the Association of College and Research Libraries (ACRL): the 2000 *Information Literacy Competency*

Standards for Higher Education (*Standards*), built on discrete objectives for learners; and its evolution, the 2016 *Framework for Information Literacy for Higher Education* (*Framework*). These are in turn supported and supplemented by various international standards, specialized audience standards (such as the 2018 American Association of School Librarians' *Standards Framework for Learners*), and additional literacy frameworks. In today's information landscape, however, these professional guidelines have fallen short. Not only do they assume a formal educational setting in which learners will be adequately instructed in these tenets (as opposed to the reality of the one-shot, hour-long sessions that constitute the majority of information literacy instruction), but many, such as the ACRL documents, tend to be utilized in classrooms with static, traditional documents; although the *Framework* does lean in to a more fluid, socially constructed information environment, the staid halls of education do not. This is borne out by the anecdotal evidence of the still-constant struggle between academic librarians and faculty regarding the often Byzantine source requirements for class projects (e.g., "five peer-reviewed articles, written by a nurse practitioner, published within the last two years," etc.).

Indeed, that has been one of the strongest criticisms of the *Framework*: It is a product of a specialized, academic environment, and although the frames attempt to breach those boundaries, the document still speaks to a hegemonic academic epistemology (Beilin 2015; Beatty 2014). To be fair, its main audience is higher education in the United States; however, the influence of the ACRL information literacy documents can be seen throughout the literature of other educational communities (Piloiu 2016). While the *Framework* attempts to broaden the scope and understanding of information literacy beyond what the *Standards* accomplished, many assert they do not go far enough to critically consider the information environment and the power structures that underlie information production, access, use, and evaluation (Beilin 2015). Indeed, along with the adherence to an academic model of information valuation, the *Framework* has also been considered by some to be neoliberal and colonialist, echoing the worst ills of the academy from which it was developed (Beilin 2015; Beatty 2014).

Still others have flagged what they see to be internal contradictions or limitations within the frames themselves (Wilkinson 2014). Commenting on an early draft of "Information Creation as a Process" (at the time it was "Format as Process"), Amanda Hovious (2014) called out the persistent focus on format, "especially now that we are entering the information convergence," preferring instead to "focus on how information is used as a tool in scholarly or popular media." Stefanie Bluemle (2018, 275) noted similar inherited concepts in the "Authority is Constructed and Contextual" frame, criticizing the pervasive reliance on peer-reviewed scholarship as an easy heuristic for "authority," and writing that "[t]he frame posits a definition of authority on which it does not entirely follow through." More damning is her assertion that the "librarian's guiding document on authority in information literacy does not prepare us to teach in a post-facts United States" (277).

Stepping away from the ACRL documents, the very concept of information literacy and what it should be, or should not be, in the current information age remains problematic. Ben Johnson (2017), reeling from the 2016 election of Donald Trump and its aftereffects, wrote that "information literacy is dead" in an age of post-truth. Even the very notion of truth is questioned by some, which leads to the question of how do we teach evaluative tactics if there is no universally accepted marker of truth? Sullivan writes of the contradiction inherent in the discipline: Information literacy constantly is championed as the answer to questions that aren't well defined in themselves; for example, with "fake news," is the problem the existence of the fake news itself or its consequences? (Sullivan 2019). And are those concepts in turn clearly and universally understood? Academe and its hangers-on have written themselves into knots, and the vast amount of literature that we can only touch on here often raises more questions than answers.

What of those who do not attend higher education and/or who left schooling before information literacy became fully incorporated into the curriculum? Those who have been thrust into our socially mediated information landscape without any understanding of how the information they engage with has been produced, how it got to their attention, and which part of reality the story reflects (or does not)? Sarah Hartman-Caverly (2019), writing in the early days of the QAnon movement, found that the problem is not necessarily an epistemological information literacy deficit. She concludes, instead, that the problem is one of hermeneutics, writing:

> Participants in the QAnon Storm conspiracy community engage with a broad range of information sources. . . . In any given thread one can find links to stories from multiple establishment newspapers of record, clips from broadcast and cable news, SEC filings and public records of financial transactions, government reports, statutes and regulations, patents, academic papers, live hearings, interviews, and expert witness testimonies— just to name a few. (189)

Indeed, those of us who teach would probably be elated should the breadth and depth of resources used by the conspiratorial community show up in students' bibliographies. Hartman-Caverly argues that the long line of actual conspiracies evidenced by those documents, along with the current polarization and bias in the mainstream media environment, make it clear that more of us should be more skeptical, more questioning, and encourage learners to be the same:

> Broadening focus from rote fact checking to epistemic choice making eases the tension around contested interpretations of reality [. . .]Talking

about epistemic ethics is an entry point to so many of the dispositions in the *Framework*, a technique for making an unconscious cognitive process open to observation, a challenge to take responsibility for the reality we cocreate, a celebration of freedom of conscience, an acknowledgment that we are going to get it wrong, and of the redemption in changing our minds. Helping students think through epistemic choices and their consequences seems a reasonable pedagogical approach in the learning context of a tainted, compromised, and weaponized information domain. (207-8)

The "reality we cocreate," the reality of internet communities, is more often than not a *response* to the rote authoritarianism of the guidelines and standards for information literacy that the educated elite champion, as Barbara Fister (2021) cautions:

Those who spend their time in the library of the unreal have an abundance of something that is scarce in college classrooms: information agency. One of the powers they feel elites have tried to withhold from them is the ability to define what constitutes knowledge. They don't simply distrust what the experts say, they distrust the social systems that create expertise. They take pleasure in claiming expertise for themselves, on their own terms.

Matthew Hannah echoes these conclusions in his discussion of the QAnon ecosystem as an information literacy practice in itself (Hannah 2023). The problems of information literacy, then, do not stem from one's ability to distinguish a scholarly article. Rather, we have an information landscape feeding the affective needs of the disaffected, championing influencers and personalities over established experts, and bombarding our psychological systems with exactly what we want over what we need. Much of the discourse about conspiracy ideation has begun to shift toward a more holistic understanding of human psychology and the complex reasoning that emerges when under the influence of conspiracy ideation. While the field of conspiracy research often still assumes a lack of critical thinking, there is now more discussion about conspiracy ideation being an outcome of faulty interpretations informed by myriad life experiences and influences. A whole host of factors may play a role in whether one adheres to a conspiratorial worldview, including education, socioeconomic status, exposure to new ideas and beliefs that challenge one's own, and more.

Throughout our research over the past four years, we have observed specific information behaviors that elucidate gaps in various literacies. In our article from 2023, we observed specific instances of faulty visual, digital, and scientific literacies within conspiracy communities; anyone who spends any time on social media, conspiracy-adjacent or not, will easily find additional examples. A lack, or a collapse of knowledge, combines with the use of faulty reasoning, faulty hermeneutics, and emotionally driven engagement to craft the story that the user wants to see. The Frameworks and Standards that have structured our thinking for the past generation are not equipped to address these issues.

BROADENING OUR HORIZONS

First, a caveat: We do not advocate for the abandonment of the *Framework*. It provides an excellent starting point for thinking about information literacy, and to acknowledge its gaps and the unique challenges of the social media environment can only serve to make our discipline stronger. The existence of numerous companion documents, such as the *Framework for Visual Literacy for Higher Education* (Beene et al. 2022) enumerates how a holistic approach to information literacy can be fluid and expansive, rather than restrictive. The following sections serve to highlight various other approaches that can be used alone or in tandem with the *Framework*, with the acknowledgment that this is only a small sample; as Amanda Hovious (2014) encourages, if the frames don't work for you, make your own!

CRITICAL PEDAGOGIES

Critical pedagogies serve as a base upon which we can frame the problematization of information literacy documents, practice, and discourse. Librarians may perhaps be most familiar with critical information literacy (CIL), a movement within IL that has been embraced over the past two decades, and which derives from the work of Paolo Freire (Díaz 2024). Eamon Tewell (2015), a major scholar in this area, writes of critical IL:

> It is this critical appraisal of information literacy's conventions and norms—from a lack of involvement with the sociopolitical dynamics that shape student learning and scholarly information to the notion that IL is an educational obstacle that can be conquered—that in part distinguishes critical information literacy from traditional conceptions of IL and makes it an important perspective to consider. (25)

Tewell further opines that critical source evaluation, which is often prioritized in IL instruction and understanding, "can only get us so far, since some people refuse to have their mind changed"; trust, power, and openness are salient concepts that we must deconstruct in order to move forward (Schneider, Borges, and Bezerr, n.d.).

CIL is only one of the many critical pedagogies that have sprung up in Freire's legacy. To our purposes, Sarah Amsler (2011, 58) envisions a critical affective pedagogy that would problematize emotion itself, rather than viewing it as the objective end, "to enable people to understand why they have certain feelings, desires, and needs; why, perhaps, they do not have or are not 'supposed' to have others; and to critically imagine conditions in which radical alternatives may be possible." In this she draws from Zembylas and Boler (2002, 6), who critique the shortcomings of critical information literacy and media literacy as they examine patriotism in post-9/11 America. The rational discourse and objective inquiry inherent to these literacies, they argue, neglects the "emotional investments [. . .] in relation to particular symbols." The authors argue for a "pedagogy of discomfort" that "particularly emphasizes a critical inquiry that recognizes "how emotions define how and what one chooses to see, and conversely, not to see" (6, citing A. Roy, "The Algebra of Infinite Justice"). Affective semiotics from the patriotic, the political, and all other facets of humanity are utilized without fail in social media and news media to drive emotion and engagement. Their pedagogy derives from the work of Foucault in encouraging learners to create a "genealogy of emotions" (20) to interrogate the formational basis of emotions associated with symbols. By tracing back one's emotional development, therefore, the original affective assumptions or motivators can be critically analyzed, compared against other knowledge, and understood within the larger hegemonic society.

A MODEL OF CARE

In her professional work, Katie teaches an online, asynchronous general education course. Those who teach online can attest that it takes a great deal of effort to engage students, especially when the learning management system mediates all your interactions with them. (For those who are not educators, a learning management system is the tool used to deliver the courses; the most common in higher education are Canvas, Blackboard, and Moodle.) Katie has always been interested in online pedagogies and critical pedagogies, but around the time of the pandemic, she added pedagogies of care to her repertoire—teaching modalities that emphasize the student as a whole person and active participant in their learning, which relies on relationship building to structure the classroom and its content. The work of Nel Noddings (1984) and her "ethic of caring" was an inspiration to her specifically, as well as bell hooks (1994) and Paolo Freire (1984), as pedagogies of care draw from feminist, critical, and trauma-informed pedagogies, alongside other models.

The application of care ethics is often seen in the literature of nursing, medical education, and K-12 education, which makes sense as those are caring-focused professions. Librarianship, especially the more publicly focused roles, also has ontological components of care; in our research, we have heard from many librarians who express fatigue and exasperation with their patrons—but also a great deal of care and concern for their well-being.

Pedagogies of care should not involve overbearing insertion into learners' personal lives and feelings, as some critics have framed Noddings's work (Hoagland 1990); rather, the focus should be on respectful, bounded concern for learners' needs and creating a community of learners (including the instructor). The notion of "care" itself has been problematized and explored thoroughly by Sally Baker and Rachel Burke (2023) in their book *Questioning Care in Higher Education*. Their introductory chapter, "What is Care," delves deeply into the meanings and functions of care, concluding that

> [c]are is deeply context-dependent, cultural, relational, and ontological and is, thus, inherently complex and fluid; simultaneously, care is also made invisible by silences, and it is culturally situated, contested, and slippery, all of which makes debates about care difficult to navigate. (53)

Importantly, we must distinguish between care and empathy. While empathy involves positioning oneself along with others in an affective state, Kitayama, Hashizaki, and Osler (2022) caution against conflating care with empathy. They note that even Noddings discouraged this: "She maintains that those caring need to set aside a temptation to analyse and project upon the other, and instead develop receptive attention to perceive the other" (34).

The benefits of utilizing a pedagogy of care, in Katie's experience, have been many, including increased engagement and deeper learning. In this book, we explore numerous intersections of affect, mostly in terms of mood and emotion, with learning and information behaviors. Mary Helen Immordino-Yang (2016, 18) crystallizes the current state of research on these intersections when she writes, "It is literally neurobiologically impossible to build memories, engage complex thoughts, or make meaningful decisions without emotion." A pedagogy of care, by foregrounding relationships, an understanding of how affective states contribute to learning, and care for each individual's unique needs, provides support for the learner and can strengthen connections between the learner and the educator or mentor. In a recent article, Katie also explored how a pedagogy of care might promote metaliteracy objectives by supporting the affective and metacognitive domains of learning (Greer 2023).

Those who are not educators may be tempted to dismiss this section, but pedagogies of care do not require a dedicated classroom. Many of our interactions with patrons and learners, of course, are exceedingly brief (e.g., information literacy instruction sessions, reference interviews, consultations). Noddings's (1984) framework for care ethics could be adapted to various settings; her framework consists of four components:

1. **Modeling:** How is care modeled in your interactions? This is done not just through the educator or authority figure showing care when encountering others but also through course or service design that anticipates those encounters. For example, Katie utilizes universal design for learning principles (http://udlguidelines.cast.org) and a trauma-aware teaching checklist (https://bit.ly/traumachecklist) to help her think through the obstacles her learners might face. What obstacles might your patrons or learners encounter at service points or in your educational settings? How could those be addressed to show support for their needs?

2. **Dialogue:** This component prioritizes open, nonjudgmental communication that expresses care and builds on what has been done through modeling. This doesn't just take place through the conversations you have with patrons or learners when they are seeking help or information, however. By actively seeking input on what their needs are (which can then inform the modeling component of care) and providing affirmative feedback as appropriate, dialogue enacts care. If you only have short interactions, how might you assess if the person's needs are being met during those interactions and afterward? How might your word choices indicate care for them?

3. **Practice:** In Noddings's model, practice "refers to the ability for learners to enact care themselves" (Greer 2023, 4). Because care is a relationship construct, it should not be one-sided. Ideally, the modeling and the dialogue that you structure will encourage the other person to reciprocate care in some way. In education, we structure opportunities for this practice through assignments such as peer-to-peer feedback or collaborative tasks. It is important to mention here that practice in care should also include self-care. Caring pedagogy, if done without proper boundaries, can be very draining and lead to burnout. Caring for others takes a lot of energy, and the wisdom of "you can't care for others if you aren't caring for yourself" has its place not only for traditional caregivers but for those of us in service-oriented professions. Structure self-care into your schedule and your routines. You deserve it, and it will help you to be your professional best as well.

4. **Confirmation:** Noddings described confirmation as "see[ing] the cared-for as he is and as he might be—as he envisions his best self—in order to confirm him" (1984, 67). In the educational environment, assessment (grading) often serves as confirmation; specifically, assessment that provides individual and detailed feedback to the learner on how they are succeeding or where they are still growing. Confirmation can occur during the dialogue of a reference interview, for example, as you tailor the conversation to reflect and appreciate the "cared-for" and their interests. If this seems daunting when you consider interacting with members of the public who are agitated or expressing deeply seated conspiracy beliefs, consider

the underlying motivations for their belief. QAnon, for example, has at its core a concern for children's safety. Through using "I" statements, such as "I agree that we as a society must care for our children," or even just "I hear what you are saying," you can position yourself as someone who confirms the core beliefs of the person while moving the conversation into what could be a more productive space.

Much of Noddings's framework probably seems intuitive to many of us in our service-oriented practice. The formal structure that such a framework provides, however, can help us to see where there might be gaps or where we can improve. With this background of care ethics, we can anticipate and prepare for the hard conversations as we strive to dislodge others' assumptions and anxieties.

EXPANDING THE INFORMATION LITERACY SPECTRUM

As we consider the gaps in our information literacy praxis and how we might build an information-literate learner for our current information environment, it helps to consider how other learning communities, both within North America and globally, have approached information literacy. Common information literacy standards, such as the ACRL documents or the American Association of School Libraries (AASL) *Learner Framework* (2018), have been used in conjunction with indigenous ways of knowing, for example, to direct information literacy projects that acknowledge traditional values and enhance the understanding of knowledge practices for those communities (Montague, Reyes, and Meyer 2020; Chong 2022; Ford 2022). Other practices and epistemologies can inform and extend our own, as they often emphasize the importance of community and cultural knowledge, the affective connections to information, and expand the concept of information in and of itself. Looking to communities outside of that which created the *Framework* will also help address the criticized shortcomings, noted above, of it being a product of hegemonic culture.

Writing from Germany, Rares Piloiu pointed out that "much of the American information literacy scholarship is almost exclusively self-referential" (2016, 79). Our myopia results in a conception of information literacy that, while influential around the world, does not reflect the richness of global information literacy scholarship and praxis. For example, Piloiu writes of the German concept of *Bibliothekspädagogik*, "the pedagogy of the library," which addresses learning that takes place within the library setting at exhibits, programs, etc. Piloiu extends this concept to instruction, asking, "[W]hat kinds of teaching methods should be developed to address learning modes that transgress the traditional types of learning associated with academic communication and research practices?" (82) The German acknowledgment that different types of learning occur within different contexts highlights the non-universality of our information literacy models that are tailored for academic contexts, and encourages an expansion of our practices to better serve learners. This is reinforced by another German concept that Piloiu explores, that of *Informationskultur*, which "suggests that our approach to information and communication is informed by cultural assumptions about information creation and ownership, by dissemination systems that reflect technological and intellectual practices rooted in individual histories and in distinct worldviews" (86). The practice of *Informationskultur* requires a metacognition and an epistemic awareness that echoes the advice of Hartman-Caverly, above, and the tenets of metaliteracy, discussed below.

By considering how others around the globe are approaching the same information problems, we can enrich our own praxis. Broadening out from specific countries, examples include the European Commission on Media Literacy (https://digital-strategy.ec.europa.eu/en/policies/media-literacy), which conducts research and sets policies for member countries; resources and connections from UNESCO's Media and Information Literacy Alliance (https://www.unesco.org/en/media-information-literacy/alliance); and the IFLA's Information Literacy Section (https://www.ifla.org/units/information-literacy/).

ENGAGING METALITERACY

In the first iteration of the *Framework*, metaliteracy, a then-recent addition to the information literacy literature, served a large role. Criticism about the unclear nature of metaliteracy and its role in the *Framework*,[1] however, resulted in the concept being removed by name and its influence downplayed in the final version; in their response, Fulkerson, Ariew, and Jacobson (2017) argue that the removal of metaliteracy (and with it, knowledge practices and dispositions that emphasized metacognition) significantly weakened the effectiveness of the *Framework*.

Effectively divorced from the hegemonic information literacy model, then, metaliteracy evolved from being a re-conception and extension of information literacy to a mature pedagogy that poses critical questions of and responsibilities focusing on the learner as a consumer and producer of knowledge. Mackey and Jacobson (2022) acknowledge several key influences on metaliteracy, drawing from educational psychology and learning theories. Metaliteracy not only fills the gaps in the *Framework* that were left when it was removed, its tenets embrace an information-filled world that is not conceived of as a product of or an activity within the academy. Crucially, the information user, not the information itself, is the central component of the model. As Mackey and Jacobson (2022) argue, echoing many of the concerns with today's information environment highlighted in earlier chapters:

Learners are often connected within social media environments [...] that rely on the production of original and repurposed content to maintain the continued engagement within the interface. These proprietary systems enable wide-ranging participation by individuals and also reinforce deep-seated political and societal divisions. In today's polarizing information environment, learners must be able to investigate these commercial platforms and understand how the systems work. They also need to analyze their biases in these spaces and to think beyond their communities of influence. (6)

In their recent books *Metaliterate Learning for the Post-Truth World* (2019) and *Metaliteracy in a Connected World* (2022), Mackey and Jacobson expand upon these ideas and the role that metaliteracy can play in fighting information disorder. Much of the literature exploring metaliteracy in practice has focused on the cognitive and behavioral domains of learning, as learners engage with and produce information content in communal multimodal learning environments (Carlito 2018; Mortimore and Baker 2019), a trend that possibly reflects the traditional information literacy zeitgeist; however, the metacognitive and affective domains as exhibited by the metaliterate learner can play a larger role in the fight against information disorder. In many ways, metaliteracy complements the work of other information literacy theorists who conceive of it as a sociocultural practice. For example, Lloyd (2010) reframes information literacy as a messy, social, participatory, and affective process through which meaning is made and shared. Her conception of an "information landscape," which she defines as "the communicative space through which people develop identities and form relationships based on shared practices and ways of doing and saying things" (9), is especially salient. Lloyd's definition of information landscapes provides a useful descriptor for how information and meaning are enacted and interacted with in the social web. Given how information spreads among trusted authorities, explored previously in this book, if we consider the metaliterate role of teacher, it can be assumed that an individual who attains metaliteracy skills will model and help pass those skills on to others throughout their social networks.

Trust and affect are key tools for our battle against information disorder. Metaliteracy remains one of the only models to acknowledge and utilize the affective domain, how information impacts the user, as a main component. Zembylas (2023) explored "reparative pedagogies," which seek to disrupt racist narratives and understandings to promote cultural healing after historical trauma and injustice. The post-truth climate of our information landscape, as Zembylas illustrates with examples from Donald Trump's political rhetoric, is often interwoven with racism; both for those affected by racism and for White audiences who may not want to confront systemic racism, emotions—which he elucidates for this purpose as "situated in social, cultural, moral and political conditions in which they are entangled with power relations" (27)—play a pivotal role. As such, purely epistemological models will not lead to the deep learning and affective wrestling with information that is needed. His assertion that this work must be done through cultivating "affective solidarity," or finding common affective ground, is illuminating:

> Although affective solidarity cannot change the world, it demonstrates that some pedagogical strategies, such as fostering affective solidarity, have the potential to, at least, disrupt the taken-for-granted means through which post-truth and racism manifest and become normalised. (40)

Confronting difficult knowledge in our information-disordered landscape require an enormous effort that goes far beyond fact-checking. Recalling chapter 10 and the use of narrative or storytelling within the inoculation method, one strategy to help learners engage affectively is to use fictional narratives; Partyka (2019) advocates for the use of fiction as "part of the solution" (186); she has seen how it

> invites [students] to emotionally engage with the characters in productive ways . . . Fiction offers the metaliterate learner a way to experience the kind of active border crossing between character, author, and reader. . . . To identify with a fictional character is akin to actively reframing an understanding of oneself and others. (193)

We must prioritize the "active border crossing" between ourselves, our experiences of information, and the experiences of others to together find the affective solid ground upon which to build a more sustainable and productive information future.

FINAL THOUGHTS

This chapter, indeed, this book, began with the tolling of a warning bell: We live in an information-disordered world, and information literacy, as it has been conceived of and implemented, has not been able to sufficiently prepare learners to function in the contemporary information environment. While we wish we could wrap up this tome with a neat solution, there is none. The complex, multi-faceted problems of information disorder and the spread of conspiracy ideation that we are confronting will require multi-pronged efforts, new thinking, and new partnerships.

Although the additional frameworks and pedagogical models that we include here are mentioned only briefly, we hope that they will inspire readers to think of their praxis as holistic and fluid, incorporating numerous resources to respond to our changing information society. Each offers unique strengths; none can be used alone to conquer our current disinformation problems. By utilizing the wealth of interesting challenges that each provide to the other, and the richness of other approaches we were not able to include, however, we hope that our work will serve to inspire new and responsive models in the future, to further confront and heal our societal and cultural relationships with and understandings of information.

NOTE

1. Brian Berg (2014) wrote, "More confusing is whether the concept of metaliteracy is one of the anchors of the new framework, or if it is a desired outcome. As presently envisioned, metaliteracy is both an independent and dependent variable, which runs the risk of making the framework a tautology."

References

Aaronovitch, David. 2010. *Voodoo Histories: The Role of the Conspiracy Theory in Shaping Modern History*. New York: Riverhead Books.

Abdeljawad, Camille. 2023. "HOAX: How Perceived Authority of Information Sources Affects Students' Likeliness to Disseminate Misinformation." *Journal of New Librarianship* 8 (1): 183–205. https://doi.org/10.33011/newlibs/13/18.

Aberman, Jonathan. 2021, October 24. "Are You Ever Curious? Here's Why." *Washington Post*. https://www.washingtonpost.com/news/capital-business/wp/2017/07/17/are-you-ever-curious-heres-why/.

Adjin-Tettey, Theodora Dame. 2022. "Combating Fake News, Disinformation, and Misinformation: Experimental Evidence for Media Literacy Education." *Cogent Arts & Humanities* 9, no. 1: 2037229.

Adorno, Theodor. 1967. "Education after Auschwitz." Available from https://josswinn.org/wp-content/uploads/2014/12/AdornoEducation.pdf.

Aguilar, Gabrielle, Sofia Ompolasvili, Luisa Garcia Amaya, and Sophie Kerstens. 2021. "True Crime TikTok: Affording Criminal Investigation and Media Visibility in the Gabby Petito Case." *Masters of Media* (blog). https://mastersofmedia.hum.uva.nl/blog/2021/10/29/true-crime-tiktok-affording-criminal-investigation-and-media-visibility-in-the-gabby-petito-case/.

Aïmeur, Esma, Sabrine Amri, and Gilles Brassard. 2023. "Fake News, Disinformation and Misinformation in Social Media: A Review." *Social Network Analysis and Mining* 13, no. 30. https://doi.org/10.1007/s13278-023-01028-5.

Alba, Davey. 2022, December 8. "OpenAI Chatbot Spits Out Biased Musings, Despite Guardrails." *Bloomberg*. https://www.bloomberg.com/news/newsletters/2022-12-08/chatgpt-open-ai-s-chatbot-is-spitting-out-biased-sexist-results.

Al-Heeti, Abrar. 2013, December 4. "Microsoft's Seeing AI App Is Now Available on Android." CNET. https://www.cnet.com/tech/mobile/microsofts-seeing-ai-app-is-now-available-on-android/.

Allen, Kelly-Ann, Zoe A. Morris, Margaret L. Kern, Chrisopher Boyle, and Caomban McGlinchey. 2023. "The Need to Belong: The Appeal, Benefits, and Dangers of QAnon and Similar Groups." In *The Social Science of QAnon*, edited by Monica K. Miller, 176–94. New York: Cambridge University Press.

Allyn, Bobby. 2023, May 30. "Mitigating the Risk of AI Should Be a Global Priority, Open Letter Says." NPR. https://www.npr.org/2023/05/30/1178919245/mitigating-the-risk-of-ai-should-be-a-global-priority-open-letter-says.

Alonso, Miguel A., David Vilares, Carlos Gómez-Rodríguez, and Jesús Vilares. 2021. "Sentiment Analysis for Fake News Detection." *Electronics* 10: 1348.

Alsaleh, Hamad. 2022. "An Evidence-Based Digital Nudging in Support of Health Misinformation Assessment on Social Media Sites." PhD thesis, University of North Carolina at Charlotte.

Amarasingam, Amarnath, Marc-Andre Argentino, Dakota Johnson, and Sharday Mosurinjohn. 2023. "Categorizing QAnon: Is This a New Religious Movement?" In *The Social Science of QAnon*, edited by Monica K. Miller, 271–90. New York: Cambridge University Press,

American Association of School Librarians. *AASL Standards Framework for Learners*. 2018. https://standards.aasl.org/wp-content/uploads/2017/11/AASL-Standards-Framework-for-Learners-pamphlet.pdf.

American Association of University Professors (AAUP). (n.d.) "Advancing Academic Freedom." Accessed March 25, 2024. https://www.aaup.org/our-work/protecting-academic-freedom.

American Library Association (ALA). 1986. "Mission, Priority Areas, Goals." https://www.ala.org/ala/ourassociation/governingdocs/policymanual/mission.htm.

American Library Association. 2011, January 25. "Resolution to Condemn White Supremacy and Fascism as Antithetical to Library Work." https://www.ala.org/aboutala/sites/ala.org.aboutala/files/content/Resolution%20to%20Condemn%20White%20Supremacy%20and%20Fascism%20as%20Antithetical%20to%20Library%20Work%20FINAL.pdf.

American Library Association. (n.d.) "Professional Ethics." Amended June 29, 2021. https://www.ala.org/tools/ethics.

Amsler, Sarah S. 2011. "From 'Therapeutic' to Political Education: The Centrality of Affective Sensibility in Critical Pedagogy." *Critical Studies in Education* 52, no. 1: 47–63. https://doi.org/10.1080/17508487.2011.536512.

Andersen, Jack. 2005. "Information Criticism: Where Is It." *Progressive Librarian* 25: 12–22.

Anderson, Lorin, David Krathwohl, Peter Airasian, Kathleen Cruikshank, Richard Mayer, Paul Pintrich, James Raths, and Merlin Wittrock. 2000. *Taxonomy for Learning, Teaching, and Assessing, A: A Revision of Bloom's Taxonomy of Educational Objectives, Abridged Edition*. 1st edition. New York: Pearson.

Andrews, Nicola, Sunny Kim, and Josie Watanabe. 2018. "Cultural Humility as a Transformative Framework for Librarians, Tutors, and Youth Volunteers: Applying a Lens of Cultural Responsiveness in Training Library Staff and Volunteers." *Young Adult Library Services* 16, no. 2: 19–22.

Anonymous. 2018. "Are Libraries Neutral?" *American Libraries* 49, no. 6: 32–39.

Argentino, Marc-André. 2020, May 18. "The Church of QAnon: Will Conspiracy Theories Form the Basis of a New Religious Movement?" The

Conversation. https://theconversation.com/the-church-of-qanon-will-con-spiracy-theories-form-the-basis-of-a-new-religious-movement-137859.

Arieti, James A. 2016, December. "Magical Thinking in Medieval Anti-Semi-tism: Usury and the Blood Libel." *Medieval Studies* 24, no. 2: 193–218.

Arisoy, Cagri, Anuradha Mandal, and Nitesh Saxena. 2022. "Human Brains Can't Detect Fake News: A Neuro-Cognitive Study of Textual Disin-formation Susceptibility." 19th Annual International Conference on Pri-vacy, Security & Trust (Fredericton, New Brunswick): 1–12. doi:10.1109/PST55820.2022.9851990.

Arkes, Hal, Catherine Hackett, and Larry Boehm. 1989. "The Generality of the Relation Between Familiarity and Judged Validity." *Journal of Behavioral Deci-sion Making* 2, no. 2: 81–94.

Armstrong, Amy J., Courtney M. Holmes, and Denise Henning. 2020. "A Changing World, Again. How Appreciative Inquiry Can Guide Our Growth." *Social Sciences & Humanities Open* 2, no. 1: 100038. https://doi.org/10.1016/j.ssaho.2020.100038.

Associated Press. 2022, November 10. "Hateful Slurs Soared on Twitter after Musk Took Over, Says Digital Anti-Hate Watchdog." *CBS News.* https://www.cbc.ca/news/world/twitter-racial-slurs-hate-musk-1.6647974.

Associated Press. 2023, May 5. "WHO Downgrades COVID Pandemic, Says It's No Longer a Global Emergency." CBC. May 5, 2023. https://www.cbc.ca/news/health/who-pandemic-not-emergency-1.6833321.

Association of College and Research Libraries (ACRL). 2016. *Framework for Information Literacy for Higher Education.* https://www.ala.org/acrl/stan-dards/ilframework.

Association of College and Research Libraries. 2000. "Information Literacy Competency Standards for Higher Education." *ACRL College & Research Libraries News* 61, no. 3. https://crln.acrl.org/index.php/crlnews/article/view/19242/22395.

Australian National University Newsroom. 2022, October 26. "How Twitter Fuelled the Black Lives Matter Movement." https://www.anu.edu.au/news/all-news/how-twitter-fuelled-the-black-lives-matter-movement.

Bačić, Edita. 2018. "Neutrality versus Proactivity in Libraries during Turbulent Times." IFLA WLIC (conference paper). https://library.ifla.org/id/eprint/2209/1/150-bacic-en.pdf.

Badke, William. 2015. "Expertise and Authority in an Age of Crowdsourcing." In *Not Just Where to Click : Teaching Students How to Think About Information*, edited by Troy A. Swanson and Heather Jagman, 191–215. Chicago: Ameri-can Library Association.

Badke, William. 2019, September–October. "Metaliteracy, the Framework, and All Those Other Statements." *Online Searcher*: 55–57.

Baer, Andrea, and Daniel Kipnis. 2023. "Navigating Online Information Spaces with Lateral Reading: Lessons Learned from Two Librarians Working with Students and Educators." *Libraries Scholarship*, September. https://rdw.rowan.edu/lib_scholarship/47.

Bailey, Moya. 2021. *Misogynoir Transformed: Black Women's Digital Resistance.* New York: NYU Press.

Baker, Sally, and Rachel Burke. 2023. *Questioning Care in Higher Education: Resisting Definitions as Radical.* New York: Palgrave MacMillan.

Baker, Stephanie Alice. 2022. "Alt. Health Influencers: How Wellness Culture and Web Culture Have Been Weaponised to Promote Conspiracy Theories and Far-Right Extremism during the COVID-19 Pandemic." *European Journal of Cultural Studies* 25, no. 1: 3-24. https://doi.org/10.1177/13675494211062623.

Baker, Stephanie Alice, and Alexia Maddox. 2022, March 21. "From COVID-19 Treatment to Miracle Cure: The Role of Influencers and Public Figures in Amplifying the Hydroxychloroquine and Ivermectin Conspiracy Theories during the Pandemic." *M/C Journal* 25, no. 1. https://doi.org/10.5204/mcj.2872.

Balasubramaniyan, Vijay. 2024, January 25. "Pindrop Reveals TTS Engine Behind Biden AI Robocall." Pindrop. https://www.pindrop.com/blog/pindrop-reveals-tts-engine-behind-biden-ai-robocall.

Balz, Dan, and Clara Ence Morse. August 18, 2023. "American Democracy Is Cracking. These Forces Help Explain Why." *Washington Post.* https://www.washingtonpost.com/politics/2023/08/18/american-democracy-political-system-failures/.

Balzer, Cass. 2022. January 3. "Uptick in First Amendment Audits: Public Libraries Report Recent Rise of Encounters." *American Libraries Magazine.* https://americanlibrariesmagazine.org/2022/01/03/uptick-in-first-amendment-audits-2/.

Banas, John A., and Adam S. Richards. 2017. "Apprehension or Motivation to Defend Attitudes? Exploring the Underlying Threat Mechanism in Inoculation-Induced Resistance to Persuasion." *Communication Monographs* 84, no. 2: 164-78.

Banas, John A., and Elena Bessarabova. 2023. "Debunking and Preventing Conspiracies: Special Challenges of QAnon." In *The Social Science of QAnon: A New Social and Political Phenomenon*, edited by Monica K. Miller, 252-70. Cambridge University Press.

Banas, John A., and Gregory Miller. 2013, April. "Inducing Resistance to Conspiracy Theory Propaganda: Testing Inoculation and Metainoculation Strategies." *Human Communication Research* 39, no. 2: 184-207. https://doi.org/10.1111/hcre.12000.

Banas, John A., and Stephen A. Rains. 2010. "A Meta-Analysis of Research on Inoculation Theory." *Communication Monographs* 77, no. 3: 281-311. https://doi.org/10.1080/03637751003758193.

Bancchor, Komal. September 19, 2023. "YouTuber PewDiePie's $90 Million Net Worth Proves the Power of Content; Here's How He Earned It." Market Realist. https://marketrealist.com/what-is-pew-die-pies-net-worth/.

Barbara Bush Foundation for Family Literacy. (n.d.) "Why Literacy." Accessed March 26, 2024. https://www.barbarabush.org/why-literacy/.

Barbati, Juliana L., Stephen A. Rains, Bobi Ivanov, and John A. Banas. 2021. "Evaluating Classic and Contemporary Ideas About Persuasion Resistance in Inoculation Theory: Argument Strength, Refutation Strength, and Forewarning." *Communication Research Reports* 38, no. 4: 272–81. https://doi.org/10.1080/08824096.2021.1956450.

Barkun, Michael. 2003. *A Culture of Conspiracy: Apocalyptic Visions in Contemporary America*. Berkeley: University of California Press.

Barrett, Lisa Feldman. 2006. "Solving the Emotion Paradox: Categorization and the Experience of Emotion." *Personality and Social Psychology Review: An Official Journal of the Society for Personality and Social Psychology* 10, no. 1: 20–46.
https://doi.org/10.1207/s15327957pspr1001_2.

Bartholomew, Ronald E. 2001. *Little Green Men, Meowing Nuns and Head-Hunting Panics: A Study of Mass Psychogenic Illness and Social Delusion*. Jefferson, NC: McFarland & Company.

Barzilay, Tzafrir. 2022. *Poisoned Wells: Accusations, Persecution, and Minorities in Medieval Europe, 1321–1422*. Philadelphia: University of Pennsylvania Press.

Basol, Melissa, Jon Roozenbeek, and Sander van der Linden. 2020. "Good News About Bad News: Gamified Inoculation Boosts Confidence and Cognitive Immunity Against Fake News." *Journal of Cognition* 3, no. 1. https://doi.org/10.5334/joc.91.

Basu, Tanya. 2020, July 15. "How to Talk to Conspiracy Theorists—and Still Be Kind." *MIT Technology Review*. https://www.technologyreview.com/2020/07/15/1004950/how-to-talk-to-conspiracy-theorists-and-still-be-kind/.

Baughan, Amanda, Justin Petelka, Catherine Jaekyung Yoo, Jack Lo, Shiyue Wang, Amulya Paramasivam, Ashley Zhou, and Alexis Hiniker. 2021. "Someone Is Wrong on the Internet: Having Hard Conversations in Online Spaces." *Proceedings of the ACM on Human-Computer Interaction* 5: 156:2. https://doi.org/10.1145/3449230.

Beane, James A. 1990. *Affect in the Curriculum: Toward Democracy, Dignity, and Diversity*. New York: Teachers College Press.

Beatty, Joshua. 2014, September 24. "Locating Information Literacy within Institutional Oppression." *In the Library with the Lead Pipe*. http://www.inthelibrarywiththeleadpipe.org/2014/locating-information-literacy-within-institutional-oppression/.

Beauchamp, Zack. 2021, January 30. "Marjorie Taylor Greene's Space Laser and the Age-Old Problem of Blaming the Jews." Vox. https://www.vox.com/22256258/marjorie-taylor-greene-jewish-space-laser-anti-semitism-conspiracy-theories.

Beck, Richard. 2015. *We Believe the Children: A Moral Panic in the 1980s*. New York: Public Affairs.

Beene, Stephanie, and Katie Greer. 2021. "A Call to Action for Librarians: Countering Conspiracy Theories in the Age of QAnon." *Journal of Academic Librarianship* 47, no. 1: 102292, 1–8. https://doi.org/10.1016/j.acalib.2020.102292.

Beene, Stephanie, and Katie Greer. 2023. "Library Workers on the Front Lines of Conspiracy Theories in the US: One Nationwide Survey." *Reference Services Review* 51, no. 3/4: 251–72. https://doi.org/10.1108/RSR-11-2022-0056.

Beene, Stephanie, Millicent Fullmer, Katie Greer, Maggie Murphy, Tiffany Saulter, Sara Schumacher, Dana Statton Thompson, and Mary Wegman. 2022. *The Framework for Visual Literacy for Higher Education.* Association of College and Research Libraries. https://www.ala.org/acrl/sites/ala.org.acrl/files/content/standards/Framework_Companion_Visual_Literacy.pdf.

Beilin, Ian G. February 25, 2015. "Beyond the Threshold: Conformity, Resistance, and the ACRL Information Literacy Framework for Higher Education." *In the Library with the Lead Pipe.* http://www.inthelibrarywiththeleadpipe.org/2015/beyond-the-threshold-conformity-resistance-and-the-aclr-information-literacy-framework-for-higher-education/.

Bell, Emily. 2023, March 10. "A Fake News Frenzy: Why ChatGPT Could Be Disastrous for Truth in Journalism." *The Guardian.* https://www.theguardian.com/commentisfree/2023/mar/03/fake-news-chatgpt-truth-journalism-disinformation.

Bennett, Kate, and Evan Perez. 2020, April 2. "Nation's Top Coronavirus Expert Dr. Anthony Fauci Forced to Beef Up Security as Death Threats Increase." CNN. https://www.cnn.com/2020/04/01/politics/anthony-fauci-security-detail/index.html.

Beran, Dale. 2019. *It Came from Something Awful: How a Toxic Troll Army Accidentally Memed Donald Trump into Office.* New York: All Points Books.

Beres, Derek, Matthew Remski, Julian Walker, and Mallory DeMille. 2023, May 18. "The Truth Wars (with Renée DiResta)," *Conspirituality* (podcast): 33:00. https://www.conspirituality.net/episodes/154-the-truth-wars-renee-diresta.

Berg, Brian. 2014, February 25. "The Draft Framework for Information Literacy for Higher Education: Some Initial Thoughts." *BeerBrarian* (blog). https://beerbrarian.blogspot.com/2014/02/the-draft-framework-for-information.html.

Bergen, Mark. 2022. *Like, Comment, Subscribe: Inside YouTube's Chaotic Rise to World Domination.* New York: Viking.

Berkeley, Edmund Callis. 1956. *Giant Brains; or Machines That Think.* 5th ed. New York: Wiley.

Berkowitz, Reed [Rabbit Rabbit]. 2020, September 30. "A Game Designer's Analysis of QAnon." Medium. https://medium.com/curiouserinstitute/a-game-designers-analysis-of-QAnon-580972548be5.

Bernstein, William J. 2021. *The Delusions of Crowds: Why People Go Mad in Groups.* New York: Atlantic Monthly Press.

Bertolotti, Mauro, and Patrizia Catellani. 2023. "Counterfactual Thinking as a Prebunking Strategy to Contrast Misinformation on COVID-19." *Journal of Experimental Social Psychology* 104. https://doi.org/10.1016/j.jesp.2022.104404.

Bertsou, Eri. 2019. "Rethinking Political Distrust." *European Political Science Review* 11, no. 2: 213. doi:10.1017/S1755773919000080.

Bessarabova, Elena, and John A. Banas. 2023. "Emotions and the QAnon Conspiracy Theory." In *The Social Science of QAnon: A New Social and Political Phenomenon*, edited by Monica K. Miller, 87–103. Cambridge University Press.

Biddlestone, Mikey, Jon Roozenbeek, and Sander van der Linden. 2023. "Once (But Not Twice) Upon a Time: Narrative Inoculation Against Conjunction Errors Indirectly Reduces Conspiracy Beliefs and Improves Truth Discernment." *Applied Cognitive Psychology* 3, no. 2: 304–18. https://doi.org/10.1002/acp.4025.

Binnquist, Ashley L., Stephanie Y. Dolbier, Macrina C. Dieffenbach, and Matthew D. Lieberman. 2022. "The Zoom Solution: Promoting Effective Cross-Ideological Communication Online. *PloS One*. https://doi.org/10.1371/journal.pone.0270355.

Blair, Alexandra. 2023. "Amateur Sleuths and Online Truths: Defamation Lawsuits in the Internet Age of True Crime" (unpublished manuscript). https://papers.ssrn.com/sol3/papers.cfm?abstract_id=4666365.

Blechinger, Joel. 2023. "Reflections on Information Literacy in the ChatGPT Era." *Pathfinder: A Canadian Journal for Information Science Students and Early Career Professionals* 4 (1): 163–72.

Bless, Herbert, and Klaus Fiedler. 2012. "Mood and the Regulation of Information Processing Behavior." In *Affect in Social Thinking and Behavior*, edited by Joseph P. Forgas, 65–84. New York: Psychology Press.

Bloom, Mia, and Sophia Moskaleno. 2021. *Pastels and Pedophiles: Inside the Mind of QAnon*. Stanford, CA: Redwood Press.

Bluemle, Stefanie R. 2018. "Post-Facts: Information Literacy and Authority after the 2016 Election." *portal: Libraries and the Academy* 18, no. 2: 262–82. https://digitalcommons.augustana.edu/libscifaculty/10.

Bohannon, Molly. June 8, 2023. "Lawyer Used ChatGPT in Court—And Cited Fake Cases. A Judge Is Considering Sanctions." *Forbes*. https://www.forbes.com/sites/mollybohannon/2023/06/08/lawyer-used-chatgpt-in-court-and-cited-fake-cases-a-judge-is-considering-sanctions/.

Bortnick, Justin A. 2023, September 20. "Play and Misinformation: How America's Conspiracy Culture Became Gamified." *Games and Culture*. https://doi.org/10.1177/15554120231203859.

Bracewell, Lorna. 2020. "Gender, Populism, and the QAnon Conspiracy Movement." *Frontiers in Sociology* 5, no. 615727. https://doi.org/10.3389%2Ffsoc.2020.615727.

Bray, Sergi D., Shane D. Johnson, and Bennett Kleinberg. 2023. "Testing Human Ability to Detect 'Deepfake' Images of Human Faces." *Journal of Cybersecurity* 9, no. 1.

Breithaupt, Fritz. 2018, April 3. "The Bad Things We Do Because of Empathy." *Interdisciplinary Science Reviews* 43, no. 2: 166–74.

Brennan, Megan, and Jeffrey M. Jones. 2024, January 22. "Ethics Ratings of Nearly All Professions Down in U.S." Gallup. https://news.gallup.com/poll/608903/ethics-ratings-nearly-professions-down.aspx.

Briggs, Tim, and Robert Moran. 2021, June 2. "What Is a Deep Fake and How Can You Spot One?" *Sydney Morning Herald*. https://www.smh.com

.au/technology/what-is-the-difference-between-a-fake-and-a-deepfake
-20200729-p55ghi.html.

Broderick, Ryan. 2022, February 28. "The Bird Site Demands Content." *Garbage Day*. https://www.garbageday.email/p/the-bird-site-demands-content?utm_source=url.

Bronner, Stephen Eric. 2003. *A Rumor About the Jews: Antisemitism, Conspiracy, and the Protocols of Zion*. New York: Oxford University Press.

Brooks, A., LaFrance, A., Uscinski, J. E., & Lytvynenko, J. (2020, August 4). QAnon: A Look Inside The Online Conspiracy. *WBUR OnPoint Radio* [podcast]. https://www.wbur.org/onpoint/2020/08/04/qanon-what-to -know-online-conspiracy.

Brooks, David. 2024, January 4. "What Biden Needs to Tell Us." *New York Times*._https://www.nytimes.com/2024/01/04/opinion/populism-trump -liberalism.html.

Brooks, Ryan, and Amber Jamieson. 2021, March 11. "CrossFit Is Finally Fed Up with Marjorie Taylor Greene." *BuzzFeed News*. https://www.buzzfeednews .com/article/ryancbrooks/marjorie-taylor-greene-QAnon-crossfit.

Brotherton, Rob. 2020. *Bad News: Why We Fall for Fake News*. London: Bloomsbury Sigma.

Brotherton, Rob. 2013, September. "Towards a Definition of 'Conspiracy Theory.'" *The British Psychology Society's Quarterly Magazine Special Issue: The Psychology of Conspiracy Theories* 88, no. 3: 20–37.

Brotherton, Rob. 2017. *Suspicious Minds: Why We Believe Conspiracy Theories*. London: Bloomsbury Sigma.

Brotherton, Rob, and Christoper C. French. 2015, May 13. "Intention Seekers: Conspiracist Ideation and Biased Attributions of Intentionality." *PLOS One*: 1–14. https://doi.org/10.1371/journal.pone.0124125.

Brown, Jennifer, and Nora Mulligan. 2022. "When First Amendment Auditors Visit Your Library." *Public Libraries* 61, no. 1 (2022): 24–30.

Bruni, Frank. "The Marketing of a Massacre." 2023, October 19. *New York Times*. https://www.nytimes.com/2023/10/19/opinion/israel-hamas -attacks-palestinians.html.

Buchanan, Ben, Andrew Lohn, Micah Musser, and Katerina Sedova. 2021. "Truth, Lies, and Automation: How Language Models Could Change Disinformation." Center for Security and Emerging Technology, Georgetown University, 2021. https://doi.org/10.51593/2021CA003.

Buratto, Luciano G., William J. Matthews, and Koen Lamberts. 2009. "When Are Moving Images Remembered Better? Study-Test Congruence and the Dynamic Superiority Effect." *Quarterly Journal of Experimental Psychology* 62, no. 10: 1896–1903. https://doi.org/10.1080/17470210902883263.

Burnham, Sarah L. F., and Miriam R. Arbeit. 2023. "Social Media Literacy to Confront Far-Right Content: Saying 'No' to Neutrality." *Human Development* 67, no. 3: 117–34.

Burton, Robert. 2009. *On Being Certain: Believing You Are Right Even When You're Not*. New York: St. Martin's Griffin.

Butler, Judith. 1990. *Gender Trouble: Feminism and the Subversion of Identity*. London and New York: Routledge.

Buttigieg, Pete. 2020. *Trust: America's Best Chance*. New York: Liverlight Publishing.

Buttry, Steve. 2014. "Verification Fundamentals: Rules to Live By." In *Verification Handbook: A Definitive Guide to Verifying Digital Content for Emergency Coverage*, non-paginated. Ed. Craig Silverman. Maastricht, NL: European Journalism Centre. http://verificationhandbook.com.

Byford, Jovan. 2011. "Towards a Definition of Conspiracy Theories." In Jovan Byford, ed., *Conspiracy Theories: A Critical Introduction*, 20–37. London: Palgrave Macmillan. https://doi.org/10.1057/9780230349216_2.

Caldwell-Stone, Deborah. 2019, October 2. "Auditing the First Amendment at Your Public Library." American Library Association, *Intellectual Freedom Blog*. https://www.oif.ala.org/auditing-the-first-amendment-at-your-public-library/.

Callero, Peter L. 2007. "Social Identity Theory." In *The Blackwell Encyclopedia of Sociology*, edited by George Ritzer. Malden, MA: Blackwell. doi:10.1002/9781405165518.

Carey, Matthew. 2017. *Mistrust: An Ethnographic Theory*. Chicago: Hau Books.

Carlito, M. Dolores. 2018. "Supporting Multimodal Literacy in Library Instruction." *Reference Services Review* 46, no. 2: 164–77.

Caulfield, Mike. 2017. *Web Literacy for Student Fact-Checkers*. Vancouver, Washington: Washington State University Vancouver. https://open.umn.edu/opentextbooks/textbooks/454.

CBS News. 2021, September 23. "How Conspiracy Theories 'Infiltrated' the Wellness Community." https://www.cbsnews.com/news/covid-19-vaccine-conspiracy-theories-online-wellness-communities/.

Center for Disease Control and Prevention. 2021, April 19. "Loneliness and Social Isolation Linked to Serious Health Conditions." https://www.cdc.gov/aging/publications/features/lonely-older-adults.html.

Chabris, Christopher, and Daniel Simons. 2010. *The Invisible Gorilla: How Our Intuitions Deceive Us*. New York: Harmony.

Chang, Clio. 2021, January 12. "The Unlikely Connection Between Wellness Influencers and the Pro-Trump Rioters." *Cosmopolitan*. https://www.cosmopolitan.com/health-fitness/a35056548/wellness-fitness-influencers-QAnon-conspiracy-theories/.

Chaudhary, Adnan Ali, Umer Ayub, Ahsan Riaz, Farhan Mirza, and Sadaf Latif. 2022. "Weaponising Social Media, Mental Health and Surveillance Capitalism." *Journal of History and Social Sciences* 13, no. 2. https://doi.org/10.46422/jhss.v13i2.226.

Chayka, Kyle. 2023, February 10. "Is A.I. Art Stealing from Artists?" *The New Yorker*. https://www.newyorker.com/culture/infinite-scroll/is-ai-art-stealing-from-artists.

Chen, Zhiyuan, and Bing Liu. 2018. *Lifelong Machine Learning*, 2nd ed. Springer.

Chesterman, Simon. 2023. "Good Models Borrow, Great Models Steal: Intellectual Property Rights and Generative AI." *Social Science Research Network*. https://doi.org/10.2139/ssrn.4590006.

Cheney-Lippold, John. 2017. *We Are Data: Algorithms and the Making of Our Digital Selves.* New York: NYU Press.

Chong, Rachel. 2022. *Indigenous Information Literacy.* Kwantlen Polytechnic University Pressbooks. https://kpu.pressbooks.pub/indigenousinformationliteracy/.

Choraś, Michał, Konstantinos Demestichas, Agata Giełczyk, Álvaro Herrero, Paweł Ksieniewicz, Konstantina Remoundou, Daniel Urda, and Michał Woźniak. 2021. "Advanced Machine Learning Techniques for Fake News (Online Disinformation) Detection: A Systematic Mapping Study." *Applied Soft Computing* 101: 107050.

Church, Ian, and Peter Samuelson. 2016. *Intellectual Humility: An Introduction to the Philosophy and Science.* London, UK: Bloomsbury Academic.

Ciampaglia, Giovanni Luca, Alessandro Flammini, and Filippo Menczer. 2015. "The Production of Information in the Attention Economy." *Scientific Reports* 5, no. 1: 9452. https://doi.org/ 10.1038/srep09452: 9452.

Citrin, Jack, and Laura Stoker. 2018. "Political Trust in a Cynical Age." *Annual Review of Political Science* 21: 49–70. https://doi.org/10.1146/annurev-polisci-050316-092550.

Clear, Sarah E., James A. Dimmock, Josh Compton, and Ben Jackson. 2021, March 4. "How Do Inoculation Messages Work? A Two-Study Mixed-Method Investigation into Inoculation Mechanisms." *Asian Journal of Communication* 31, no. 2: 83–104. https://doi.org/10.1080/01292986.2021.1888306.

Clegg, Nick. 2024, February 6. "Labeling AI-Generated Images on Facebook, Instagram, and Threads." Meta. https://about.fb.com/news/2024/02/labeling-ai-generated-images-on-facebook-instagram-and-threads/.

Coaston, Jane. 2018, October 31. "How the Rise of Conspiracy Theory Politics Emboldens Antisemitism." Vox. https://www.vox.com/identities/2018/10/31/18034256/anti-semitism-pittsburgh-synagogue-shooting-prejudice-right.

Cole, Richard. 2020. *The Death of Tidericus the Organist: Plague and Conspiracy Theory in Hanseatic Visby.* Exeter: Short Run Press Ltd.

Compton, Josh. 2019. "Inoculation Theory and Metaliterate Learning." In *Metaliterate Learning for the Post-Truth World*, edited by Thomas P. Mackey and Trudi E. Jacobson, 63–80. Chicago: ALA Neal-Schuman.

Compton, Josh. 2021. "Threat and/in Inoculation Theory." *International Journal of Communication* 15: 4294–4306. https://ijoc.org/index.php/ijoc/article/view/17634/3565.

Compton, Josh, Sander van der Linden, John Cook, and Melisa Basol. 2021. "Inoculation Theory in the Post-Truth Era: Extant Findings and New Frontiers for Contested Science, Misinformation, and Conspiracy Theories." *Social and Social Personality Psychology Compass* 15, no. 6: e12602. https://doi.org/10.1111/spc3.12602.

Computer History Museum (n.d.) "Computer History Timeline: 1942." Accessed March 1, 2024. https://www.computerhistory.org/timeline/1942/.

Conner, Christopher T. 2023. "Qanon, Authoritarianism, and Conspiracy within American Alternative Spiritual Spaces." *Frontiers in Sociology* 8. https://doi.org/10.3389/fsoc.2023.1136333.

Connery, Catherine, and Christina Curran. 2014. "A Cultural-Historical Teacher Starts the School Year: A Novel Perspective on Teaching and Learning." In *The Educational Psychology Reader*, rev. ed., edited by Greg S. Goodman, 150–64. New York: Peter Lang.

Cook, Dani Brecher, and Kevin Michael Klipfel. 2015. "How Do Our Students Learn? An Outline of a Cognitive Psychological Model for Information Literacy Instruction." *Reference & User Services Quarterly* 55, no. 1: 34–41.

Cook, John. 2021. "Cranky Uncle: A Game Building Resilience Against Climate Misinformation." *Plus Lucis* 3: 13–16.

Cooke, Nicole A. 2017. "Posttruth, Truthiness, and Alternative Facts: Information Behavior and Critical Information Consumption for a New Age," *The Library Quarterly* 87 (3): 211–21, https://doi.org/10.1086/692298

Cover, Rob. 2012. "Performing and Undoing Identity Online: Social Networking, Identity Theories and the Incompatibility of Online Profiles and Friendship Regimes." *Convergence* 18, no. 2: 177–93.

Cowall, Alan. 2024, February 26. "Jacob Rothschild, Banker Who Broke from Dynasty, Dies at 87." *New York Times*. https://www.nytimes.com/2024/02/26/business/jacob-rothschild-dead.html.

Crenshaw, Kimberlé Williams, Luke Charles Harris, Daniel Martinez HoSang, and George

Lipsitz. 2019. *Seeing Race Again: Countering Colorblindness across the Disciplines*. Berkeley: University of California Press.

Crockett, M. J. 2017. "Moral Outrage in the Digital Age." *Nature Human Behaviour* 1:769–71. https://doi.org/10.1038/s41562-017-0213-3.

D'Angelo, Chris D. 2024. "Extremism Is Rampant in This Part of the U.S.—And There's a Toxic Reason for It." *HuffPost*. https://www.huffpost.com/entry/true-west-book-interview-betsy-gaines-quammen_n_65a7e37be4b041f1ce644683.

Das, Anubrata, Houjiang Liu, Venelin Kovatchev, and Matthew Lease. 2023. "The State of Human-Centered NLP Technology for Fact-Checking." *Information Processing & Management* 60, no. 2: 103219. https://doi.org/10.48550/arXiv.2301.03056.

Davidson, Richard J. 2003. "Affective Neuroscience and Psychophysiology: Toward a Synthesis." *Psychophysiology* 40, no. 5: 655–65. doi:10.1111/1469-8986.00067.

de Almeida, Patricia, Gomes Rêgo, Carlos Denner dos Santos, and Josivania Silva Farias. 2021. "Artificial Intelligence Regulation: A Framework for Governance." *Ethics and Information Technology* 23, no. 3: 505–25.

Deitering, Anne-Marie, and Hannah Gascho Rempel. 2017, February 22. "Sparking Curiosity—Librarians' Role in Encouraging Exploration." *In the Library with the Lead Pipe*. http://www.inthelibrarywiththeleadpipe.org/2017/sparking-curiosity/.

de jesus, nina. 2014, September 24. "Locating the Library in Institutional Oppression." *In the Library with the Lead Pipe.* https://www.int helibrarywiththeleadpipe.org/2014/locating-the-library-in-institutional -oppression/.

Della Lena, Sebastiano. 2023, May 15. "The Spread of Misinformation in Networks with Individual and Social Learning." SSRN. https://papers.ssrn.com/ sol3/papers.cfm?abstract_id=3511080.

Demartini, Gianluca, Stefano Mizzaro, and Damiano Spina. 2020. "Human-in-the-Loop Artificial Intelligence for Fighting Online Misinformation: Challenges and Opportunities." *IEEE Data Engineering Bulletin* 43, no. 3: 65–74.

Dentith, Matthew R. X. 2014. *The Philosophy of Conspiracy Theories.* London and New York: Palgrave MacMillan.

de Rancourt-Raymond, Audrey, and Nadia Smaili. 2023. "The Unethical Use of Deepfakes." *Journal of Financial Crime* 30, no. 4: 1066–77.

Dernikos, Bessie P., Nancy Lesko, Stephanie D. McCall, and Alyssa D. Niccolini. 2020. *Mapping the Affective Turn in Education: Theory, Research and Pedagogies.* New York: Routledge.

DeSteno, David. 2014. *The Truth About Trust: How It Determines Success in Life, Love, Learning and More.* New York: Hudson Street Press.

Díaz, Kim. (n.d.) "Paolo Freire." *Internet Encyclopedia of Philosophy.* Accessed March 27, 2024. https://iep.utm.edu/freire/.

Dickinson, Tim. 2021, February 10. "How the Anti-Vaxxers Got Red-Pilled." *Rolling Stone.* https://www.rollingstone.com/culture/culture-features/ QAnon-anti-vax-covid-vaccine-conspiracy-theory-1125197/.

Dickinson, Tim. 2022, March 23. "Amid War Crimes in Ukraine, American Right Winters are Applauding Russia." *Rolling Stone.* https://www.rolling-stone.com/politics/politics-news/praising-putin-roger-stone-aaron-lewis -laud-russian-war-1324749/.

DiNucci, Darcy. 1999. "Fragmented Future." *Print* 53, no. 4: 221–22.

DiResta, Renee. 2020, July 31. "AI-Generated Text Is the Scariest Deepfake of All." *Wired.* https://www.wired.com/story/ai-generated-text-is-the-scari-est-deepfake-of-all/.

DOMO 2022. "Data Never Sleeps." https://www.domo.com/data-never -sleeps#.

Donovan, Joan. 2020. "Media Manipulation Casebook." https://mediama-nipulation.org/homepage.

Douglas, Karen M., and Robbie M. Sutton. 2011, September. "Does It Take One to Know One? Endorsement of Conspiracy Theories Is Influenced by Personal Willingness to Conspire." *British Journal of Social Psychology* 50, no. 3: 544–52. doi:10.1111/j.2044-8309.2010.02018.x.

Douglas, Karen M., and Robbie M. Sutton. 2022. "What Are Conspiracy Theories? A Definitional Approach to Their Correlates, Consequences, and Communication." *Annual Review of Psychology* 74: 271–98.

Douglas, Karen M., Robbie M. Sutton, and Aleksandra Cichocka. 2019. "Belief in Conspiracy

Theories: Looking Beyond Gullibility." In *The Social Pscyhology of Gullibility: Fake News, Conspiracy Theories, and Irrational Beliefs*, edited by Joseph P. Forgas and Roy F. Baumeister, 61–76. New York and London: Routledge.

Douglas, Karen M., Robbie M. Sutton, Mitchell J. Callan, Rael J. Dawtry, and Annelie J. Harvey. 2016. "Someone Is Pulling the Strings: Hypersensitive Agency Detection and Belief in Conspiracy Theories." *Thinking & Reasoning* 22, no. 1: 56–77.

Douglas Stone, Bruce Patton, and Sheila Heen. (2023). *Difficult Conversations: How to Discuss What Matters Most* (Penguin).

Dowd, Robert C. 1990. "I Want to Find Out How to Freebase Cocaine or Yet Another Unobtrusive Test of Reference Performance." *The Reference Librarian* 11, no. 25–26: 483–93. doi:10.1300/J120v11n25_22.

Drabinski, E.mily. (2018). *Are libraries neutral?* https://www.emilydrabinski.com/are-libraries-neutral/.

Dundes, Alan, ed. 1991. *The Blood Libel Legend: A Casebook in Anti-Semitic Folklore*. Madison: University of Wisconsin Press.

Dyer, Owen. 2020, September. "Covid-19: Unvaccinated Face 11 Times Risk of Death from Delta Variant, CDC Data Show." *British Medical Journal* 374: n2282. https://doi.org/10.1136/bmj.n2282.

Ecker, Ullrich K. H., Lucy H. Butler, and Anne Hamby. 2020. "You Don't Have to Tell a Story! A Registered Report Testing the Effectiveness of Narrative versus Non-Narrative Misinformation Corrections." *Cognitive Research: Principles and Implications* 5, no. 1. https://doi.org/10.1186/s41235-020-00266-x.

Ecker, Ullrich K. H., Stephan Lewandowsky, John Cook, Philipp Schmid, Lisa K. Fazio, Nadia Brashier, Panayiota Kendeou, Emily K. Vraga, and Michelle A. Amazeen. 2022. "The Psychological Drivers of Misinformation Belief and Its Resistance to Correction." *Nature Reviews Psychology* 1, no. 1: 13–29. https://doi.org/10.1038/s44159-021-00006-y.

Egan, Paul, and Tresa Baldas. 2020, October 8. "'Deeply Disturbing': Feds Charge Extremists in Domestic Terror Plot to Kidnap Michigan Gov. Gretchen Whitmer, Create Civil War." *Detroit Free Press*. https://www.freep.com/story/news/nation/2020/10/08/militia-members-charged-plot-against-michigan-gov-gretchen-whitmer/5923650002/.

Eisenstein, Elizabeth L. 1980. *The Printing Press as an Agent of Change: Communications and Cultural Transformations in Early-Modern Europe*. Cambridge: Cambridge University Press. Available from http://archive.org/details/printingpressasa001-2eise_l3z7.

Elliott, Vittoria. 2023, December 18. "Worried About Deepfakes? Don't Forget 'Cheapfakes.'" *Wired*. https://www.wired.com/story/meta-youtube-ai-political-ads/.

Ellison, Sarah, Yvonne Wingett Sanchez, and Patrick Marley. 2024, January 11. "Violent Political Threats Surge as 2024 Begins, Haunting American Democracy." *Washington Post*. https://www.washingtonpost.com/politics/2024/01/09/public-officials-death-threats-swatting-surge/.

Emerging Technology from the arXiv. 2013, July 1. "The Anatomy of the Occupy Wall Street Movement on Twitter." *MIT Technology Review, Humans and Technology.* https://www.technologyreview.com/2013/07/01/177515/the-anatomy-of-the-occupy-wall-street-movement-on-twitter/.

Emerick, Barrett, and Shannon Dea (forthcoming). "Only Human (In the Age of Social Media)." In *Routledge Handbook of Non-Ideal Theory*, edited by Hilkje C. Hänel and Johanna Müller. https://philpapers.org/archive/EMEOHI.pdf.

Emery, David. 2018, April 16. "Frazzledrip: Is a Hillary Clinton 'Snuff Film' Circulating on the Dark Web?" Snopes. https://www.snopes.com/fact-check/hillary-clinton-snuff-film/.

Enders, Adam M., Joseph Uscinski, Casey Klofstad, and Justin Stoler. 2022a. "On the Relationship Between Conspiracy Theory Beliefs, Misinformation, and Vaccine Hesitancy." *PLOS ONE*, 17 no. 10: e0276082. https://doi.org/10.1371/journal.pone.0276082.

Enders, Adam M., Joseph E. Uscinski, Casey A. Kofstad, Stefan Wuchty, Michelle I. Seelig, John R. Funchion, Manohar N. Murthi, Kamal Premaratne, and Justin Stoler. 2022b. "Who Supports QAnon? A Case Study in Political Extremism." *Journal of Politics* 84, no. 3: 1844–49. https://doi.org/10.1086/717850.

Enis, Matt. 2022, March 7. "Holocaust Denial Materials and Other Fascist Content Removed from Library Ebook Platforms." *Library Journal.* https://www.libraryjournal.com/story/holocaust-denial-materials-and-other-fascist-content-removed-from-library-ebook-platforms.

Epstein, Ziv, and Aaron Hertzmann. 2023. "Art and the Science of Generative AI." *Science* 380, 6650: 1110–11. https://doi.org/10.1126/science.adh4451.

Erickson, Amy Gaumer, and Patricia Noonan. 2023. "Research Guide College and Career Competency: Curiosity." *College and Career Competency Framework.* https://www.cccframework.org/wp-content/uploads/Research-Guide-Curiosity.pdf.

Eshoo, Anna. 2022, September 20. "Unsafe Release of Model AI." https://eshoo.house.gov/sites/evo-subsites/eshoo-evo.house.gov/files/9.20.22LettertoNSCandOSTPonStabilityAI.pdf.

Ettarh, Fobazi. 2018, January 10. "Vocational Awe and Librarianship: The Lies We Tell Ourselves." *In the Library with the Lead Pipe.* https://www.inthelibrarywiththeleadpipe.org/2018/vocational-awe/.

Evli, Mahmut. 2023. "Compassion Fatigue, Empathy, and Emotional Contagion in Nursing Students." *Journal of Education and Research in Nursing* 20, no. 2. https://doi.org/10.14744/jern.2021.833127.

Farhart, Christina E., Ella Douglas-Durham, Krissy Lunz Trujillo, and Joseph A Vitriol. 2022. "Vax Attacks: How Conspiracy Theory Belief Undermines Vaccine Support." *Progress in Molecular Biology and Translational Science* 188, no. 1: 135–69. https://doi.org/10.1016/bs.pmbts.2021.11.001.

Fazio, Lisa K. 2020, February 10. "Pausing to Consider Why a Headline Is True or False Can Help Reduce the Sharing of False News." *Harvard Kennedy*

School Mis/Information Review. https://misinforeview.hks.harvard.edu/article/pausing-reduce-false-news/.

Feeld, Julian, Travis View, and Jake Rockatansky. 2022. "Episode 143: Jim Caviezel: Enter the Cavortex, Featuring Dave Anthony." *QAnon Anonymous* (podcast). 1:21:25. https://soundcloud.com/qanonanonymous/episode-143-jim-caviezel-enter-the-cavortex-feat-dave-anthony.

Feeld, Julian, Travis View, Jake Rockatansky, and Mike Rothschild. 2023. "Episode 229: Devolution Theory Hits the Road, Featuring Mike Rothschild." *QAnon Anonymous* (podcast). https://soundcloud.com/qanonanonymous/episode-229-devolution-theory-hits-the-road-feat-mike-rothschild.

Feemster, Kristen A., and Claire Szipsky. 2020. "Resurgence of Measles in the United States: How Did We Get Here?" *Current Opinion in Pediatrics* 32, no. 1: 139–44. doi:10.1097/MOP.0000000000000845.

Filimowicz, Michael. 2023. *Information Disorder: Algorithms and Society*. London: Taylor & Francis.

Fischer, Charles. 2021. "Socratic Method." *Salem Press Encyclopedia*. Hackensack, NJ: Salem Press.

Fisher, Max. 2022a. *The Chaos Machine: The Inside Story of How Social Media Rewired Our Minds and Our World*. New York: Little, Brown and Company.

Fisher, Max. 2022b, August 19. "How Democracy Is Under Threat across the Globe." *New York Times*. https://www.nytimes.com/2022/08/19/world/democracy-threat.html.

Fister, Barbara. 2017, March 13. "Practicing Freedom for the Post-Truth Era." *Barbara Fister* (blog). https://barbarafister.net/political/practicing-freedom-for-the-post-truth-era/.

Fister, Barbara. 2021, February 3. "Lizard People in the Library." Project Information Literacy: PIL Provocation Series. https://projectinfolit.org/pubs/provocation-series/essays/lizard-people-in-the-library.html.

Fitzgerald, James. 2022, May 2. "Conspiracy, Anxiety, Ontology: Theorising QAnon." *First Monday*. https://doi.org/10.5210/fm.v27i5.12618.

Foer, Franklin. 2024, April. "The End of the Golden Age." *The Atlantic* 333, no. 3: 20–45.

Ford, Jason T. 2022. "Indigenous Voices Informing Academic Information Literacy: Critical Discourses, Relationality, and Indigeneity for the Good of the Whole." MLIS thesis, University of Hawai'i at Manoa.

Forgas, Joseph P. 1995. "Mood and Judgment: The Affect Infusion Model (AIM)." *Psychological Bulletin* 117, no. 1: 39–66.

Forgas, Joseph P. 2002. "Feeling and Doing: Affective Influences on Interpersonal Behavior." *Psychological Inquiry* 13 (1): 1–28. https://www.jstor.org/stable/1449534.

Forgas, Joseph P. 2019. "On the Role of Affect in Gullibility: Can Positive Mood Increase, and Negative Mood Reduce Credulity?" In *The Social Psychology of Gullibility: Fake News, Conspiracy Theories, and Irrational Beliefs*, edited by Joseph P. Forgas and Roy F. Baumeister, 179–97. New York: Routledge.

Forgas, Joseph P., and Rebekah East. 2008. "On Being Happy and Gullible: Mood Effects on Skepticism and the Detection of Deception." *Journal of Experimental Social Psychology* 40, no. 5: 1362–67.

Forgas, Joseph P., Carrie L. Wyland, and Simon M. Laham. 2012. "Hearts and Minds: An Introduction to the Role of Affect in Social Cognition and Behavior." In *Affect in Social Thinking and Behavior*, edited by Joseph P. Forgas, 3–18. New York: Psychology Press.

Fox, Mira. 2022, August 15. "Why Conspiracy Theorists Keep Turning to Jewish Mysticism—From Early Nazis to Modern-Day MAGA," Forward. https://forward.com/culture/514455/gematria-daily-show-trump-kabbalah-maga-mysticism-conspiracy-theorist/.

Franks, Bradley, Adrian Bangerter, Martin W. Bauer, Matthew Hall, and Mark C. Noort. 2017. "Beyond 'Monologicality'? Exploring Conspiracist Worldviews." *Frontiers in Psychology* 8: 1–16. https://doi.org/10.3389/fpsyg.2017.00861.

Fredericks, Bronwyn, Abraham Bradfield, Sue McAvoy, James Ward, Shea Spierings, Troy Combo, and Agnes Toth-Peter. 2022. "The Burden of the Beast: Countering Conspiracies and Misinformation within Indigenous Communities in Australia." *M/C Journal* 25, no. 1. https://doi.org/10.5204/mcj.2862.

Freedom House. 2021. "New Report: The Global Decline in Democracy Has Accelerated." https://freedomhouse.org/article/new-report-global-decline-democracy-has-accelerated.

Freire, Paolo. 1984. *Pedagogy of the Oppressed*, trans. M. Bergman Ramos. New York: Herder and Herder.

Frosolini, Andrea, Paolo Gennaro, Flavia Cascino, and Guido Gabriele. 2023. "In Reference to 'Role of Chat GPT in Public Health,' to Highlight the AI's Incorrect Reference Generation." *Annals of Biomedical Engineering* 51, no. 10: 2120–22.

Fulkerson, Diane M., Susan Andriette Ariew, and Trudi E. Jacobson. 2017. "Revisiting Metacognition and Metaliteracy in the ACRL Framework." *Communications in Information Literacy* 11, no. 1: 21–41. https://doi.org/10.15760/comminfolit.2017.11.1.45.

Fung, Brian. 2023, August 9. "Pope Francis Warns About AI's Dangers." CNN. https://edition.cnn.com/2023/08/09/tech/pope-francis-ai/index.html.

Galea, Sandro. 2023, October 21. "10 seconds: on creating space for reflection about the right response to tragedies." *The Healthiest Goldfish Newsletter*. https://sandrogalea.substack.com/p/10-seconds.

Gamage, Dilrukshu, Piyush Ghasiya, Vamshi Bonagiri, Mark E. Whiting, and Kazutoshi Sasahara. 2022. "Are Deepfakes Concerning? Analyzing Conversations of Deepfakes on Reddit and Exploring Societal Implications." *CHI Conference on Human Factors in Computing Systems*: 1–19.

Garibay, Ozlem, Brent Winslow, Salvatore Andolina, Margherita Antona, Anja Bodenschatz, Constantinos Coursaris, Gregory Falco, et al. 2023. "Six

Human-Centered Artificial Intelligence Grand Challenges." *International Journal of Human–Computer Interaction* 39, no. 3: 391–437.

Gatehouse, Gabriel. 2022. *The Coming Storm* (podcast). https://www.bbc.co .uk/programmes/m001324r/episodes/downloads.

Geary, Jade, and Brittany Hickey. 2016, October 29. "When Does Burnout Begin? The Relationship Between Graduate School Employment and Burnout Amongst Librarians." *In the Library with the Lead Pipe*. https://www.intheli brarywiththeleadpipe.org/2019/when-does-burnout-begin/.

Gerolami, Natasha. 2020. "No Faith in the Library: Challenging Secularism and Neutrality in Librarianship." *Canadian Journal of Information and Library Science* 43, no. 2: 172–92.

Gilbert, David. 2022, February 3. "I Lost My Mom to QAnon. Wordle Is Bringing Her Back." *VICE News*. https://www.vice.com/en/article/88gva5/ wordle-QAnon-mom.

Gilbert, David. 2023, May 30. "The QAnon Shaman Is Out of Prison and Selling Yoga Leggings Now." *Vice* (blog). https://www.vice.com/en/article /4a3xm9/qanon-shaman-out-of-jail-selling-leggings.

Gilligan, Carol, and Jessica Eddy. 2021. "The Listening Guide: Replacing Judgment with Curiosity." *Qualitative Psychology* 8, no. 2: 141–51. https://doi.org /10.1037/qup0000213.

Gilroy-Ware, Marcus. 2017. *Filling the Void: Emotion, Capitalism & Social Media.* London: Repeater Books.

Gladstone, Rick, and Megan Specia. 2021, March 25. "What to Know About the Suez Canal and the Cargo Ship That Was Stuck There." *New York Times.* https://www.nytimes.com/2021/03/25/world/middleeast/suez-canal -container-ship.html.

Gleick, James. 2012. *The Information: A History, A Theory, A Flood.* London: Vintage.

Glisson, Lane. 2019. "Breaking the Spin Cycle: Teaching Complexity in the Age of Fake News." *portal: Libraries and the Academy* 19, no. 3: 461–84.

Godfrey-Smith, Peter, and Benjamin Kerr. 2019. "Tolerance: A Hierarchical Analysis." *Journal of Political Philosophy* 27, no. 4: 403–21.

Godin, Benoît. 2008. "The Information Economy: The History of a Concept through Its Measurement, 1949–2005." *History and Technology* 24, no. 3: 255–87. https://doi.org/ 10.1080/07341510801900334.

Goertzel, Ted. 1994. "Belief in Conspiracy Theories." *Political Psychology* 15, no. 4: 731–42, https://doi.org/10.2307/3791630.

Goertzel, Ted. 2010. "Conspiracy Theories in Science." *EMBO Reports* 1, no. 7: 493–99. doi:10.1038/embor.2010.84.

Goldberg, Jeffrey. 2020. "Shadowland: The Conspiracy Theorists Are Winning." *The Atlantic*. https://www.theatlantic.com/shadowland/.

Golding, Yona Tr. 2023, December 13. "Q&A: Alexa Koenig on the Potential and Pitfalls of Open Source Investigations." *Columbia Journalism Review*. https://www.cjr.org/the_media_today/qa-alexa-koenig.php.

Goldman, Alex, and P. J. Vogt. 2018, May 31. "The QAnon Code." *Reply All* (podcast). https://gimletmedia.com:443/shows/reply-all/n8homa.

Goldstein, Stéphane. 2020. *Informed Societies: Why Information Literacy Matters for Citizenship, Participation and Democracy.* UK: Facet Publishing.

Golino, Maria Alessandra. 2021, April 24. "Algorithms in Social Media Platforms." Institute for Internet & the Just Society. https://www.internetjust-society.org/algorithms-in-social-media-platforms.

Gonzalez, Nina. 2022. "Reproducing for the Race: Eugenics, "Race Suicide," and the Origins of White Replacement Conspiracy Theories, 1882–1924." PhD thesis, University of California, Davis. https://escholarship.org/content/qt0v38s4hm/qt0v38s4hm.pdf.

Gozalo-Brizuela, Roberto, and Eduardo C. Garrido-Merchán. 2023, January 11. "ChatGPT Is Not All You Need. A State of the Art Review of Large Generative AI Models." arXiv.org. https://doi.org/10.48550/arxiv.2301.04655.

Gradoń, Kacper T., Janusz A. Hołyst, Wesley R. Moy, Julian Sienkiewicz, and Krzysztof Suchecki. 2021. "Countering Misinformation: A Multidisciplinary Approach." *Big Data & Society* 8, no. 1: 20539517211013848.

Graham, Megan E., Brittany Skov, Zoë Gilson, Calvin Heise, Kaitlyn M. Fallow, Eric Y. Mach, and D. Stephen Lindsay. 2023. "Mixed News About the Bad News Game." *Journal of Cognition* 6, no. 1. https://doi.org/10.5334/joc.324.

Gramlich, John. 2021, June 1. "10 Facts About Americans and Facebook." *Pew Research Center.* https://www.pewresearch.org/short-reads/2021/06/01/facts-about-americans-and-facebook/.

Graves, Lucas, and Michelle A. Amazeen. 2019, February 25. "Fact-Checking as Idea and Practice in Journalism." *Oxford Research Encyclopedia of Communication.*

Green, Ricky, Carolina Trella, Mikey Biddlestone, Karen M. Douglas, and Robbie M. Sutton. 2023. "Psychological Motives of QAnon Followers," in *The Social Science of QAnon,* edited by Monica K. Miller, 33–48. New York: Cambridge University Press.

Greenhill, Kelly M. 2019. "Cognitive Hacking and the Role of Extra-Factual Information." *The Fletcher Forum of World Affairs* 43, no. 1: 121–26.

Greenhill, Kelly M. 2020. "Fear and Present Danger: Extra Factual Sources of Threat Conception and Proliferation." https://www.hoover.org/sites/default/files/research/docs/trinkunas_threetweetstomidnight_113-136_ch.6.pdf.

Greer, Katie S. 2023. "A Pedagogy of Care for Information Literacy and Metaliteracy Asynchronous Online Instruction." *Journal of Academic Librarianship* 49, no. 3: 102676.

Greer, Katie, and Shawn McCann. 2018. "Everything Online Is a Website: Information Format Confusion in Student Citation Behaviors." *Communications in Information Literacy* 12, no. 2: 150–65. https://doi.org/ 10.15760/comminfolit.2018.12.2.6.

Greer, Katie S., and Stephanie Beene. 2024. "When Belief Becomes Research: Conspiracist Communities on the Social Web." *Frontiers in Communication* 9, 1345973: 1–19. https://doi.org/10.3389/fcomm.2024.1345973.

Gregg, Justin. 2022. *If Nietzsche Were a Narwal.* New York: Hachette Book Group.

Gregg, Melissa, and Gregory J. Siegworth, eds. *The Affect Theory Reader.* Dunham, NC: Duke University Press, 2010.

Grenny, Joseph, Kerry Patterson, Ron McMillan, Al Switzler, and Emily Gregory. 2021. *Crucial Conversations: Tools for Talking When Stakes Are High*, 3rd ed. New York: McGraw Hill.

Griffin, Johnathan, and Shayan Sardarizadeh. 2021, August 23. "Nesara: The Financial Fantasy Ruining Lives." *BBC Trending* (podcast). 20:00. https://www.bbc.co.uk/programmes/w3ct1xzv.

Groh, Matthew, Ziv Epstein, Chaz Firestone, and Rosalind Picard. 2022. "Deepfake Detection by Human Crowds, Machines, and Machine-Informed Crowds." *Proceedings of the National Academy of Sciences* 119, no. 1: e2110013119.

Gu, Jinjin, Xinlei Wang, Chenang Li, Junhua Zhao, Weijin Fu, Gaoqi Liang, and Jing Qui. 2022, July. "AI-Enabled Image Fraud in Scientific Publications." *Patterns* 3, no. 7: 100511. https://doi.org /10.1016/j.patter.2022.100511.

Guo, Shijiang, Michael Schlichtkrull, and Andrea Vlachos. 2022. "A Survey on Automated Fact-Checking." *Transactions of the Association for Computational Linguistics* 10: 178–206. https://doi.org/10.1162/tacl_a_00454.

Gupta, Ankur, Neeraj Kumar, Purnendu Prabhat, Rajesh Gupta, Sudeep Tanwar, Gulshan Sharma, Pitshou N. Bokoro, and Ravi Sharma. 2022. "Combating Fake News: Stakeholder Interventions and Potential Solutions." *IEEE Access* 10: 78268–89.

Gurgun, Selin, Emily Arden-Close, John McAlaney, Keith Phalp, and Raian Ali. 2023. "Can We Re-Design Social Media to Persuade People to Challenge Misinformation? An Exploratory Study." *International Conference on Persuasive Technology*: 123–41.

Haag, Stephen. 2002. *The Fourth Industrial Revolution: What Every College and High School Student Needs to Know About the Future.* San Diego, CA: Janus Press.

Haber, Jonathan. 2020. *Critical Thinking.* Cambridge, MA: MIT Press.

Hameleers, Michael. 2022. "Separating Truth from Lies: Comparing the Effects of News Media Literacy Interventions and Fact-Checkers in Response to Political Misinformation in the US and Netherlands." *Information, Communication & Society* 25, no. 1: 110–26. https://doi.org/10.1080/1369118X.2020.1764603.

Hannah, Matthew N. 2021a. "A Conspiracy of Data: QAnon, Social Media, and Information Visualization." *Social Media+ Society* 7, no. 3: 20563051211036064.

Hannah, Matthew N. 2021b. "QAnon and the Information Dark Age." *First Monday* 26, no. 2 (February). https://doi.org/10.5210/fm.v26i2.10868.

Hannah, Matthew. 2023. "Information Literacy in an Age of Internet Conspiracism." *Journal of Information Literacy* 17, no. 1: 204–20.

Hanson, Jarice. 2016. "Information Age." In *The Social Media Revolution: An Economic Encyclopedia of Friending, Following, Texting, and Connecting.* Santa Barbara, CA: ABC-CLIO.

Hartman, Darrell. 2023, June 3. "The Invention of Objectivity." *The Atlantic.* https://www.theatlantic.com/ideas/archive/2023/06/invention-objectivity/674280/.

Hartman-Caverly, Sarah. 2019. "'TRUTH Always Wins:' Dispatches from the Information War." In *Libraries Promoting Reflective Dialogue in a Time of Political Polarization*, edited by Andrea Patricia Baer, Robert Schroeder, and Ellysa Stern Cahoy, 187–233. Chicago: American Library Association. https://pure.psu.edu/en/publications/truth-always-wins-dispatches-from-the-information-war.

Hassan, Aumyo, and Sarah J. Barber. 2021. "The Effects of Repetition Frequency on the Illusory Truth Effect." *Cognitive Research* 6, 38. https://doi.org/10.1186/s41235-021-00301-5.

Hassan, Steve. 2024, January 8. "Breaking the Silence: Alva Johnson's Journey in the Cult of Trump as the 2016 Campaign's Director of Outreach and Coalitions." *The Influence Continuum* (podcast). 43:00–44:54. https://podcasts.apple.com/us/podcast/breaking-the-silence-alva-johnsons-journey-in-the/id1603773245?i=1000640886473.

Hauptman, Robert. 1976. "Professionalism or Culpability? An Experiment in Ethics." *Wilson Library Bulletin* 50: 626–27.

Head, Alison J., Barbara Fister, and Margy MacMillan. 2022. "Information Literacy in the Age of Algorithms: Student Experiences with News and Information, and the Need for Change." *Project Information Literacy Algorithm Study Final Report*, 16. https://projectinfolit.org/publications/algorithm-study/.

Heaven, Will Douglas. 2022, November 22. "Why Meta's Latest Large Language Model Survived Only Three Days Online." *MIT Technology Review.* https://www.technologyreview.com/2022/11/18/1063487/meta-large-language-model-ai-only-survived-three-days-gpt-3-science/.

Heinberg, Richard. 2020, December 18. "2020: The Year Consensus Reality Fractured." Resilience. https://www.resilience.org/stories/2020-12-18/2020-the-year-consensus-reality-fractured/.

Hellinger, Daniel C. 2023. *Conspiracies and Conspiracy Theories in the Age of Trump.* Palgrave MacMillan Cham. https://doi.org/10.1007/978-3-031-44829-4_3.

Heřmanová, Marie. 2022, March 16. "Sisterhood in 5D: Conspirituality and Instagram Aesthetics." *M/C Journal* 25, no. 1. https://doi.org/10.5204/mcj.2875.

Hernandez Aguilar, Luis M. 2023. "Memeing a Conspiracy Theory: On the Biopolitical Compression of the Great Replacement Conspiracy Theories. *Ethnography.* https://doi.org/10.1177/14661381221146983.

Herrero-Diz, Paula, and Clara López-Rufino. 2021. "Libraries Fight Disinformation: An Analysis of Online Practices to Help Users' Generations in Spotting Fake News." *Societies* 11, no. 133: 1–11.

Hess, Amanda Nichols. 2018. *Transforming Academic Library Instruction: Shifting Practices to Reflect Changed Perspectives.* Lanham, MD: Rowman & Littlefield.

Hitt, Tarpley. 2020, August 14. "How QAnon Became Obsessed with 'Adrenochrome,' an Imaginary Drug Hollywood is 'Harvesting' from Kids." The Daily

Beast. https://www.thedailybeast.com/how-qanon-became-obsessed-with
-adrenochrome-an-imaginary-drug-hollywood-is-harvesting-from-kids.

Hoagland, Sarah Lucia. 1990. "Some Concerns About Nel Noddings' Caring."
Hypatia 5, no. 1: 109–14.

Hodge, Twanna. 2018, January 17. "Addressing Cultural Humility and Implicit
Bias in Information Literacy Sessions." Webinar, www.youtube.com/watch
?v=RyWxuCMMXDA.

Hodges, James A. 2023. "Taxonomizing Information Practices in a Large
Conspiracy Movement: Using Early QAnon as a Case Study." *Information &
Culture* 58, no. 2: 129–44.

Hofstadter, Richard. 1964. "The Paranoid Style in American Politics." *Harper's Magazine*. https://harpers.org/archive/1964/11/the-paranoid-style-in
-american-politics/.

hooks, bell. 1994. *Teaching to Transgress: Education as the Practice of Freedom*.
New York: Routledge.

hooks, bell. 2003. *Teaching Community*. New York: Routledge.

Horne, Benjamin D., Mauricio Gruppi, and Sibel Adali. 2019. "Trustworthy
Misinformation Mitigation with Soft Information Nudging." *2019 First IEEE
International Conference on Trust, Privacy and Security in Intelligent Systems
and Applications (TPS-ISA)*, 245–54. https://ieeexplore.ieee.org/abstract/
document/9014346/.

Hornsey, Matthew J., Kinga Bierwiaczonek, Kai Sassenberg, and Karen M.
Douglas. 2023."Individual, Intergroup and Nation-Level Influences on Belief
in Conspiracy Theories." *Nature Reviews Psychology* 2: 85–97. https://doi.org
/10.1038/s44159-022-00133-0.

Horvitz, Eric. 2022. "On the Horizon: Interactive and Compositional Deepfakes."
Proceedings of the 2022 International Conference on Multimodal Interaction (Ben-
galuru, India): 653–61. https://erichorvitz.com/blue_sky_horizon_ICMI.pdf.

Hosier, Alison. 2019. "First, Teach Students to Be Wrong." In *Metaliterate
Learning for the Post-Truth World*, edited by Thomas P. Mackey and Trudi
Jacobson, 159–80. Chicago: ALA Neal-Schuman.

House Subcommittee on Cybersecurity, Information Technology, and Government Innovation. 2023, March 23. "Mace: We Must Have Reliable Safe-
guards Against Malicious Cyber Activity." https://oversight.house.gov/
release/mace-we-must-have-reliable-safeguards-against-malicious-cyber
-activity%ef%bf%bc/.

Hovious, Amanda. 2014, March 11. "The Information Literacy Threshold Concepts." *Designer Librarian* (blog). https://designerlibrarian.wordpress.com
/2014/03/11/the-information-literacy-threshold-concepts/.

Howard, Jeffrey G. 2023. "Fostering Reflection and Empathy: Narratives as
Pedagogical Tools in Writing Consultation Preparation." *WLN: A Journal of
Writing Center Scholarship* 48, no. 1: 3–6.

Hsu, Tiffany, and Stuart A. Thompson. 2023, June 20. "Disinformation Researchers Raise Alarms About A.I. Chatbots." *New York Times*. https://www.nytimes
.com/2023/02/08/technology/ai-chatbots-disinformation.html.

Huang, Carol. 2011, June 6. "Facebook and Twitter Key to Arab Spring Uprisings: Report." *The National*. https://www.thenationalnews.com/uae/facebook-and-twitter-key-to-arab-spring-uprisings-report-1.428773.

Hund, Emily. 2023. *The Influencer Industry: The Quest for Authenticity on Social Media*. Princeton, NJ: Princeton University Press.

Hurley, David A., Sarah R. Kostelecky, and Lori Townsend. 2019. "Cultural Humility in Libraries." *Reference Services Review* 47, no. 4: 544–55. https://doi.org/10.1108/RSR-06-2019-0042.

Huynh, Ho Phi, and Bryan Bayles. 2022. "Secure Yet Flexible: Can Intellectual Humility Protect Against Belief in Conspiracy Theories?" *North American Journal of Psychology* 24, no. 4: 561–70.

Immordino-Yang, Mary Helen. 2016. *Emotions, Learning, and the Brain*. New York: W.W. Norton & Company.

Inform (Information Network Focus on Religious Movements). 2023, August 7. "Online Cultic Milieus: QAnon and Anti-Vax Conspiracy Movements." *Global Network on Extremism & Technology*. https://gnet-research.org/2023/08/07/online-cultic-milieus-QAnon-and-anti-vax-conspiracy-movements/.

International Federation of Library Associations and Institutions (IFLA). 2012. "IFLA Code of Ethics for Librarians and Other Information Workers (full version)." https://www.ifla.org/publications/ifla-code-of-ethics-for-librarians-and-other-information-workers-full-version/.

Jacobson, Trudi, Thomas Mackey, Kelsey O'Brien, Michelle Forte, and Emer O'Keefe. 2018. "Metaliteracy Goals and Learning Objectives." *Metaliteracy*. https://metaliteracy.org/learning-objectives/2018-metaliteracy-goals-and-learning-objectives/.

Jacovi, Alon, and Yoav Goldberg. 2020. "Towards Faithfully Interpretable NLP Systems: How Should We Define and Evaluate Faithfulness?" *Proceedings of the 58th Annual Meeting of the Association for Computational Linguistics*, 4198–4205. https://aclanthology.org/2020.acl-main.386.

JAMA Network. (n.d.). *Instructions for Authors*. https://jamanetwork.com/journals/jama/pages/instructions-for-authors.

Jardine, David. 2014. "Jean Piaget and the Origins of Intelligence: A Return to 'Life Itself.'" In *The Educational Psychology Reader*, rev. ed., edited by Greg S. Goodman, 132–49. New York: Peter Lang.

Jeantet, Diane, and Mauricio Savarese. 2023, November 30. "Brazillian City Enacts an Ordinance That Was Written by ChatGPT." AP News. https://apnews.com/article/brazil-artificial-intelligence-porto-alegre-5afd1240afe7b6ac202bb0bbc45e08d4.

Jensen, Robert. 2008. "The Myth of the Neutral Profession." In *Questioning Library Neutrality: Essays from Progressive Librarian*, edited by Alison Lewis, 89–96. Sacramento, CA: Library Juice Press.

Jhaver, Shagun, Pranil Vora, and Amy Bruckman. 2017, December 12. "Designing for Civil Conversations: Lessons Learned from ChangeMyView. *GVU Technical Report*. https://shagunjhaver.com/research/tech-reports/jhaver-2017-cmv/jhaver-2017-cmv.pdf.

Johnson, Ben. 2017, March. "Information Literacy Is Dead: The Role of Libraries in a Post-Truth World. *Computers in Libraries* 37, no. 2.

Johnson, Eric J. 2021. *The Elements of Choice: Why the Way We Decide Matters*. New York: Riverhead Books.

Johnson, Steven. 2007. *The Ghost Map: The Story of London's Most Terrifying Epidemic—and How It Changed Science, Cities, and the Modern World*. New York: Riverhead Books.

Jones, Barbara M. 2009. *Protecting Intellectual Freedom in Your Academic Library: Scenarios from the Front Lines*. American Library Association, 2009.

Jones, Bethan. 2022. "Websleuthing, Participatory Culture and the Ethics of True Crime Content." *Ethical Space: The International Journal of Communication Ethics* 19, no. 3/4: 52–59.

Jones, Callum. 2023, March 6. "'We the People, not the Sheeple': QAnon and the Transnational Mobilisation of Millennialist Far-Right Conspiracy Theories." *First Monday* 28, no. 3. https://firstmonday.org/ojs/index.php/fm/article/view/12854.

Jones, Ja'han. 2023, June 7. "Deepfakes of Purported Putin Declaring Martial Law Fits Disturbing Pattern." MSNBC. https://www.msnbc.com/the-reidout/reidout-blog/putin-deepfake-russia-rcna88014

Joseph, Cameron. 2024, February 2. "How the Collapse of Local Newsrooms Made All Politics National." *Columbia Journalism Review*. https://www.cjr.org/the_media_today/local_media_collapse_presidential_primaries.php.

Kahneman, Daniel. 2013. *Thinking, Fast and Slow*. New York: Farrar, Straus and Giroux.

Kahneman, Daniel, Oliver Sibony, and Cass R. Sunstein. 2021. *Noise: A Flaw in Human Judgment*. New York: Little, Brown Spark.

Kaplan, Alex. 2022, June 28. "QAnon Community Celebrates the Return of 'Q' after an 18-Month Absence." Media Matters for America. https://www.mediamatters.org/QAnon-conspiracy-theory/QAnon-community-celebrates-return-q-after-18-month-absence.

Kardefelt-Winther, Daniel. 2014. "A Conceptual and Methodological Critique of Internet Addiction Research: Towards a Model of Compensatory Internet Use. *Computers in Human Behavior* 31: 351–54. https://doi.org/10.1016/j.chb.2013.10.059.

Kaskazi, Amana. 2014, March 3. "Social Network Identity: Facebook, Twitter, and Identity Negotiation Theory." Poster presented at the 2014 iConference at the University of Illinois at Urbana-Champaign. https://hdl.handle.net/2142/47365.

Kassen, Maxat. 2023. "Curbing the COVID-19 Digital Infodemic: Strategies and Tools." *Journal of Public Health Policy* 44: 643–57. https://doi.org/10.1057/s41271-023-00437-2.

Katsara, Ourania, and Kristof De Witte. 2019. "How to Use Socratic Questioning in Order to Promote Adults' Self-Directed Learning." *Studies in the Education of Adults* 51, no. 1: 109–29. https://doi.org/10.1080/02660830.2018.1526446.

Kay, Aaron C., Danielle Gaucher, Jamie L. Napier, Mitchell J. Callan, and Kristin Laurin. 2008. "God and the Government: Testing a Compensatory Control Mechanism for the Support of External Systems." *Journal of Personality and Social Psychology* 95, no. 1: 18–35. https://doi.org/10.1037/0022-3514.95.1.18.

Kelleher, Kara. 2023, August 10. "Revenge Porn and Deep Fake Technology: The Latest Iteration of Online Abuse." *Boston University School of Law Dome* (blog). https://sites.bu.edu/dome/2023/08/10/revenge-porn-and-deep-fake-technology-the-latest-iteration-of-online-abuse/.

Kelly, Meg, and Elyse Samules. 2019, November 18. "How Russia Weaponized Social Media, Got Caught, and Escaped Consequences." *Washington Post.* https://www.washingtonpost.com/politics/2019/11/18/how-russia-weaponized-social-media-got-caught-escaped-consequences/.

Keyes, Scott. 2014, June 10. "What the 1984 Rajneeshee Bioterror Attack Can Teach About Voter Fraud." *The Atlantic.* https://www.theatlantic.com/politics/archive/2014/06/a-strange-but-true-tale-of-voter-fraud-and-bio-terrorism/372445/.

Khardori, Ankush. 2024, January 30. "The Crisis within Texas' Border Crisis." POLITICO. https://www.politico.com/newsletters/politico-nightly/2024/01/30/the-crisis-within-texas-border-crisis-00138691.

Kierkegaard, Soren. 2014. *The Concept of Anxiety.* New York: Liverlight.

Kim, Juliana. 2023, March 31. "U.S. Capitol Rioter the 'QAnon Shaman' Is Released Early from Federal Prison." NPR. https://www.npr.org/2023/03/31/1167319814/qanon-shaman-jacob-chansley-capitol-riot-early-release-reentry.

Kim, Yoo Jung. 2020, June 19. "Med School Taught Me How to Talk to Conspiracy Theorists." Medscape. http://www.medscape.com/viewarticle/932592.

Kirkland, Anita Brooks. 2021, November 8. "Library Neutrality as Radical Practice." *Canadian School Libraries Journal.* https://journal.canadianschoollibraries.ca/library-neutrality-as-radical-practice/.

Kitayama, Yuka, Yoriko Hashizaki, and Audrey Osler. 2022. "The Ethics of Care as a Pedagogical Approach: Implications for Education for Democratic Citizenship." *Educational Studies in Japan: International Yearbook* 16: 31–43.

Klein, Ezra. 2022, February 25. "A Philosophy of Games That Is Really a Philosophy of Life." *New York Times.* https://www.nytimes.com/2022/02/25/opinion/ezra-klein-podcast-c-thi-nguyen.html.

Klein, Tim V. 2019. "'Single Out the Rascals for Distinction from Their Fellows': Realist, Prosecutorial, Yellow, and Radical Muckraking in the Progressive Era." *Media History Monographs* 21, no. 1: 1–73.

Kleinfeld, Rachel. 2023, September 5. "Polarization, Democracy, and Political Violence in the United States: What the Research Says." Carnegie Endowment for International Peace. https://carnegieendowment.org/2023/09/05/polarization-democracy-and-political-violence-in-united-states-what-research-says-pub-90457.

Klepper, David. 2024, January 31. "Days of Darkness: How One Woman Escaped the Conspiracy Trip That Has Ensnared Millions." ABC News. https://abcnews.go.com/US/wireStory/days-darkness-woman-escaped -conspiracy-theory-trap-ensnared-106827810.

Klepper, David. 2024, January 31. "Grave Peril of Digital Conspiracy Theories: 'What Happens When No One Believes Anything Anymore?'" AP News. https://apnews.com/article/dangers-of-digital-conspiracy-theories-ec2 1024be1ed377a35fb235d9fa2af36.

Kline, Robert R. 2015. *The Cybernetics Moment: Or Why We Call Our Age the Information Age*. Baltimore, MD: John Hopkins University Press.

Klipfel, Kevin Michael, and Dani Brecher Cook. 2017. *Learner-Centered Pedagogy: Principles and Practice*. Chicago: ALA Editions.

Knight, Will. 2023, April 27. "Met ChatGPT's Right-Wing Alter Ego." *Wired*. https://www.wired.com/story/fast-forward-meet-chatgpts-right-wing -alter-ego/.

Köbis, Nils C., Barbora Doležalová, and Ivan Soraperra. 2021. "Fooled Twice: People Cannot Detect Deepfakes but Think They Can." *Iscience* 24, no. 11.

Kocergina, Lija. 2022, March 21. "The Republic: Understanding Censorship in Plato's Ideal City-State." Arcadia. https://www.byarcadia.org/post/the -republic-understanding-censorship-in-plato-s-ideal-city-state.

Kos, Denis, and Sonja Špiranec. 2014. "Debating Transformative Approaches to Information Literacy Education: A Critical Look at the Transformative Learning Theory." In *Information Literacy: Lifelong Learning and Digital Citizenship in the 21st Century*, 427–35, doi:10.1007/978-3-319-14136-7_45.

Kotsonis, Stefano, and Anthony Brooks. 2020, August 4. "QAnon: A Look Inside the Online Conspiracy," WBUR OnPoint Radio. 31:30–31:51. https://www .wbur.org/onpoint/2020/08/04/qanon-what-to-know-online-conspiracy.

Kranich, Nancy. 2020, March 25. "Libraries and Democracy Revisited." *The Library Quarterly* 90, no. 2: 121–53. https://doi.org/10.1086/707670.

Kreps, Sarah, R. Miles McCain, and Miles Brundage. 2022. "All the News that's Fit to Fabricate: AI-Generated Text as a Tool of Media Misinformation." *Journal of Experimental Political Science* 9, no. 1: 104–17.

Kruger, Justin, and David Dunning. 1999, December. "Unskilled and Unaware of It: How Difficulties in Recognizing One's Own Incompetence Lead to Inflated Self-Assessments." *Journal of Personality and Social Psychology* 77, no. 6: 1121–34.

Kuehn, Evan F. 2023. "The Information Ecosystem Concept in Information Literacy: A Theoretical Approach and Definition." *Journal of the Association for Information Science and Technology* 74, no. 4: 434–43.

Kuglitsch, Rebecca Z. "Teaching for transfer: Reconciling the framework with disciplinary information literacy." portal: Libraries and the Academy 15, no. 3 (2015): 457–470.

LaFrance, Adrienne. 2020, June. "The Prophecies of Q." *The Atlantic*. https:// www.theatlantic.com/magazine/archive/2020/06/qanon-nothing-can -stop-what-is-coming/610567/.

Lajante, Mathieu, Marzia Del Prete, Beatrice Sasseville, Geneviève Rouleau, Marie-Pierre Gagnon, and Normand Pelletier. 2023. "Empathy Training for Service Employees: A Mixed-Methods Systematic Review." *PLoS ONE* 18, no. 8: e0289793, 1–32. http://dx.doi.org/10.1371/journal.pone.0289793.

Lankes, R. David. 2011. *The Atlas of New Librarianship.* Cambridge: Massachusetts Institute of Technology.

Lankes, R. David. 2012, August 29. "Beyond the Bullet Points: IFLA Code of Ethics." *R. David Lankes* (blog). https://davidlankes.org/beyond-the-bullet-points-ifla-code-of-ethics/.

Lantian, Anthony, Dominique Muller, Cecile Nurra, and Karen M. Douglas. 2017, July. "I Know Things They Don't Know! The Role of Need for Uniqueness in Belief in Conspiracy Theories." *Social Psychology* 48, no. 3: 160–73.

Larson, Heidi J. 2020. *Stuck: How Vaccine Rumors Start—and Why They Don't Go Away.* Oxford University Press.

Larson, Heidi J., and Leesa Lin. 2024, January 16. "Generative Artificial Intelligence Can Have a Role in Combating Vaccine Hesitancy." *BMJ* 384: q69. https://doi.org/10.1136/bmj.q69.

LaRue, James. 2018, April 29. "Yes, There Was a Holocaust." *My LibBlog* (blog). https://jaslarue.blogspot.com/2018/04/yes-there-was-holocaust.html.

Lawal, Vicki, and Connie Bitso. 2020. "Constructionists' Approaches to Information Literacy: Exploring Savolainen's Everyday Life Information Seeking in Information Literacy Research." *Annals of Library and Information Studies* 67: 231–39.

Leavey, Sean T. 2022. "'We're Just Here Working on a Story': First Amendment Auditors, Political Culture, and the Mediated Public Sphere." *Communication and Democracy* 56, no. 1: 71–89. https://doi.org/10.1080/27671127.2022.2049451.

LeBeau, Chris. 2017. "Entitled to the Facts: A Fact-Checking Role for Librarians." *Reference and User Services Quarterly* 57, no. 2: 76–78.

Lee, Ken Jen, Adrian Davila, Hanlin Cheng, Joslin Goh, Elizabeth Nilsen, and Edith Law. 2023. "'We Need to do More . . . I Need to Do More': Augmenting Digital Media Consumption via Critical Reflection to Increase Compassion and Promote Prosocial Attitudes and Behaviors." *Proceedings of the 2023 CHI Conference on Human Factors in Computing Systems.* https://doi.org/10.1145/3544548.3581355.

Legal Information Institute. (2022). *Conspiracy.* https://www.law.cornell.edu/wex/conspiracy

Legum, Judd. 2020, September 22. "Trump Courts Cult." Popular Information. https://popular.info/p/trump-courts-cult.

Legum, Judd. 2024, January 23. "The Tide Turns on Florida Book Bans." Popular Information. https://popular.info/p/the-tide-turns-on-florida-book-bans.

Legum, Judd. 2024, January 29. "The Second Insurrection." Popular Information. https://popular.info/p/the-second-insurrection?post_id=141136473&r=fgot.

Leonard Mlodinow, *Emotional: How Feelings Shape Our Thinking* (New York: Vintage, 2023).

Lewandowsky, Stephan, Ullrich K. H. Ecker, Colleen M. Seifart, Norbert Schwarz, and John Cook. 2012. "Misinformation and Its Correction: Continued Influence and Successful Debiasing." *Psychological Science in the Public Interest* 13, no. 3: 106–31.

Lewandowsky, Stephan, Gilles E. Gignac, and Klaus Oberauer. 2013, October 2. "The Role of Conspiracist Ideation and Worldviews in Predicting Rejection of Science." *PLOS ONE* 8, no. 10: e75637. https://doi.org/10.1371/journal.pone .0075637.

Lewandowsky, Stephan, John Cook, Ullrich Ecker, Doug Lombardi, et al. 2020. *Debunking Handbook 2020.* Center for Climate Change Communication. https://doi.org/10.17910/b7.1182.

Lewandowsky, Stephan, and Sander van der Linden. 2021. "Countering Misinformation and Fake News through Inoculation and Prebunking." *European Review of Social Pscyhology* 32, no. 2: 348–84. https://doi.org/10.1080 /10463283.2021.1876983.

Lewandowsky, Stephan, Ullrich K. H. Ecker, John Cook, Sander van der Linden, Jon Roozenbeek, and Naomi Oreskes. 2023. "Misinformation and the Epistemic Integrity of Democracy." *Current Opinion in Psychology*: 101711. https:// doi.org/10.1016/j.copsyc.2023.101711.

Liebers, Nicole, and Holger Schramm. 2019. "Parasocial Interactions and Relationships with Media Characters-An Inventory of 60 Years of Research." *Communication Research Trends* 38 (2).

Lim, Rachel Esther, and So Young Lee. 2023. "'You Are a Virtual Influencer!': Understanding the Impact of Origin Disclosure and Emotional Narratives on Parasocial Relationships and Virtual Influencer Credibility." *Computers in Human Behavior* 148 (November): abstract. https://doi.org/10.1016/j. chb.2023.107897.

Lindemann, Hilde. 2014. *Holding and Letting Go: The Social Practice of Personal Identities.* Oxford University Press.

Lindquist Kristen A., Tor D. Wagner, Hedy Kober, Eliza Bliss-Moreau, and Lisa Feldman Barrett. 2012, June. "The Brain Basis of Emotion: A Meta-Analytic Review." *Behavioral and Brain Sciences* 35, no. 3: 121–43. https://doi.org/10 .1017/S0140525X11000446.

Litman, Jordan A., and Mark V. Pezzo. 2012. "Interpersonal Curiosity." In *Encyclopedia of the Sciences of Learning*, edited by Norbert M. Seel, 1634–35. Boston: Springer. https://doi.org/10.1007/978-1-4419-1428-6_1644.

Lloyd, Annemaree. 2006. "Information Literacy Landscapes: An Emerging Picture." *Journal of Documentation* 62, no. 5: 570–83. https://doi.org/10.1108 /00220410610688723.

Lloyd, Annemaree. 2010. *Information Literacy Landscapes: Information Literacy in Education, Workplace, and Everyday Contexts.* Oxford: Chandos Publishing.

Lovelace Jr., H. Timothy. 2022. "Xenophobic Conspiracy Theories and the Long Roots of January Sixth." *Law and Contemporary Problems* 85, no. 19: 19–68.

Lüders, Adrian, Alejandro Dinkelberg, and Michael Quayle. 2022. "Becoming 'Us' in Digital Spaces: How Online Users Creatively and Strategically Exploit Social Media Affordances to Build up Social Identity." *Acta Psychologica* 228: 103643.

Lundskow, George, and Sarah Louise MacMillen. 2024. *QAnon and Other Replacement Realities*. Lanham, MD: Lexington Books.

Lyngs, Ulrik, Kai Lukoff, Reuben Binns, Michael Inzlicht, Max Van Kleek, Adam Slack, Petr Slovak, and Nigel Shadbolt. 2019. "Self-Control in Cyberspace: Applying Dual Systems Theory to a Review of Digital Self-Control Tools." *Proceedings of CHI Conference on Human Factors in Computing Systems*. https://doi.org/10.1145/3290605.3300361.

Ma, Yanni, and Jay D. Hmielowski. 2022. "Are You Threatening Me? Identity Threat, Resistance to Persuasion, and Boomerang Effects in Environmental Communication." *Environmental Communication* 16, no. 2: 225–42. doi:10.1080/17524032.2021.1994442.

Mackey, Thomas P., and Trudi E. Jacobson. 2014. *Metaliteracy: Reinventing Information Literacy to Empower Learners*. Chicago: ALA Neal-Schuman.

Mackey, Thomas P., and Trudi E. Jacobson. 2018. *Metaliterate Learning for the Post-Truth World*. Chicago: ALA Neal-Schuman.

Mackey, Thomas P., and Trudi E. Jacobson. 2022. *Metaliteracy in a Connected World: Developing Learners as Producers*. Chicago: ALA Neal-Schuman.

Madrigal, Alexis C. 2018, October 3. "Raised by YouTube." *The Atlantic*. https://www.theatlantic.com/magazine/archive/2018/11/raised-by-youtube/570838/.

Maerten, Rakoen, Jon Roozenbeek, Melisa Basol, and Sander van der Linden. 2021. "Long-term Effectiveness of Inoculation Against Misinformation: Three Longitudinal Experiments." *Journal of Experimental Psychology: Applied* 27, no. 1: 1–16. https://doi.org/10.1037/xap0000315.

Mai, Kimberly T., Sergi Bray, Toby Davies, and Lewis D. Griffin. 2023. "Warning: Humans Cannot Reliably Detect Speech Deepfakes." *PLoS ONE* 18, no. 8: e0285333. https://doi.org/10.1371/journal.pone.0285333.

Marotta, Thomas. 2023. "Feeling, Thinking, and Not Seeing: How Images Engage and Disengage in an Information-Saturated World—a Neurophenomenological Perspective." *Media Practice and Education*: 1–21. https://doi.org/10.1080/25741136.2023.2243376.

Martin, Christine. 2009, December. "Library Burnout: Causes, Symptoms, Solutions." *Library Worklife* (blog). https://ala-apa.org/newsletter/2009/12/01/spotlight-2/.

Martin, Jennifer L., and Sarah E. Torok-Gerard. 2019. *Educational Psychology: History, Practice, Research, and the Future*. Praeger/ABC-CLIO.

Martin, Michael. 2020, September 26. "Author Interview: Adapting to Social Media's Disruptions in 'The Hype Machine.'" *All Things Considered* (podcast). NPR. https://www.npr.org/2020/09/26/917311280/author-interview-adapting-to-social-medias-disruptions-in-the-hype-machine.

Martiny, Clara, and Sabine Lawrence. 2023. *A Year of Hate: Anti-Drag Mobilization Efforts Targeting LGBTQ+ People in the US*. London: Institute for Strategic Dialogue. https://www.isdglobal.org/wp-content/uploads/2023/06/Anti-drag-Mobilization-Efforts-Targeting-LGBTQ-People-in-the-US.pdf.

Maslow, Abraham H. 1943. "A Theory of Human Motivation." *Psychological Review* 50, no. 4: 370–96. https://doi.org/10.1037/h0054346.

Masrani, Teale W., Jack Jamieson, Naomi Yamashita, and Helen Ai He. 2023. "Slowing It Down: Towards Facilitating Interpersonal Mindfulness in Online Polarizing Conversations Over Social Media." *Proceeds ACM Human-Computer Interaction* 7, no. CSCW1, Article 90: 1–16.

Massumi, Brian. 2010. "The Future Birth of the Affective Fact: The Political Ontology of Threat." In *The Affect Theory Reader*, edited by Melissa Gregg and Gregory J. Siegworth. Durham & London: Duke University Press.

Mathiasson, Mia Høj, and Henrik Jochumsen. 2023. "'The Soup We are In'—Reflections on Post-Neutrality Librarianship." *Public Library Quarterly* 42, no. 6: 602–21. https://doi.org/10.1080/01616846.2022.2149017.

Mathiesen, Ylva Olsen Bøgeberg. 2022. "Web Sleuths in Contemporary True Crime Documentaries." Master's thesis, University of Oslo. https://www.duo.uio.no/handle/10852/96471.

Matsa, Katerina Eva. 2023, November 15. "More Americans Are Getting News on TikTok, Bucking the Trend Seen on Most Other Social Media Sites." *Pew Research Center*. https://www.pewresearch.org/short-reads/2023/11/15/more-americans-are-getting-news-on-tiktok-bucking-the-trend-seen-on-most-other-social-media-sites/.

Matthews, Adam, Mike McLinden, and Celia Greenway. 2021. "Rising to the Pedagogical Challenges of the Fourth Industrial Age in the University of the Future: An Integrated Model of Scholarship." *Higher Education Pedagogies* 6, no. 1: 1–21.

Mauk, Marlene, and Max Grömping. 2023, September 16. "Online Disinformation Predicts Inaccurate Beliefs About Election Fairness Among Both Winners and Losers." *Comparative Political Studies*. https://doi.org/10.1177/00104140231193008.

McAfee, David G. 2020. *The Curious Person's Guide to Fighting Fake News*. Durham, NC: Pitchstone Publishing.

McBurney, Shawn. 1999. "Staging War (Staged Photographs of Battle Taken during the US Civil War)." *American Heritage* 50, no. 5: 102.

McCarthy, John, M. L. Minsky, N. Rochester, and Claude Shannon. 1955, August 31. "A Proposal for the Dartmouth Summer Research Project on Artificial Intelligence." https://www-formal.stanford.edu/jmc/history/dartmouth/dartmouth.html.

McCulloh, John M. 1997. "Jewish Ritual Murder: William of Norwich, Thomas of Monmouth, and the Early Dissemination of the Myth." *Speculum* 72, no. 3: 698–740. doi:10.2307/3040759.

McDaniel, Justine, and Hannah Natanson. 2024, January 1. "Florida Law Led School District to Pull 1,600 Books—Including Dictionaries." *Washington Post.* https://www.washingtonpost.com/education/2024/01/11/escambia-dictionaries-removed/.

McDowell, Kate. 2024. "Storytelling and/as Misinformation: Storytelling Dynamics and Narrative Structures for Three Cases of COVID-19 Viral Misinformation." *Cambridge Studies on Governing Knowledge Commons.* https://www.ideals.illinois.edu/items/126223.

McGuire, Molly. 2024. "Remix Literacy and Digital Cultural Heritage Collections." In *Unframing the Visual: Visual Literacy Pedagogy in Academic Libraries and Information Spaces*, edited by Maggie Murphy, Stephanie Beene, Katie Greer, Sara Schumacher, and Dana Statton Thompson, 9–22. Chicago: ACRL.

McGuire, William J. 1964. "Inducing Resistance to Persuasion: Some Contemporary Approaches." *Advances in Experimental Social Psychology* I: 191–229.

McIntyre, Lee, ed. 2018. *Post-Truth.* Cambridge, MA: The MIT Press.

McIntyre, Lee. 2021. *How to Talk to a Science Denier: Conversations with Flat Earthers, Climate Deniers, and Others Who Defy Reason.* Cambridge, MA: The MIT Press.

McKay, Spencer, and Chris Tenove. 2021, September 1. "Disinformation as a Threat to Deliberative Democracy." *Political Research Quarterly* 74, no. 3: 703–17. https://doi.org/10.1177/1065912920938143.

McPhedran, Robert, Michael Raatjczak, Max Mawby, Emily King, Yuchen Yang, and Natalie Gold. 2023. "Psychological Inoculation Protects Against the Social Media Infodemic." *Scientific Reports* 13. https://doi.org/10.1038/s41598-023-32962-1.

Meehan, Kasey, and Jonathan Friedman. 2023, April 20. "Banned in the USA: State Laws Supercharge Book Suppression in Schools." Pen America. https://pen.org/report/banned-in-the-usa-state-laws-supercharge-book-suppression-in-schools/.

Mehta, Hemant. 2024, February 24. "GOP Lawmaker Pushes Anti-Abortion Propaganda Bill with Scientific, Antisemitic Lies." Friendly Atheist. https://www.friendlyatheist.com/p/gop-lawmaker-pushes-anti-abortion.

Meister, Stefan. 2016. *Research Report: Isolation and Propaganda: The Roots and Instruments of Russia's Disinformation Campaign.* German Marshall Fund of the United States.

Meltzer, Marisa. 2021, March 29. "How New Age Spirituality and Sensitive Masculinity Led to QAnon." *Washington Post Magazine.* https://www.washingtonpost.com/magazine/2021/03/29/qanon-new-age-spirituality/.

Mercier, Hugo, and Dan Sperber. 2018. *Enigma of Reason: A New Theory of Human Understanding.* New York: Penguin Books.

Metz, Cade, Karen Weise, Nico Grant, and Mike Isaac. 2024, March 4. "How Elon Musk and Larry Page's AI Debate Led to OpenAI and an Industry Boom." *New York Times.* https://www.nytimes.com/2023/12/03/technology/ai-openai-musk-page-altman.html.

Meyer, Jan, and Ray Land, *Threshold Concepts and Troublesome Knowledge: Linkages to Ways of Thinking and Practising Within the Disciplines.* (Edinburgh: ETL Project, 2003). https://kennslumidstod.hi.is/wp-content/uploads/2016/04/meyerandland.pdf.

Miller, Carolyn R. 1984. "Genre as Social Action." *Quarterly Journal of Speech* 70 (2): 151–67. https://doi.org/10.1080/00335638409383686.

Miller, Joanne M., Kyle L. Saunders, and Christina E. Farhart. 2016. "Conspiracy Endorsement as Motivated Reasoning: The Moderating Roles of Political Knowledge and Trust." *American Journal of Political Science* 60, no. 4: 824–44. https://doi.org/10.1111/ajps.12234.

Mitchell, Amy, Mark Jurkowitz, J. Baxter Oliphant, and Elisa Shearer. 2020, September 16. "Most Americans Who Have Heard of QAnon Conspiracy Theories Say They Are Bad for the Country and That Trump Seems to Support People Who Promote Them." American Trends Survey, Pew Research Center. https://www.journalism.org/2020/09/16/most-americans-who-have-heard-of-qanon-conspiracy-theories-say-they-are-bad-for-the-country-and-that-trump-seems-to-support-people-who-promote-them/.

Modirrousta-Galian, Ariana, and Philip A. Higham. 2023. "Gamified Inoculation Interventions Do Not Improve Discrimination Between True and Fake News; Reanalyzing Existing Research with Receiver Operating Characteristic Analysis." *Journal of Experimental Psychology: General* 152, no. 9: 2411–37. doi:10.1037/xge0001395.

Mogul, Joey L., Andrea J. Ritchie, and Kay Whitlock. 2012. *Queer (In)Justice: The Criminalization of LGBT People in the United States.* Boston: Beacon Press.

Montague, Rae-Anne, Kuuleilani Reyes, and Keikilani Meyer. 2020. "Nānā I Ke Kumu - Look to the Source." *School Libraries Worldwide* 26, no. 1 (2020): 99–109. doi:10.14265.26.1.004.

Montasari, Reza. 2024. *Cyberspace, Cyberterrorism and the International Security in the Fourth Industrial Revolution: Threats, Assessment and Responses.* Springer International Publishing.

Morie, Kristen P. Michael J. Crowley, Linda C. Mayes, and Marc N. Potenza. 2022, April. "The Process of Emotion Identification: Considerations for Psychiatric Disorders." *Journal of Psychiatric Research* 148: 264–74. https://doi.org/10.1016/j.jpsychires.2022.01.053.

Mortimore, Jeffrey M., and Ruth L. Baker. 2019. "Supporting Student-Led Content Creation in the Distance Learning Environment with Libguides CMS." *Journal of Library & Information Services in Distance Learning* 13, nos. 1–2: 88–103.

Mutz, Diana C. 2018. "Status Threat, Not Economic Hardship, Explains the 2016 Presidential Vote." *PNAS* 115, no. 19: E4331. https://doi.org/10.1073/pnas.1718155115.

Myers, Mary E. 2021. "Propaganda, Fake News, and Deepfaking." In *Understanding Media Psychology*, edited by Gayle S. Stever, David C. Giles, J. David Cohen, and Mary E. Myers, 161–81. New York: Routledge.

Natanson, Hannah. 2024, February 2. "Students Reported Her for a Lesson on Race. Then She Taught It Again." *Washington Post*. https://www.washingtonpost.com/education/2024/02/01/south-carolina-teacher-racism-lesson-revised/?wpisrc=nl_most.

Nature Editors. 2023, July 7. "Why *Nature* Will Not Allow the Use of Generative AI in Images and Video." https://www.nature.com/articles/d41586-023-01546-4.

Neely, Teresa Y., and Margie Montañez, eds. 2022. *Dismantling Constructs of Whiteness in Higher Education*. New York: Routledge.

Neuman, Scott. 2020, May 8. "Seen 'Plandemic'? We Take a Close Look at the Viral Conspiracy Video's Claims." NPR. https://www.npr.org/2020/05/08/852451652/seen-plandemic-we-take-a-close-look-at-the-viral-conspiracy-video-s-claims.

Noddings, Nel. 1984. *Caring: A Feminine Approach to Ethics and Moral Education*. Berkeley: University of California Press.

Nour, Nika, and Julia Gelfand. 2022. "Deepfakes: A Digital Transformation Leads to Misinformation," In *GL-Conference Series: Conference Proceedings*, 11.

Oberlo. 2023, June 20. "10 YouTube Statistics That You Need to Know in 2023." https://www.oberlo.com/blog/youtube-statistics.

O'Connor, Cailin, and James Owen Weatherall. 2019. *The Misinformation Age: How False Beliefs Spread*. New Haven, CT: Yale University Press.

Odell, Jenny. 2019. *How to Do Nothing: Resisting the Attention Economy*. Brooklyn, NY: Melville House.

Oliver, J. Eric, and Thomas J. Wood. 2014. "Conspiracy Theories and the Paranoid Style(s) of Mass Opinion." *American Journal of Political Science* 58, no. 4: 952–66. https://doi.org/10.1111/ajps.12084.

O'Neil, Cathy. 2016. *Weapons of Math Destruction: How Big Data Increases Inequality and Threatens Democracy*. Ontario: Crown.

Orbach, Israel, Mario Mikulincer, Pinhas Sirota, and Eva Gilboa-Schechtman. 2003. "Mental Pain: A Multidimensional Operationalization and Definition." *Suicide & Life-Threatening Behavior* 33, no. 3: 219–30. https://doi.org/10.1521/suli.33.3.219.23219.

Oreck, Alden. 2024. "Modern Jewish History: The Golem." Jewish Virtual Library. https://www.jewishvirtuallibrary.org/the-golem.

Oremus, Will, and Jeremy B. Merrill. 2021, October 26. "Five Points for Anger, One for a 'Like': How Facebook's Formula Fostered Rage and Misinformation." *The Seattle Times*. https://www.seattletimes.com/nation-world/five-points-for-anger-one-for-a-like-how-facebooks-formula-fostered-rage-and-misinformation/.

Orenstein, Walter A., Mark J. Papania, and Melinda E. Wharton. 2004. "Measles Elimination in the United States." *Journal of Infectious Diseases* 189, Supplement 1: S1–S3.

Ortutay, Barbara, and Matt O'Brien. 2022, November 15. "Twitter Layoffs Slash Content Moderation Staff as New CEO Elon Musk Looks to Outsource." *USA Today*. https://www.usatoday.com/story/tech/2022/11/15/

elon-musk-cuts-twitter-content-moderation-staff/10706732002/. Oxford English Dictionary. 2023. https://www.oed.com.

Palmer, Ewan. 2023, May 2. "Trump's Military Record Set Straight with Note from Twitter." *Newsweek.* https://www.washingtonpost.com/news/morning-mix/wp/2017/10/20/retired-navy-seal-praising-trump-on-fox-news-was-a-fake/.

Palmer, Thomas. 2019. "When Stories and Pictures Lie Together—And You Do Not Even Know It." In *Metaliterate Learning for the Post-Truth World*, edited by Thomas P. Mackey and Trudi E. Jacobson, 103–42. Chicago: ALA Neal-Schuman.

Paris, Britt, and Joan Donovan. 2019, September. "Deepfakes and Cheap Fakes." https://datasociety.net/wp-content/uploads/2019/09/DS_Deepfakes_Cheap_FakesFinal-1-1.pdf.

Parry, Douglas A., Jacob T. Fisher, Hannah Mieczkowski, Craig J. R. Sewall, and Britanny I. Davidson. 2022. "Social Media and Well-Being: A Methodological Perspective." *Current Opinions in Psychology* 45, 101285.

Parsons, Sharon, William Simmons, Frankie Shinhoster, and John Kilburn. 1999. "A Test of the Grapevine: An Empirical Examination of Conspiracy Theories Among African Americans." *Sociological Spectrum*, no. 2: 201–22

Partyka, Jaclyn. (2019). Fictional affect and metaliterate learning through genre. In *Metaliterate Learning for the Post-Truth World*, edited by Thomas P. Mackey and Trudi E. Jacobson, 181–200. Chicago: ALA Neal-Schuman

Passanante, Aly, Ed Pertwee, Leesa Lin, Kristi Yoonsup Lee, Joseph T. Wu, and Heidi J. Larson. 2023. "Conversational AI and Vaccine Communication: Systematic Review of the Evidence." *Journal of Medical Internet Research* 25, no. 1: e42758. https://doi.org/10.2196/42758.

Patel, Nadya Shaznay. 2023. "Empathetic and Dialogic Interactions: Modelling Intellectual Empathy and Communicating Care." *International Journal of TESOL Studies* 5, no. 3: 51–70. https://doi.org/10.58304/ijts.20230305.

Petrov, Alexander. 2021. "Is Inoculation Effective Against Fake News? A Mathematical Model." In *2021 14th International Conference Management of Large-Scale System Development (MLSD)*: 1–4. https://doi.org/10.1109/MLSD52249.2021.9600188.

Pettegree, Andrew. 2014. *The Invention of News.* New Haven, CT: Yale University Press.

Pew Research Center. 2020, November 16. "5 Facts About the QAnon Conspiracy Theories." https://www.pewresearch.org/fact-tank/2020/11/16/5-facts-about-the-qanon-conspiracy-theories/.

Pew Research Center. 2023, September 19. "Public Trust in Government: 1958-2023." *Pew Research Center—U.S. Politics & Policy* (blog). https://www.pewresearch.org/politics/2023/09/19/public-trust-in-government-1958-2023/.

Pfeiffer, Dan. 2022. *Battling the Big Lie: How Fox, Facebook, and the MAGA Media are Destroying America.* New York: Twelve Books.

Phelps-Roper, Megan. 2017. "I Grew Up in the Westboro Baptist Church. Here's Why I Left." TED. https://www.youtube.com/watch?v=bVV2Zk88beY.

Pierre, Joe. 2020, August 21. "How Far Down the QAnon Rabbit Hole Did Your Loved One Fall?" *Psychology Today*. https://www.psychologytoday.com/blog/psych-unseen/202008/how-far-down-the-qanon-rabbit-hole-did-your-loved-one-fall.

Pierre, Joseph M. 2020. "Mistrust and Misinformation: A Two-Component, Socio-Epistemic Model of Belief in Conspiracy Theories. *Journal of Social and Political Psychology* 8, no. 2. https://doi.org/10.5964/jsppv8i2.1362.

Pierre, Joseph. 2023. "Down the Conspiracy Rabbit Hole: How Does One Become a Follower of QAnon?" In *The Social Science of QAnon: A New Social and Political Phenomenon*, edited by Monica K. Miller, 17–32. Cambridge University Press.

Pillai, Raunak M., and Lisa K. Fazio. 2023. "Explaining Why Headlines Are True or False Reduces Intentions to Share False Information." *Collabra:Psychology* 9, no. 1: 87617. https://doi.org/10.1525/collabra.87617.

Pillai, Raunak M., Eunji Kim, and Lisa K Fazio. 2023. "All the President's Lies: Repeated False Claims and Public Opinion." *Public Opinion Quarterly* 87, no. 3: 764–802. https://doi.org/10.1093/poq/nfad032.

Piloiu, Rares. 2016. "Rethinking the Concept of 'Information Literacy': A German Perspective." *Journal of Information Literacy* 10, no. 2: 78–93. http://dx.doi.org/10.11645/10.2.2126.

Pinker, Steven. 2001. *Rationality: What It Is, Why It Seems Scarce, Why It Matters.* New York: Viking.

Plohl, Nejc, and Bojan Musil. 2023. "Assessing the Incremental Value of Intellectual Humility and Cognitive Reflection in Predicting Trust in Science." *Personality and Individual Differences* 214: 112340. https://doi.org/10.1016/j.paid.2023.112340.

Popovich, Sam. 2021. "The Problem of Neutrality and Intellectual Freedom: The Case of Libraries." In *The Free Speech Wars: How Did We Get Here and Why Does It Matter?*, edited by Charlotte Lydia Riley. Manchester, UK: Manchester University Press.

Popper, Karl. 1950. *The Open Society and Its Enemies*. Princeton, NJ: Princeton University Press.

Prescott, Virginia, Pria Mahadevan, and Associated Press. 2020. "How QAnon Is Migrating from the Dark Web into Georgia Politics." *On Second Thought*. https://www.gpb.org/news/2020/07/16/how-qanon-migrating-the-dark-web-georgia-politics.

PRRI (Public Religion Research Institute). 2021. "Understanding QAnon's Connection to American Politics, Religion, and Media Consumption." https://www.prri.org/research/qanon-conspiracy-american-politics-report/.

PRRI (Public Religion Research Institute). 2022, October 27. "Challenges in Moving Toward a More Inclusive Democracy: Findings from the 2022 American Values Survey." https://www.prri.org/research/challenges-in-moving-toward-a-more-inclusive-democracy-findings-from-the-2022-american-values-survey/.

Pscyhology Today. 2023. "Developing Empathy," *Psychology Today*. https://www.psychologytoday.com/intl/basics/empathy#developing-empathy.

Quinn, Michael J. 2023. "The Development of Online Participatory Cultures: From Baseball Analytics to Covid Conspiracy." *Atlantic Journal of Communication*: 1–17. https://doi.org/10.1080/15456870.2023.2259532.

Radtke, Theda, Theresa Apel, Konstantin Schenkel, Jan Keller, and Eike von Lindern. 2021. "Digital Detox: An Effective Solution in the Smartphone Era? A Systematic Literature Review." *Mobile Media & Communication* 10, no. 2, 190–215. https://doi.org/10.1177/20501579211028647.

Rahman, Md. Luftor, Daniel Timko, Hamid Wali, and Ajaya Neupane. 2023. "Users Really Do Respond to Smishing." *Proceedings of the Thirteenth ACM Conference on Data and Application Security and Privacy*: 49–60. doi:10.1145/3577923.3583640.

Raihani, Nichola J., and Vaughan Bell. 2019. "An Evolutionary Perspective on Paranoia." *Nature Human Behavior* 3: 114–21.

Rapucci, Sarah. 2023, May 31. "Reversing the Decline of Democracy in the United States." *Freedom House*. https://freedomhouse.org/report/freedom-world/2022/global-expansion-authoritarian-rule/reversing-decline-democracy-united-states.

Ratzabi, Hila. (n.d.) "What is Gematria? Hebrew Numerology, and the Secrets of the Torah." My Jewish Learning. https://www.myjewishlearning.com/article/gematria/.

Reiner, Rob. 1987. *The Princess Bride* (film). 20th Century Fox.

Remski, Matthew, and Julian Brave NoiseCat. 2023, November 4. "Special Report: QAnon Fantasies Look like Colonial Realities." *Conspirituality* (podcast). https://www.conspirituality.net/episodes/special-report-julian-brave-noisecat.

Revez, Jorge, and Luís Corujo. 2021. "Librarians Against Fake News: A Systematic Literature Review of Library Practices (Jan. 2018–Sept. 2020)." *Journal of Academic Librarianship* 47, no. 2: 102304.

Revez, Jorge, and Luís Corujo. 2022. "Infodemic, Disinformation and Fake News." *Boletim Do Arquivo Da Universidade de Coimbra* 35, no. extra 1: 31–53. https://doi.org/10.14195/2182-7974_extra2022_1_2.

Rieh, Soo Young. 2010. "Credibility and Cognitive Authority of Information." In *Encyclopedia of Library and Information Sciences*, 3rd ed., 1337–44. New York: Taylor and Francis Group. https://deepblue.lib.umich.edu/handle/2027.42/106416.

Robinson, Shannon Marie. 2017. "Socratic Questioning: A Teaching Philosophy for the Student Research Consultation." *In the Library with the Lead Pipe*. https://www.inthelibrarywiththeleadpipe.org/2017/socratic-questioning/.

Rohlinger, Kasey. 2020, August 28. "How to Talk to Family Members About Conspiracy Theories so They Actually Listen." Popsugar. https://www.popsugar.com/family/how-to-talk-to-family-members-about-conspiracy-theories-47730400.

Roose, Kevin. 2020a, September 15. "Yoga Teachers Take On QAnon." *New York Times*. https://www.nytimes.com/2020/09/15/technology/yoga-teachers-take-on-QAnon.html.

Roose, Kevin. 2020b, September 28. "How 'Save the Children' Is Keeping QAnon Alive." *New York Times*. https://www.nytimes.com/2020/09/28/technology/save-the-children-qanon.html.

Roose, Kevin. 2023, May 30. "A.I. Poses 'Risk of Extinction,' Industry Leaders Warn." *New York Times*. https://www.nytimes.com/2023/05/30/technology/ai-threat-warning.html.

Roozenbeek, Jon, and Sander van der Linden. 2020. "Breaking Harmony Square: A Game That 'Inoculates' Against Political Misinformation." *Harvard Kennedy School Misinformation Review* 1, no. 8. doi:10.37016/mr-2020-47.

Rose, Todd. 2022. *Collective Illusions: Conformity, Complicity and the Science of Why We Make Bad Decisions.* New York: Hachette Books.

Rosenberg, Stacy. 2019, July 22. "Trust and Distrust in America." *Pew Research Center*. https://www.pewresearch.org/politics/2019/07/22/trust-and-distrust-in-america/.

Rothschild, Mike. 2021. *The Storm Is Upon Us: How QAnon Became a Movement, Cult, and Conspiracy Theory of Everything*. Brooklyn: Melville House.

Rothschild, Mike. 2023. *Jewish Space Lasers: The Rothschilds and 200 Years of Conspiracy Theories*. Brooklyn and London: Melville House.

Rotter, Julian B. 1966. "Generalized Expectancies for Internal Versus External Control of Reinforcement." *Psychological Monographs: General and Applied* 80, no. 1.

Rousis, Gregory J., F. Dan Richard, and Dong-Yuan Debbie Wang. 2022. "The Truth Is Out There: The Prevalence of Conspiracy Theory Use by Radical Violent Extremist Organizations." *Terrorism and Political Violence* 34, no. 8: 1739–57.

Roy, Barsha. 2024, November. "'QAnon Shaman'Jacob Chansley Files to Run for Office in Arizona, Internet Calls It 'Funniest Thing DC Has Ever Seen.'" MSN. https://www.msn.com/en-us/news/politics/qanon-shaman-jacob-chansley-files-to-run-for-office-in-arizona-internet-calls-it-funniest-thing-dc-has-ever-seen/.

Russo, Alyssa, Amy Jankowski, Stephanie Beene, and Lori Townsend. 2019. "Strategic Source Evaluation: Addressing the Container Conundrum." *Reference Services Review* 47, no. 3, 294–313.

Russonello, Giovanni. 2021, May 27. "QAnon Now as Popular in U.S. as Some Major Religions, Poll Suggests." *New York Times*.https://www.nytimes.com/2021/05/27/us/politics/qanon-republicans-trump.html.

Saad, Lydia. 2023, July 6. "Historically Low Faith in U.S. Institutions Continues." Gallup. https://news.gallup.com/poll/508169/historically-low-faith-institutions-continues.aspx.

Salman, Javeria. 2024, January 8. "How the Anti-CRT Push Has Unraveled Local Support for Schools." The Hechinger Report. https://hechingerreport.org/anti-crt-push-has-weakened-support-for-schools-led-to-districts-circling-the-wagons/.

Santos, Fátima C. Carrilho. 2023. "Artificial Intelligence in Automated Detection of Disinformation: A Thematic Analysis." *Journalism and Media* 4, no. 2: 679–87.

Saul, Jennifer. 2021. "Someone Is Wrong on the Internet: Is There an Obligation to Correct False and Oppressive Speech on Social Media?" In *The Epistemology of Deceit in a Postdigital Age: Dupery by Design*, edited by Alison MacKenzie, Jennifer Rose, and Ibrar Bhatt, 139–57. New York: Springer.

Savolainen, Reijo. 2021. "Information Landscapes as Contexts of Information Practices." *Journal of Librarianship and Information Science* 53, no. 4: 655–67. https://doi.org/10.1177/0961000620982359.

Scavnicky-Yaekle, Liz. 2015, June 9. "Disagree Agreeably—Three Ways to Say 'No' Nicely." *Dale Carnegie Training of Central & Southern New Jersey* (blog). https://dalecarnegiewaynj.com/2015/06/19/disagree-agreeably-three -ways-say-no-nicely/.

Scherbina, Anna, and Bernd Schlusche. 2023, June. "The Effect of Malicious Cyber Activity on the US Corporate Sector." American Enterprise Institute Working Paper. https://www.aei.org/wp-content/uploads/2023/06/ Scherbina-Schlusche-The-Effect-of-Malicious-Cyber-Activity-WP-updated .pdf?x91208.

Schneider, Marco, Ana Lúcia Alexandre Borges, and Arthur Coelho Bezerr. (n.d.) "Interview with Eamon Tewell." Accessed March 27, 2024. https:// eamontewell.files.wordpress.com/2022/03/interview-with-eamon-tewell .pdf.

Schiff, Daniel. 2022. "Education for AI, Not AI for Education: The Role of Education and Ethics in National AI Policy Strategies." *International Journal of Artificial Intelligence in Education* 32, no. 3: 527–63.

Schiff, Kaylyn Jackson, Daniel S. Schiff, and Natalia S. Bueno. 2024. "The Liar's Dividend: Can Politicians Claim Misinformation to Evade Accountability?" *American Political Science Review*: 1–20. https://doi.org/10.1017/ S0003055423001454.

Schilke, Oliver, Martin Reimann, and Karen S. Cook. 2021. "Trust in Social Relations." *Annual Review of Sociology* 47, no. 1: 239–59. https://doi.org/10.1146 /annurev-soc-082120-082850.

Schlechter, Pascal, Thole H. Hoppen, and Nexhmedin Morina. 2023. "Counterfactual Comparisons and Affective Styles in the Aftermath of Traumatic Events." *Current Psychology* 42: 32147. https://doi.org/10.1007/s12144-022 -04193-6.

Scott, Dani, and Laura Saunders. 2021. "Neutrality in Public Libraries: How Are We Defining One of Our Core Values?" *Journal of Librarianship and Information Science* 53, no. 1: 153–66. https://doi.org/ 10.1177/0961000620935501.

Serafini, Frank. 2013. *Reading the Visual: An Introduction to Teaching Multimodal Literacy*. New York: Teachers College Press.

Serafini, Frank. 2022. *Beyond the Visual: An Introduction to Researching Multimodal Phenomena*. New York: Teachers College Press.

Shaftel, Holly. (n.d.) "Overview: Weather, Global Warming and Climate Change." Climate Change: Vital Signs of the Planet. Accessed June 1, 2023. https://climate.nasa.gov/global-warming-vs-climate-change.

Sharlet, Jeff. 2023. *The Undertow: Scenes from a Slow Civil War.* New York: W.W. Norton & Company.

Shahzad, Khurram, and Shakeel Ahmad Khan. 2022. "Relationship Between New Media Literacy (NML) and Web-Based Fake News Epidemic Control: A Systematic Literature Review." *Global Knowledge, Memory and Communication.* https://doi.org/10.1108/GKMC-08-2022-0197.

Shneiderman, Ben. 2022. *Human-Centered AI.* Oxford University Press.

Shu, Kai, Deepak Mahudeswaran, Suhang Wang, Dongwon Lee, and Huan Liu. 2020. "FakeNewsNet: A Data Repository with News Content, Social Context, and Spatiotemporal Information for Studying Fake News on Social Media." *Big Data* 8, no. 3: 171–88. doi:10.1089/big.2020.0062.

Simmons, William Paul, and Sharon Parsons. 2005. "Beliefs in Conspiracy Theories Among African Americans: A Comparison of Elites and Masses." *Social Science Quarterly* 86, no. 3: 582–98.

Singh, Prakhar, Anubrata Das, Junyi Jessy Li, and Matthew Lease. 2022, Feburary. "The Case for Claim Difficulty Assessment in Automatic Fact Checking." Arxiv.org. https://arxiv.org/abs/2109.09689.

Singh, Vivek K., Isha Ghosh, and Darshan Sonagara. 2021. "Detecting Fake News Stories via Multimodal Analysis." *Journal of the Association for Information Science and Technology* 72: 3–17.

Sloman, Steven, and Philip Fernbach. 2017. *The Knowledge Illusion: Why We Never Think Alone.* New York: Riverhead Books.

Smith, K. Annabelle. 2013, August 13. "A WWII Propaganda Campaign Popularized the Myth That Carrots Help You See in the Dark." *Smithsonian.* https://www.smithsonianmag.com/arts-culture/a-wwii-propaganda-campaign-popularized-the-myth-that-carrots-help-you-see-in-the-dark-28812484/.

"Socratic Dialog Method: How Philosophy Can Help Your Teams and Your Organization. 2022, November 2. *Management* 30. https://management30.com/blog/socratic-dialog-method/

Sofer, Oren Jay, and Joseph Goldstein. 2018. *Say What You Mean: A Mindful Approach to Nonviolent Communication.* Boulder, CO: Shambhala.

Solaiman, Irene, Miles Brundage, Jack Clark, Amanda Askell, Ariel Herbert-Voss, Jeff Wu, Alec Radford, et al. 2019, August 24. "Release Strategies and the Social Impacts of Language Models." arXiv.org. https://arxiv.org/abs/1908.09203.

Sommer, Will. 2023. *Trust the Plan: The Rise of QAnon and the Conspiracy That Unhinged America.* New York: Harper.

Soule, Douglas. 2024, January 16. "Bill O'Reilly Wants DeSantis to Respond after 'Killing' Books Pulled from Florida Shelves." *USA Today.* https://www.usatoday.com/story/news/politics/2024/01/16/bill-oreilly-decries-removal-of-two-of-his-books-in-florida/72241216007/.

Spring, Marianna. 2024, March 4. "Trump Supporters Target Voters with Faked AI Images." BBC. https://www.bbc.com/news/world-us-canada-68440150.

Stanovich, Keith E., Richard F. West, and Maggie E. Toplak. 2013. "Myside Bias, Rational Thinking, and Intelligence." *Current Directions in Psychological Science* 22, no. 4: 259–64.

Stephens, Monica, Jessie P. H. Poon, and Gordon K. S. Tan. 2023. *Misinformation in the Digital Age: An American Infodemic*. Northampton, MA: Edward Elgar Publishing.

Sterling, Christopher, and John Michael Kittross. 2001. *Stay Tuned: A History of American Broadcasting*. 3rd ed. Mahwah, NJ: Lawernce Erlbaum Associates.

Sternisko, Anna, Aleksandra Cichocka, and Jay J. Van Bavel. 2020. "The Dark Side of Social Movements: Social Identity, Non-Conformity, and the Lure of Conspiracy Theories." *Current Opinions in Psychology* 35, no. 1: 1–6.

Stone, Douglas, Bruce Patton, and Sheila Heen. 2023. *Difficult Conversations: How to Discuss What Matters Most*. New York: Penguin.

Stracqualursi, Veronica. 2022, August 5. "Man Who Threatened Anthony Fauci Sentenced to Over 3 Years in Federal Prison." CNN. https://www.cnn.com/2022/08/05/politics/fauci-threatened/index.html.

Stray, Jonathan. 2022, May 2. "Designing Recommender Systems to Depolarize." *First Monday*. https://doi.org/10.5210/fm.v27i5.12604.

Stray, Jonathan, Ravi Iyer, and Helena Puig Larrauri. 2023, August 22. "The Algorithmic Management of Polarization and Violence on Social Media. *Algorithmic Amplification and Society*. Knight First Amendment Institute at Columbia University. https://knightcolumbia.org/content/the-algorithmic-management-of-polarization-and-violence-on-social-media.

Stupp, Catherine. 2019. "Fraudsters Used AI to Mimic CEO's Voice in Unusual Cybercrime Case." *Wall Street Journal*. https://www.wsj.com/articles/fraudsters-use-ai-to-mimic-ceos-voice-in-unusual-cybercrime-case-11567157402.

Sullivan, Daniel, Mark J. Landau, and Zachary K. Rothschild. 2010. "An Existential Function of Enemyship: Evidence That People Attribute Influence to Personal and Political Enemies to Compensate for Threats to Control." *Journal of Personality and Social Psychology* 98, no. 3: 434–49.

Sullivan, Larry E., Johnson R. Burke, Cynthia Calkins Mercado, and Karen J. Terry, eds., 2009. "Confirmation Bias." In *The SAGE Glossary of the Social and Behavioral Sciences*. Sage Publications.

Sullivan, Margaret. 2021, November 30. "What Happens to Democracy When Local Journalism Dries Up? The End Result Is Disastrous." *Washington Post Magazine*. https://www.washingtonpost.com/magazine/2021/11/30/margaret-sullivan-the-local-news-crisis/.

Sullivan, Matthew C. 2019. "Libraries and Fake News: What's the Problem? What's the Plan?" *Communications in Information Literacy* 13, no. 1: 91–113. https://doi.org/10.15760/comminfolit.2019.13.1.7.

Sullivan, Mor. 2019. "Why Librarians Can't Fight Fake News." *Journal of Librarianship and Information Science* 51, no. 4: 1146–56.

Sunstein, Cass R., and Adrian Vermeule. 2009. "Conspiracy Theories: Causes and Cures." *Journal of Political Philosophy* 17, no. 2: 202–27.

Susman, Mark W., and Duane T. Wegener. 2021. "The Role of Discomfort in the Continued Influence Effect of Misinformation." *Memory and Cognition* 50: 435–48.

Sutton, Jeremy. 2020, June 19. "Socratic Questioning in Philosophy: Examples and Techniques." *Positive Psychology.* https://positivepsychology.com/socratic-questioning/.

Swanson, Cecilia P. 1992. "Assessment of Stress and Burnout in Youth Librarians." Master's thesis, Kent State University. https://eric.ed.gov/?id=ED355955.

Swanson, Troy. 2006. "Information Literacy, Personal Epistemology, and Knowledge Construction: Potential and Possibilities." *College & Undergraduate Libraries* 13, no. 3: 93–112.

Swanson, Troy A. 2023. *Knowledge as a Feeling: How Neuroscience and Psychology Impact Human Information Behavior.* Lanham, MD: Rowman & Littlefield.

Swenson, Ali, and Will Weissert. 2024, January 22. "New Hampshire Investigating Fake Biden Robocall Meant to Discourage Voters Ahead of Primary." AP News. https://apnews.com/article/new-hampshire-primary-biden-ai-deepfake-robocall-f3469ceb6dd613079092287994663db5.

Syvertsen, Trine. 2020. *Digital Detox: The Politics of Disconnecting.* New York: Emerald Publishing.

Taub, Amanda, and Lauren Leatherby. 2024, February 2. "How Shrinking Populations Fuel Divisive Politics." *New York Times.* https://www.nytimes.com/2024/02/02/world/europe/interpreter-shrinking-populations-fuel-divisive-politics.html.

Tavernise, Sabrina. 2019, November 15. "Planned Parenthood Awarded $2 Million in Lawsuit over Secret Videos." *New York Times.* https://www.nytimes.com/2019/11/15/us/planned-parenthood-lawsuit-secret-videos.html.

Teter, Magda. 2020. *Blood Libel: On the Trail of an Antisemitic Myth.* Cambridge, MA: Harvard University Press.

Tewell, Eamon. 2015. "A Decade of Critical Information Literacy: A Review of the Literature." *Communications in Information Literacy* 9, no. 1: 24–43.

Thaler, Richard H., and Cass R. Sunstein. 2009. *Nudge: Improving Decisions About Health, Wealth, and Happiness.* New York: Penguin Books.

Thinknetic. (n.d.) *Critical Thinking & Socratic Questioning Mastery.*

Thorburn, Luke. 2023, April 17. "From 'Filter Bubbles,' 'Echo Chambers,' and 'Rabbit Holes' to 'Feedback Loops.'" Tech Policy Press. https://techpolicy.press/from-filter-bubbles-echo-chambers-and-rabbit-holes-to-feedback-loops/.

Todd, Chuck, Mark Murray, and Carrie Dann. 2021, May 27. "Study Finds Nearly One-in-Five Americans Believe QAnon Conspiracy Theories." *NBC News.* https://www.nbcnews.com/politics/meet-the-press/study-finds-nearly-one-five-americans-believe-qanon-conspiracy-theories-n1268722.

Tolentino, Jia. 2019. *Trick Mirror: Reflections on Self-Delusion.* New York: Random House.

Topor, Lev. 2022. *Phishing for Nazis: Conspiracies, Anonymous Communications and White Supremacy Networks on the Dark Web*. London: Routledge.

Tufekci, Zeynep. 2019, April 1. "YouTube's Recommendation Algorithm Has a Dark Side." *Scientific American*. https://doi.org/10.1038/scientificameri can0419-77.

Tuquero, Loreben. 2024, March 20. "AI-Generated Audio Deepfakes Are Increasing. We Tested Four Tools Designed to Detect Them." Politifact. https://www.politifact.com/article/2024/mar/20/ai-generated-audio -deepfakes-increasing-we-tested/.

Turchin, Peter. 2023, June 2. "America Is Headed Toward Collapse." *The Atlantic*. https://www.theatlantic.com/ideas/archive/2023/06/us-soci- etal-trends-institutional-trust-economy/674260/.

University of California–Los Angeles (UCLA). 2007, June 22. "Putting Feel- ings into Words Produces Therapeutic Effects in the Brain." Science Research News, ScienceDaily. June 22, 2007. https://www.sciencedaily .com/releases/2007/06/070622090727.htm.

Unknown. 2021, May 5. "This Week in Fascism #107: Violence from Proud Boys Still Welcomed at Rallies Alongside Trump Supporters; Given Free Pass by Police." *It's Going Down*. https://itsgoingdown.org/this-week-in-fascism-107/.

Uscinski, Joseph E. 2018. *Conspiracy Theories and the People Who Believe Them*. Oxford University Press.

Uscinski, Joseph E., and Joseph M. Parent. 2014. *American Conspiracy Theories*. Oxford University Press.

Van Bavel, Jay J., Katherine Baicker, Paulo S. Boggio, Valerio Capraro, Alek- sandra Cichocka, Mina Cikara, Molly J. Crocket, et al. 2020. "Using Social and Behavioral Science to Support COVID-19 Pandemic Response." *Nature Human Behavior* 4: 460–71. https://doi.org/10.1038/s41562-020-0884-z.

Vanden Abeele, Mariek M. P., Annabel Halfmann, and Edmund W. J. Lee. 2022. "Drug, Demon, or Donut? Theorizing the Relationship Between Social Media Use, Digital Well-Being and Digital Disconnection." *Current Opinion in Psychology* 45: 101295.

Van der Linden, Sander. 2023. *Foolproof: Why Misinformation Infects Our Minds and How to Build Immunity*. New York: W.W. Norton & Company.

Van der Linden, Sander, Graham Dixon, Chris Clarke, and John Cook. 2021. "Inoculating Against COVID-19 Vaccine Misinformation." *EClinicalMedicine* 33. https://doi.org/10.1016/j.eclinm.2021.100772.

Van Prooijen, Jan-Willem. 2019, November 4. "Suspicion Make Us Human." *Aeon*. https://aeon.co/essays/how-conspiracy-theories-evolved-from-our -drive-for-survival.

Van Prooijen, Jan-Willem. 2020. "An Existential Threat Model of Conspiracy Theories." *European Psychologist* 25, no. 1: 16–25.

Van Prooijen, Jan-Willem, Giuliana Spadaro, and Haiyan Wang. 2022. "Sus- picion of Institutions: How Distrust and Conspiracy Theories Deteriorate Social Relationships." *Current Opinion in Psychology* 43: 65–69. https://doi .org/10.1016/j.copsyc.2021.06.013.

Van Prooijen, Jan-Willem, Taila Cohen Rodrigues, Carlotta Bunzel, Oana Georgescu, Dániel Komáromy, and André P. M. Krouwel. 2022. "Populist Gullibility: Conspiracy Theories, News Credibility, Bullshit Receptivity, and Paranormal Belief." *Political Psychology* 43: 1061–79. https://doi.org/10.1111/pops.12802.

Velie, Elaine, and Rhea Nayyar. 2024, January 9. "Ethical Questions Arise after AI 'Completes' Keith Haring Painting." *Hyperallergic*. https://hyperallergic.com/865291/ethical-questions-arise-after-ai-completes-keith-haring-painting/.

Vellani, Valentina, Sarah Zheng, Dilay Ercelik, and Tali Sharot. 2023, July. "The Illusory Truth Effect Leads to the Spread of Misinformation." *Cognition* 236: 105421. https://doi.org/10.1016/j.cognition.2023.105421.

Veltman, Chloe. 2023, April 21. "When You Realize Your Favorite New Song Was Written and Performed by . . . AI." NPR. https://www.npr.org/2023/04/21/1171032649/ai-music-heart-on-my-sleeve-drake-the-weeknd.

View, Travis, Jake Rockatansky, and Julian Feeld. 2022. "Episode 175: Attending the Arizona Trump Rally." *QAnon Anonymous* (podcast). https://soundcloud.com/qanonanonymous/episode-175-attending-the-arizona-trump-rally.

View, Travis, Jake Rockatansky, and Julian Feeld. 2023. "Episode 234: Jacob Chansley, America's Shaman." *QAnon Anonymous* (podcast). Accessed June 12, 2023. https://open.spotify.com/episode/4kBwwatVAc9ASi7GxktdRK.

Villasenor, John. 2022, January 4. "The Vital Role of Twitter in Responding to Covid." Washington, DC: Brookings Institution. https://www.brookings.edu/articles/the-vital-role-of-twitter-in-responding-to-covid/.

Vinhas, Otávio, and Marco Bastos. 2022. "Fact-Checking Misinformation: Eight Notes on Consensus Reality." *Journalism Studies* 23, no. 4: 448–68.

Vogt, P. J., and Alex Goldman. 2020, September 18. "Episode 166: Country of Liars, Feat. Frederick Brennan and Mike Rothschild." *Reply All* (podcast) 58, no. 26. https://gimletmedia.com:443/shows/reply-all/llhe5nm.

Wagner-Egger, Pascal, Sylvain Delouvée, Nicolas Gauvrit, and Sebastian Dieguez. 2018. "Creationism and Conspiracism Share a Common Teleological Bias." *Current Biology* 28, no. 16: R867–68, https://doi.org/10.1016/j.cub.2018.06.072.

Walker, Jesse. 2013. *The United States of Paranoia: A Conspiracy Theory*. New York: Harper.

Wang, Shuo, Leandro L. Minku, and Xin Yao. 2015. "Resampling-Based Ensemble Methods for Online Class Imbalance Learning." *IEEE Transactions on Knowledge and Data Engineering* 27: 1356–68.

Wang, Yuping, Chen Ling, and Gianluca Stringhini. 2023. "Understanding the Use of Images to Spread COVID-19 Misinformation on Twitter." *Proceedings of the ACM on Human-Computer Interaction* 7, no. CSCW1: 1–32.

Wardle, Claire, and Hossein Derakshan. 2017. *Information Disorder: Toward an Interdisciplinary Framework for Research and Policy Making*. Council of Europe Report 5. https://edoc.coe.int/en/media/7495-information-disorder-toward-an-interdisciplinary-framework-for-research-and-policy-making.html.

Wasike, Ben. 2023. "You've Been Fact-Checked! Examining the Effectiveness of Social Media Fact-Checking Against the Spread of Misinformation." *Telematics and Informatics Reports* 11: 100090.

Weise, Karen, Cade Metz, Nico Grant, and Mike Isaac. 2023, December 12. "One Year of ChatGPT: How A.I. Changed Silicon Valley Forever." *New York Times*. https://www.nytimes.com/2023/12/05/technology/ai-chat-gpt-google-meta.html.

Wenzler, John. 2019. "Neutrality and Its Discontents: An Essay on the Ethics of Librarianship." *portal: Libraries and the Academy* 19, no. 1: 55–78.

Wheeler, Tom. 2019. *From Gutenberg to Google: The History of Our Future*. Washington, DC: Brookings Institution Press.

Wilkinson, Lane. 2014, June 19. "The Problem with Threshold Concepts." *Sense and Reference* (blog). https://senseandreference.wordpress.com/2014/06/19/the-problem-with-threshold-concepts/.

Wilson, Patrick. 1983. *Second-Hand Knowledge: An Inquiry into Cognitive Authority*. Westport, CT: Greenwood Press.

Wineburg, Sam, Sarah McGrew, Joel Breakstone, and Teresa Ortega. 2016. "Evaluating Information: The Cornerstone of Civic Online Reasoning." Stanford Digital Repository. https://purl.stanford.edu/fv751yt5934.

Wood, Michelle L. M. 2007. "Rethinking the Inoculation Analogy: Effects on Subjects with Differing Preexisting Attitudes." *Human Communication Research* 33, no. 3: 357–78.

World Health Organization (WHO). 2021, May 20. "The True Death Toll of Covid-19: Estimating Global Excess Mortality." Accessed March 13, 2024. https://www.who.int/data/stories/the-true-death-toll-of-covid-19-estimating-global-excess-mortality.

Xie, Wei. 2021. "Information Disorder Behavior on Social Media: A Moral Intensity Perspective." PhD dissertation, University of North Carolina at Greensboro.

Yallop, Olivia. 2021. *Break the Internet: In Pursuit of Influence*. San Francisco: Scribe.

Yasmin, Seema, and Craig Spencer. 2020, August 28. "'But I Saw It on Facebook': Hoaxes Are Making Doctors' Jobs Harder." *New York Times*. https://www.nytimes.com/2020/08/28/opinion/sunday/coronavirus-misinformation-faceboook.html.

Yong Jin, Dal. 2021. *Artificial Intelligence in Cultural Production: Critical Perspectives on Digital Platforms*. London: Routledge.

Zagni, Giovanni, and Tommaso Canetta. 2023, April 5. "Generative AI Marks the Beginning of a New Era for Disinformation." European Digital Media Observatory. https://edmo.eu/2023/04/05/generative-ai-marks-the-beginning-of-a-new-era-for-disinformation/.

Zak, Dan, and Roxanne Roberts. 2022, January 27. "Anthony Fauci Is Up Against More than a Virus." *Washington Post*. https://www.washingtonpost.com/lifestyle/2022/01/27/fauci-pandemic-threats.

Zarouali, Brahim, Tom Dobber, Guy De Pauw, and Claes de Vreese. 2022. "Using a Personality-Profiling Algorithm to Investigate Political Microtargeting: Assessing the Persuasion Effects of Personality-Tailored Ads on Social Media." *Communication Research* 49, no. 8: 1066–91. https://doi.org/10.1177/0093650220961965.

Zelizer, Julian E. 2017. "How Washington Helped Create the Contemporary Media: Ending the Fairness Doctrine in 1987." In *Media Nation: The Political History of News in Modern America*, edited by Bruce J. Schulman and Julian E. Zelizer, 176–89. Philadelphia:University of Pennsylvania Press.

Zembylas, Michalinos. 2023. "Post-Truth, Difficult Knowledge, and Reparative Futures." In *Reparative Futures and Transformative Learning Spaces*, edited by Melanie Walker, Alejandra Boni, and Diana Velasco, 25–44. Springer Link.

Zembylas, Michalinos, and Megan Boler, 2002. "On the Spirit of Patriotism: Challenges of a 'Pedagogy of Discomfort.'" *Teachers College Record* 104, no. 5.

Zhao, Nan, and Guangyu Zhou. 2021. "COVID-19 Stress and Addictive Social Media Use (SMU): Mediating Role of Active Use and Social Media Flow. *Frontiers in Psychiatry* 12: 635546. https://doi.org/10.3389/fpsyt.2021.635546.

Zhou, Jiawei, Yixuan Zhang, Qianni Luo, Andrea G. Parker, and Munmun De Choudhury. 2023. "Synthetic Lies: Understanding AI-Generated Misinformation and Evaluating Algorithmic and Human Solutions." *Proceedings of the 2023 CHI Conference on Human Factors in Computing Systems*. Hamburg, Germany. https://doi.org/10.1145/3544548.3581318.

Zuboff, Shoshana. 2019. *The Age of Surveillance Capitalism: The Fight for a Human Future at the New Frontier of Power.* New York: PublicAffairs.

Zurkowski, Paul G. 1974. *The Information Service Environment Relationships and Priorities.* Related Paper No. 5. https://eric.ed.gov/?id=ED100391.

Index

Capitol insurrection (January 6, 2021), U.S., 25–26, 30, 32, 55, 58, 112–13
care, 69, 76, 162–65
Carey, Matthew, 56
Catellani, Patrizia, 129
Catholicism, 32, 90
Caulfield, Mike, 65
censorship, 118–19, 138–39, 141
"Change My View" Reddit community, 81
Chansley, Jacob ("QAnon Shaman"), 25, 32
ChatGPT, 23, 147–48, 151–52
cherry-picking information, 15, 20, 79, *132*
child pornography, 30, 99
children, 49, 92–94, *93*, 118; QAnon on, 30, 87, 96, 102, 107, 165; Satanic Panic and, 7, 87, 96–97
China, 22, 88–89
Christianity, 22, 25, 89–90, 92–93, *93*, 108; evangelical, 95, 106–7
Church, Ian, 72–73
Churchill, Winston, 98
Cichocka, Aleksandra, 40, 46, 105
CIE. *See* "continued influence effect"
CIL. *See* critical information literacy
Civil War, U.S., 22
climate change denialism, 79, 131, *132*
Clinton, Hillary, 30–31, 94, 102
cognitive, *44*, 49–50, *66*, 70, 112, *128*; authority, 3, 11, 15, 55–56, 61–63, 65, 79, 127; bias, 20, 41–42, *128*; processes, 40, 51, 59–63, 82, 100, 159–60
Cole, Richard, 89
collusion, 26, 31, 38, 46, 112
colonialism, 115, 145, 158
Comet Ping Pong (pizzaria), 30
The Coming Storm (podcast), 103
communities, conspiracy, 41, 45–46, 94–95, 102–3, 107, 159–61. *See also specific communities*
compassion fatigue, 70–71

Compton, Josh, 127, 133
computing, 4, 6, 7–8
Conner, Christopher T., 42
consent, 120, 150
conservatism, 21–22, 51
conspiracies *vs.* conspiracy theories, 25–28
conspiracism, 26, 52, 103, 105–9, 112, 114; rise of, 32–33
conspiracy theories. *See specific topics*
constructivism, 50
Cook, Dani Brecher, 49
Cook, John, 131
corroboration, information, 4–6, 26
counterfactual thinking, 129
Cover, Rob, 104–5
COVID-19 pandemic, 20, 29, 71, 112, 127–28, 162; conspiracy theories, 13, 88–89, 103, 116–17; QAnon on, 45, 69
Cranky Uncle, 129
credibility, 3, 11, 61–62, 100, 149, 155
critical information literacy (CIL), 50, 155–56, 161–62
Critical Race Theory, 118
critical thinking, 33, 78, 141, 160
CrossFit, 107–8
crowdsourcing, 61–62, 101–3
crucial conversations, 69–70, 73–75
cultural humility, 70–72
A Culture of Conspiracy (Barkun), 27
cybersecurity, 120, 151, 154

Daily Mail, 18
DALL-E, 148
Dea, Shannon, 80, 82
Debunking Handbook (Lewandowsky), 130
debunking misinformation, 79, 123, 128, 130–31
decision-making, 48, 54
deepfakes, 21–23, 149–52, 156
deep learning, 148, 155
deep state, 116–18

deficit model for conspiracy ideation, 40, 51

The Delusions of Crowds (Berstein), 46

democratic society, threats to, 14, 33, 111–17, 120–21

Denial101x lectures, 131, *132*

Dentith, Matthew R. X., 51

Derakshan, Hossein, 14–16

Dewey, John, 66, 121

digital citizens, 103, 137–46

Digital Detox (Syvertsen), 109

Dinkelberg, Alejandro, 21

DiResta, Renée, 15

discrimination, employment, 118

disinformation, 11, 14–17, 113–14, 120–21, 137, 144; AI-generated, 22, 147–49; QAnon and, 31–32

dismissal, 124, 137

distrust, 28–29, 57, 58, 102, 114, 160

Donovan, Joan, 31–32

doomscrolling, 13, 109

Douglas, Karen, 26–28, 40, 42–43, 46

Drabinski, Emily, 145

Dunning, David, 47–48, 67

Dunning-Kruger effect, 47–48

ebooks, 141–42

echo chambers, 11, 21, 112

Ecker, Ullrich K. H., 128

economic recession (2008), U.S., 10–11

Edison, Thomas, 6

educated citizenry, 95, 139, 157

"Education after Auschwitz" (Adorno), 143–44

educators, 50–51, 63–64, 76–77, 121, 137

8chan (imageboard), 9, 30

ELIS. *See* Everyday Life Information Seeking

Emerick, Barrett, 80, 82

emotions, mood and, 5, 70, 73–74, 100, 125, 162–63; affect and, 16–17, 106; in cognitive processes, 59–61; in decision-making, 54; flattening of, 10; in information behavior, 64; negative, 127, 153; physiology and, 76; polarization, 154

empathy, 16, 72, 76, 109, 124–25, 128, 163; affective, 70, 144

Enders, Adam M., 105

epistemic, 40–43, 76–77, 159–60

Eshoo, Anna, 150

ethics, 139–40, 154, 156

Europe, 5, 14, 88–90, 120, 165

evangelical movements, 33, 95, 106–7

Everyday Life Information Seeking (ELIS) model, 50

Evli, Mahmut, 70–71

exclusion, 139

experts, expertise and, 11, 15, 22–23, 42–43, 140, 159–60; crowdsourced, 61–62, 101–3

extra-factual information, AI-generated, 148–49, 152–56

extremism, 82–83, 97, 112–14, 120, 144, 149

Facebook, 4, 9–11, 31, 105; AI-generated content on, 152; growth of, 56; social identity and, 21

fact-checking, 63–64, 157, 159–60, 168; AI and, 152–53, 155–56; formula, 130–31; influencers and, 11; social media and, 14

Fact-Myth-Fallacy structure, 131, *132*

Fairness Doctrine, U.S., 18

fake news, 14, 127, 159

false information, 14, 23, 100–101, 131–33

fascism, 97, 114, 146

Fauci, Anthony, 45, 116–17

federal government, U.S., 116–17

feedback loops, 11, 21, 162

feminism, 97, 162

nudging, 33, 78–80, 107, 123–24, 130
numerology, 42, 90

Oberauer, Klaus, 108
objectivity, 4–6, 22, 162
online, 8, 21, 31, 80–83, 104, 144;
    conspiracy theory assessment,
    125–26; education, 162–65. *See
    also* social media
open-access research, 155
OpenAI, 147–48, 151
The Open Society and Its Enemies
    (Popper), 143
open-source investigations, 101–3
O'Reilly, Bill, 119
Osler, Audrey, 163
the Other, 22, 89–90, 98, 115
outgroup, 21–22, 42, 81
Overdrive (ebook provider), 141

Page, Larry, 9
Palmer, Thomas, 100
paradoxes, 3, 143
paranoia, 28, 33, 38–40
parasocial relationships, 55, 61–63
pareidolia, 41, *41*
participatory game, conspiracy
    ideation as a, 99–104, 108
pattern-seeking, 28, 38, *41*, 41–42,
    53, 104, 123–24
pedagogies, pedagogical approaches
    and, 51, 71, 159–65
pedophiles, satanic, 29, 87, 94,
    96–97, 114
peer-reviewed scholarship, 158
peer-to-peer feedback, 164
Pelosi, Nancy, 150
Perplexity.ai, 148
personal computing, 4, 7–8
persuasion-immune response, 127
Petito, Gabby, 99
Petrov, Alexander, 131
Pettegree, Andrew, 3, 5
Pfeffer, Dan, 18, 112–13
Phelps-Roper, Megan, 80, 82

photography, 22, 100, 149–50
Photoshop, 23, 149
physiology, 38, 76
Piaget, Jean, 49–50
the picture superiority effect, 100
Pierre, Joseph, 42, *43*, 51, 54
Piloiu, Rares, 165–66
Pindrop, 152
Pinterest, 9
pizzagate, 30–31, 99
Plandemic (disinformation
    documentary), 116–17
Planned Parenthood, 119–20
Plato, 77, 141, 143
plausibility, 28
Plohl, Nejc, 72
Podesta, John, 30–31
poisoned wells, 88–89
polarization, 7, 33, 112–13, 120–21,
    153–54, 159
policy frameworks, AI related,
    154–56
political extremism, 112–13, 149
Popper, Karl, 143
popular culture, 5, 71, 95
Populism, 47, 58, 97
pornography, 7, 22, 30, 99, 150
post-truth, 4, 155, 159, 167–68
power, power structures and, 5,
    22–23, 112, 158, 160–61, 167–68;
    of conspiracy theories, 26, 31;
    of GAI, 147; libraries and, 71–72;
    QAnon and, 114–15
"Practicing Freedom for the Post-
    Trust Era" (Fister), 121
prebunking, 79, 126–29
printing press, 4–5, 92
privacy, 120, 154
privilege, 145
producers, information, 15–16, 140
Project Information Literacy
    Algorithms study, 12
Prooijen, Jan-Willem van, 39, 42
propaganda, 92–93, 114
pseudoscience, 32, 94

World War II, 6–7, 20, 22, 143
World Wide Web, 8. *See also*
  internet
wrongness, models of, 82

X. *See* Twitter
xenophobia, 97, 115
Xie, Wei, 16

Yallop, Olivia, 11
YouTube, 4, 9–11, 31, 101, 131

Zembylas, Michalinos, 162, 167
Zionism, 91
Zone of Proximal Development
  (ZPD), 50
Zurkowski, Paul, 63

About the Authors

Stephanie Beene is an associate professor and the Art, Architecture, and Planning Librarian at the University of New Mexico (UNM) in Albuquerque. She has worked as an educator within museums, K-12, and higher-education settings, in addition to her work as an information professional. Currently, she delivers instruction as a member of the UNM College of University Libraries and Learning Sciences, and supports the university and her departments through collections management, programming, governance work, and collaborative grants. Her research interests include information and visual literacy frameworks as they relate to notions of trust, the scholarship of teaching and learning within a librarianship context, and the shifting creative practices among artists and architects. She earned an MS in Information Studies from the University of Texas at Austin, an MA in Art History from the University of California, Riverside, and a BA in Art and Art History from Colorado State University.

Katie Greer is a professor in the library at Oakland University in Rochester, Michigan, where she serves as the Fine and Performing Arts Librarian, and teaches the library's general education course. Her research interests range widely; currently, when not making herself anxious about conspiracy theorists, she is pondering pedagogical models and strategies for helping the general public obtain metaliteracy skills. Katie holds a BA in English from Aquinas College, a MA in Art History from the University of Notre Dame, and a MLIS from Drexel University, and is working on a PhD in Higher Education Leadership from Oakland University. She is managed by two entitled chihuahuas.

About the Contributing Author

Shawn McCann obtained his MLIS from Wayne State University in 2003. He is currently an associate professor and business librarian at Oakland University in Rochester, Michigan. His research interests include information literacy and digital accessibility; however, as artificial intelligence rapidly intersects with the world of libraries, he finds his attention being drawn to this rapidly evolving technology.